Praise

"All Hands on Deck is a thought-provoking book about the important role that well-functioning, transparent, and connected capital markets play in driving sustainable economic development. It illustrates how higher levels of financial literacy benefit individuals, companies, and governments alike, and presents actionable ideas for how to develop and leverage capital markets to transform societies across the world."

— **Julie Becker**, Chief Executive Officer, Luxembourg Stock Exchange

"Arunma Oteh's insightful book powerfully advocates for the leadership required to build strong, resilient capital markets. At the WFE, we understand how vital these markets are for global economic growth and stability. This should be on every leader's reading list."

— **Nandini Sukumar**, Chief Executive Officer, World Federation of Exchanges

"This is a must-read from a global expert on capital markets. At IFC, we are committed to mobilizing private sector funds for development, recognizing that public sector resources alone will not meet the immense funding needs across all sectors."

— **Makhtar Diop**, Managing Director, International Finance Corporation (IFC)

"Through our work at the World Bank, we have seen firsthand the critical role world class capital markets play in raising the funds essential for global development."

— **Jorge Familiar**, Vice President and Treasurer, World Bank

"Drawing from decades of experience promoting the value of capital markets, this book is a must-read for anyone committed to sustainable development and global financial resilience. Arunma Oteh brilliantly captures how well-functioning markets can transform economies – a vision I have championed throughout my career."

— **Jingdong Hua**, Vice-Chair, International Sustainability Standards Board, and Former Vice President and Treasurer, World Bank

"I am thrilled that Arunma Oteh is sharing her expertise on capital markets in this important book. From my work, I know that capital markets play a pivotal role in spurring innovation, which is essential for societal progress. Her insights are invaluable for anyone looking to understand how finance can drive transformative change."

— **Prof. Soumitra Dutta**, Dean, Saïd Business School, University of Oxford

"Arunma Oteh's book provides profound insights into the leadership and capital markets that are essential for driving economic and social transformation. Her work offers a compelling case for how strong financial systems can shape the future of developing economies. This is an important read for anyone interested in global development."

— **Prof. Roger Goodman**, Warden, St. Antony's College, and Nissan Professor of Modern Japanese Studies, University of Oxford

"Arunma Oteh's experience as Director General of the Securities and Exchange Commission and as Vice President and Treasurer of the World Bank brings depth and power to her account of leadership, governance, and capital markets – key areas that shape global economic development. Her insights into how well-governed financial systems can drive prosperity and inclusion across the developing world make this a must-read for anyone committed to creating stronger, more resilient economies."

— **Prof. Ngaire Woods**, Founding Dean, Blavatnik School of Government, and Professor of Global Economic Governance, University of Oxford

"*All Hands on Deck* powerfully narrates anecdotes on financial inclusion, a passion we both share. Her deep insights align with my own research on the transformative impact of accessible financial systems. This is an essential read for anyone committed to expanding opportunity through financial empowerment."

> — **Prof. Peter Tufano**, Baker Foundation Professor, Harvard Business School, and former Dean, Saïd Business School, University of Oxford

"Arunma Oteh's book is a timely guide on the leadership required to mobilize the funds that will drive sustainable development in Nigeria and across Africa. Her insights are invaluable for shaping the future of our economies. I am incredibly proud of her work and this contribution to advancing the continent's prosperity."

> — **Prof. Yemi Osinbajo**, Former Vice President of the Federal Republic of Nigeria

"Arunma Oteh's unique book offers a profound exploration of leadership and capital markets, showcasing their critical roles in driving Africa's economic transformation. At Afreximbank, we understand the importance of innovative financing tools and skills, and strong markets, in unlocking trade and development across the continent. This is a must-read for anyone interested in understanding the key drivers of Africa's trade and development."

> — **Prof. Benedict Okey Oramah**, President and Chairman of the Board of Directors, African Export–Import Bank (Afreximbank)

"Arunma Oteh, a proud daughter of Abia State, Nigeria, has traversed the world and also led groundbreaking capital market reforms in Nigeria. Now, through this timely book, she shares her invaluable insights and experience with us all. I commend her for boldly challenging us to build the world class financial ecosystem we need to finance infrastructure and critical social services for our people."

— **Dr. Alex Otti**, Governor of Abia State, Nigeria

"Arunma Oteh's book is a masterclass. It articulates the transformative leadership needed to unlock the power of capital markets across Africa. Developing world class financial ecosystems in Africa will significantly enhance the African Development Bank's capacity to deliver even more on its crucial mandate of driving sustainable development for the continent."

— **Dr. Akinwumi A. Adesina**, President and Chairman of the Boards of Directors, African Development Bank Group

"*All Hands on Deck* takes you from Arunma Oteh's journey learning about financial markets as an eight-year-old in Kano, Nigeria to the commanding heights of sophisticated finance. Throughout her career, she has exemplified the courage and character that the great people of Kano have demonstrated for centuries. I witnessed this firsthand as we worked side by side to reform Nigeria's financial system, following the global financial crisis in the face of stiff opposition.

In this brilliant tome, she distills her vast experience, championing a world class financial ecosystem for our people."

— **His Highness Muhammad Sanusi II**, Emir of Kano and former Governor of the Central Bank of Nigeria

All Hands on Deck

Unleash prosperity through world class capital markets

Arunma Oteh

R^ethink

For my parents, who taught me the true meaning of living an impactful life and ignited my lifelong passion for finance and capital markets.

Contents

Foreword

In 2015, countries across the globe gathered around
the United Nations Sustainable Development Goals
to create a more inclusive, equal, and sustainable world
for all, and committed to curb global warming through
the Paris Agreement. We are now more than halfway
to 2030, and progress has been slow. The devastating
effects of climate change are affecting countries around
the world, inequality is on the rise, and geopolitical tensions and wars are wreaking havoc on many communities. Amidst these crises, some companies, industries,
and regions have decided to deprioritize their sustainability objectives. But the reality is that time is running
out fast, and we need to act now if we are to set the
world on a more sustainable path.

This forms the backdrop to Arunma Oteh's new book *All Hands on Deck* – a timely and important book that highlights the role that capital markets can and should play in enabling and accelerating sustainable development on a global scale. Global challenges require coordinated, collective responses, and finance must be at the heart of the solutions to the global crises we are currently faced with. This means that we must rethink the very mission of capital markets, and join forces across borders to unleash their full potential when it comes to driving the green transition, social progress, and sustainable economic development across the world.

Arunma Oteh is well placed to provide insights into the inner workings and potential of international capital markets. Thanks to her extraordinary career in finance, she can provide a unique and legitimate perspective on the status quo and a well-founded vision for the future, and this is precisely what makes this book so valuable. As the Treasurer of the World Bank and, earlier in her career, in her role as the Group Treasurer of the African Development Bank, Arunma Oteh helped shape important developments in international capital markets. As an example, she led innovative green and sustainable finance transactions during her tenure at the World Bank.

Throughout her career, Arunma Oteh has consistently championed the role of transparency and integrity in capital markets. Her tenure as Director-General of the Nigerian Securities and Exchange Commission saw her lead significant reforms aimed at enhancing market transparency and fostering investor confidence. Under her leadership, Nigeria's capital market became a more robust, regulated environment that encouraged both local and international investment. Her initiatives underscored the importance of a stable and transparent regulatory framework – a foundation without which capital markets cannot function effectively or attract the investment needed to foster growth and development. It is because of her impressive background and her distinctive contribution to international capital markets over several decades that we should listen when Arunma Oteh speaks.

As the CEO of the Luxembourg Stock Exchange, and the Founder of Luxembourg Green Exchange, I am a great supporter of Arunma Oteh's work, vision, and values. She has served as a source of inspiration for me and for our work at the Luxembourg Stock Exchange, especially in the field of sustainable finance. We established the Luxembourg Green Exchange (LGX) in 2016 to help mobilize capital for sustainable development and reorient these capital flows toward the regions and communities where the funding gap is the most striking. Since then, we have worked relentlessly to advance the sustainable finance agenda and strengthen transparency and accountability in capital markets, with a specific focus on fostering sustainable finance initiatives in emerging markets and growth economies. Today, LGX encompasses more than 2,100 outstanding sustainable bonds issued by 330 issuers across 60 countries, raising more than EUR 1 trillion for investments with positive green and social outcomes across the world.

Arunma Oteh has long advocated for exchanges to play a more active role in accelerating sustainable development. In 2016, in her capacity as Treasurer of the World Bank, she delivered a keynote speech at the 56th General Assembly and Annual Meeting of the World Federation of Exchanges in Cartagena, Colombia. In her speech, she called on exchanges to align their mission to the twin missions of the World Bank: to eradicate extreme poverty by 2030 and promote shared prosperity. She pointed out that exchanges are vital for the creation and the maintenance of robust, liquid, and transparent capital markets, and argued that exchanges should capitalize more on their unique role as financial infrastructure providers and help advance financing for climate action and other global development challenges. She also highlighted the need for joint action to develop the required infrastructure to establish financial markets in emerging markets. Above all, she called on exchanges as champions of innovation to come up with new solutions to tackle the world's most difficult challenges. In other words, Arunma Oteh has worked relentlessly for a number of years already to encourage exchanges to broaden their mission as market operators and pave the way for more sustainable and inclusive capital markets, capable of driving meaningful, positive change in the real world, leaving no one behind.

In September 2021, we marked the five-year anniversary of LGX, and we had the great honor to welcome

Arunma Oteh as a keynote speaker to celebrate the accomplishments we had made in the early years of our sustainable finance journey. Arunma Oteh seized the opportunity to stress the importance of making sustainable finance truly global. She highlighted how exchanges facilitate engagement and financial education among investors and the broader public alike, and she talked about the role exchanges in developed economies play in advancing green finance in emerging markets and thereby contribute to driving sustainable, economic development across different regions. Exchanges enable diversification of funding sources and can help reorient capital flows from the international investor community to new markets, and unleash the power of capital markets when it comes to advancing sustainable, long-term economic development.

At the Luxembourg Stock Exchange, we have embraced this mission and we have established partnerships and cooperation agreements with exchanges in different African countries, such as Nigeria, Cabo Verde, Rwanda, and Ivory Coast, as well as in Latin America and Asia. The objective behind this cooperation is to share our experience, build capacity and foster sustainable finance developments in new regions.

All Hands on Deck skillfully conveys Arunma Oteh's remarkable vision and commitment to the transformative potential of finance. By sharing her experiences and observations, she challenges us to rethink the role of finance, and more specifically of capital markets, and invites us to reflect over the role, responsibility, and impact capital markets should have in the real economy and in the real world. As companies move their focus from shareholder primacy to consider the impact they have on a broader range of stakeholders, and financial objectives have evolved from short-term profit maximization to long-term, sustainable value creation, capital markets are being transformed as well.

I fully share Arunma Oteh's conviction that capital markets can and must be agents of positive societal change in a transforming world. Exchanges can facilitate or condition access to market financing, and help direct capital flows toward the companies and industries that are able to come up with solutions to our global challenges. This is why exchanges should join forces and lead the transformation of capital markets everywhere, in both advanced and developing economies.

To decarbonize the world economy, we need to decarbonize capital markets. And to be successful in this, we need to create more connected and inclusive international capital markets that cover all the regions of the world and that allow capital to flow across markets, borders, and continents. Arunma Oteh is right when she says that capital markets are the backbone of any thriving economy, and that capital markets hold the power to transform societies and drive sustainable, economic development in emerging markets. By sharing the example of Nigeria's capital markets, she provides a blueprint that can serve as a source of inspiration for other growth economies as they strive to build world class capital markets in their own region. As importantly, she creates awareness of the role we all play in strengthening and broadening international capital markets.

In her book, Arunma Oteh presents four recommendations for the future of international capital markets, articulated as clear calls for action. One of these recommendations is to convene a renewed global focus on financial literacy. The book illustrates well the importance of financial education in shaping both individual lives and societies, and I share her conviction that financial knowledge is the foundation of well-functioning and efficient capital markets. Many studies suggest that financial literacy levels remain low across the line in both developed and emerging markets, and that most people do not fully understand the role they play in supporting the development of the real economy through investments in financial securities. In my view, the chapter about financial literacy is one of the most important chapters of the book. We need to create a more inclusive financial system, and it all starts with financial awareness and education.

Financial literacy is also a key aspect of women's economic empowerment, which forms the basis of gender equality, poverty eradication, and inclusive economic growth. Women are crucial to climate action and sustainable development everywhere, and especially in emerging economies. This is why gender finance and gender-lens investing, which advance financing for projects that contribute to gender equality objectives and the empowerment of women and girls, will bring benefits to all. Capital markets play a crucial role in this development.

Beyond illustrating the essential role and extraordinary potential of capital markets in driving prosperity and economic development, in this book, Arunma Oteh also describes the leadership and strategic vision required to develop and regulate robust and transparent capital markets. I found the description of her leadership style particularly compelling, which is anchored in the four "Cs" that reflect the author's values and attitude to life: character, compassion, competence, and courage. As financial sector professionals, as business leaders committed to contribute to a more sustainable and inclusive world economy, we can only take inspiration from this.

All Hands on Deck is a must-read for all stakeholders of capital markets, whether you are a policymaker, regulator, issuer, investor, or part of the broader ecosystem surrounding capital market activity. The development of world class capital markets across the planet is necessary to address our global challenges, progress toward the sustainable development goals, curb global warming, ensure a just transition, and shape a prosperous future for all.

I am convinced that one day finance will become sustainable by default, and at the Luxembourg Stock Exchange, this is the goal we work toward every day. I recommend that everyone reads and reflects over Arunma Oteh's vision and recommendations, as we all need to work together, across industries and borders, to put finance at the heart of the solutions to our global challenges and to reduce inequality.

Let's start by embracing the sense of urgency presented in the title of this book, and make sure we bring all regions together and all hands on deck to create capital markets that act as a force for good. Because as the African proverb goes, "If you want to go fast, go alone, but if you want to go far, go together."

Julie Becker
CEO of the Luxembourg Stock Exchange

Introduction

Capital markets play a transformative role in society that is often either overlooked or misunderstood. In developed economies, their critical role in elevating and sustaining the high standard of living people often take for granted is seldom fully appreciated, even when their impact is visibly evident. In developing countries, capital markets remain almost a thing of mystery, with many unaware of their potential to drive economic development and lift millions out of poverty. Throughout my adult life, I have been deeply involved in capital markets across Africa, Europe, and the United States – as an operator, regulator, and investor. Early in my career, while working as an analyst at Africa's premier multilateral development finance institution, the correlation between wealth creation and a healthy capital market became increasingly evident to me.

I was appointed by the President of Nigeria to lead Nigeria's Securities and Exchange Commission (SEC) from 2010 to 2015, during a pivotal period for Nigeria's financial markets. Amid the global uncertainty following the 2008 financial crisis, my responsibility was to lead the market's recovery, restore shattered investor confidence, and lay the groundwork for world class capital markets in Africa's most populous nation. In this book, I share my unique perspective gained from decades of observing the profound impact of capital markets in developed societies and their extraordinary potential to drive sustainable development in emerging regions such as my own. I also set out to convey, with a sense of urgency, my firm belief that we need *all hands on deck* to build and maintain such modern, world class capital markets across Africa and throughout the wider developing world to experience the prosperity such markets unleash.

Capital markets are the backbone of any thriving economy, functioning as a sophisticated system that meets the financial needs of governments, businesses, and individuals alike. These markets serve as the crucial link between the medium- to long-term capital providers – whether they are large institutional investors, pension funds, or everyday citizens – and those who need financing. Governments access capital markets to fund infrastructure, healthcare, and other public services, while businesses and entrepreneurs raise funds to expand operations, foster innovation, and create jobs. Individuals, in turn, can save and invest, building personal wealth while contributing to the economy's overall growth. Beyond finance, world class capital markets foster a meritocratic system where resources are efficiently allocated based on potential, innovation, and need. By doing so, they help build a more equitable society that rewards effort and talent.

A truly world class capital market is not just about trading stocks and bonds; it creates an environment where financial literacy and capability flourish. Citizens are empowered with the knowledge and tools to manage money effectively, save wisely, and invest for the future. Through robust educational systems and financial literacy programs, citizens understand how to engage with these markets, contributing to a broader, more inclusive financial ecosystem. Such markets also drive entrepreneurship by providing easy access to funds for new ideas and startups, ensuring that innovation and creativity are not stifled by a lack of capital. They become pillars of financial strength and catalysts for a thriving, dynamic society where economic opportunities are accessible to all.

This book is not only about the importance of capital markets. It is equally about the leadership and strategic vision required to develop and regulate such robust markets. My journey, as detailed in this book, is not about professional accomplishments; it conveys my personal commitment and passion for the role that capital markets can play in transforming society and improving the lives of millions. This passion is woven throughout the book, where I also share experiences from my five years leading Nigeria's capital markets. I recount the difficulties of leadership in some of the most difficult environments, particularly challenges that are uniquely present in the public sector of less-advanced democracies. These range from high-stakes decisions to remove the politically connected management of the stock exchange, standing firm against threats from lawmakers on live national television, and receiving a chilling revelation during a discreet meeting with the National Security Adviser regarding assassination plots on my life orchestrated by those our market-sanitizing reforms were adversely affecting. At a point, certain legislators issued an ultimatum to the President of Nigeria, demanding my dismissal and threatening that the nation's entire budget would not be approved otherwise.

The lessons I learned in navigating these challenges have deepened my appreciation of the indispensable role of strong institutions and partnerships in driving systemic change. In the book, I detail the steps we took to strengthen the SEC as the apex regulator, reposition the stock exchange as the most visible symbol of our capital market, and challenge other market participants to address their capacity gaps. Among my most gratifying achievements are the initiatives around financial literacy and inclusion. Since falling in love with finance at the age of eight, when my father made me read bulky annual reports of blue-chip companies and my mother encouraged me to save coins in a piggy bank, I have always recognized the importance of financial education in shaping both individual lives and societies. Through a series of catch-them-young initiatives, partnerships with the Nigerian movie industry, health and wealth campaigns, and even leveraging the popular Monopoly board game, we raised the level of financial literacy and inclusion across our vast country.

In reforming Nigeria's capital markets, we benchmarked ourselves against the best in the world, aligned our regulatory framework with international best practices, and implemented recommendations of a peer review of our market by colleagues from the United States SEC. We communicated clearly and firmly to the market that there would be a zero-tolerance posture to all market malfeasance. We backed that up through collaboration with the Nigeria Police and the Ministry of Justice, which strengthened our enforcement actions against bad actors, disgorging massive amounts of illegally gained profits and shutting down dozens of Ponzi schemes. Internationally, we formed partnerships that further enhanced our capacity to unleash a wave of product innovation, which deepened the market and improved its liquidity. We registered new trading platforms that are revolutionizing the Nigerian financial system and maintained policies that improved corporate governance across the market.

Exploring this book, you will encounter the delicate interplay between local challenges and global opportunities, short-term gains, and long-term sustainability. While it is a reflection on past actions, it also aims to inspire future leaders who wish to continue the work of transforming economies and improving lives through building and maintaining robust capital markets. The book is written for a broad audience, including policymakers, economists, finance professionals, investors, regulators, and anyone eager to deepen their understanding of capital markets. Given this diverse audience, certain sections of the book may seem elementary to some readers, but I have intentionally retained these definitional parts to contribute to the literature because I am unaware of any other work that brings together in one book such straightforward explanations of the numerous terms, participants, products, and policies that make up modern capital markets.

If you are a policymaker, government official, or international development partner, I hope you find valuable insights into the crucial role well-regulated and transparent capital markets play in national development, as well as ideas on the most pressing policy needs. For finance professionals and seasoned investors, the book offers thought-provoking analyses of the challenges and opportunities we face as the world grapples with the unfinished business of climate change, inequality, and sustainable development. Aspiring leaders, particularly those looking to serve in public sector roles, may discover, within these pages, lessons on leadership, preparation, resilience, and the power of vision in driving large-scale change. Economists and scholars may find case studies and analyses that contribute to the broader dialogue on capital markets' role in economic development, or perhaps also identify areas for further study.

Most importantly, this book is for Africans who aspire to see our beloved continent flourish and achieve its full potential. It is also for those in prosperous societies who believe that, with the right tools, policies, and leadership, Africa and other developing regions can emerge as equal players in the global economy. Finally, I hope the book speaks to the dreamers and doers, leaders and changemakers, aiming to convince any doubters out there that building world class capital markets is not just a goal but a necessity for shaping a prosperous future for all.

1
Homecoming

"Covered in forests…towards the sunset; it is rough…
and my heart could never forget it."
— Odysseus describing Ithaca to the Phaeacians

After over two decades of living and working abroad, I prepared to return home to lead the overhaul of the Nigerian capital market. I was acutely aware of the enormity of the task ahead, as the Nigerian capital market was still reeling from the severe repercussions of the global financial crisis. Since accepting the appointment from the President of Nigeria several months earlier, I had started to devote time to reflecting on the best ways to revitalize the tarnished image of the market, restore investor confidence, and lay the foundation for developing a world class capital market, capable of driving Nigeria's socioeconomic transformation.

I left Tunis, Tunisia, in December 2009 as I was due to assume office in Abuja, Nigeria, that same month. As the plane departed Tunis, I could not help but feel frustration that my journey would see me transit through Europe, even though my destination was Abuja, a city on the same continent from which I was taking off. Quite aside from the long additional travel time, the absurdity of it struck me deeply – two important capitals on the same continent, yet no direct flight links them. This is akin to having no direct flight between Budapest and Berlin. On the contrary, there are at least thirty flights daily between these two cities. To go from Tunis to Abuja, however, I had to make an unnecessary detour to Europe. This was a stark reminder of the challenges Africa still faces – its infrastructure, underfunded and incomplete, leaves travellers between many African cities reliant on external hubs. Resolving the challenge of infrastructure is also undermined by weak financial ecosystems that are unable to fund the robust connections that should exist between major African cities.

Still contemplating this as a flight attendant approached to hand me a bottle of water, I felt that the Parisian detour was not just a matter of inconvenience. Rather, it epitomised the niggling gaps in Africa's advancement, and the unfulfilled potential that leaves the people disconnected from one another. "Africa Rising," or Africa's enormous potential, was being undermined by very basic physical and economic barriers. How many connections never happen, how many opportunities are missed with each day that goes by without linkages between African towns? And how does this hinder Africa's capacity to strengthen the ties that bind its people, to build the networks and structures needed to tackle Africa's biggest challenges, and to unleash an era of prosperity across the continent? How pitiable is it that it is easier to get to another African capital by way of a distant European city rather than directly? How can we earnestly speak of unity, of Pan-Africanism, when African skies remain sorely fragmented and links between Africans continue to be challenged by the very past Africa is striving to overcome?

As was the case in the many days preceding this flight, my reflections on my return home to Nigeria, after twenty-two years living abroad, were laced with concerns about the magnitude of the challenge before me in respect of reforming the Nigerian capital market. I also reflected on how such an opportunity could enable me to continue to contribute my own bit to unleashing Africa's enormous potential. I went back and forth between my preoccupation with exhilarating ruminations on the possibilities for Nigeria and Africa on the one hand, and my disappointment with Africa's underperformance on the other.

Africa's infrastructure deficits

Africa, a continent famously rich in natural resources and cultural diversity, is unacceptably home to 70% of the world's poor. The United Nations Development Programme (UNDP) Human Development Index (HDI) annually reveals that twenty-seven of the thirty lowest-ranked countries are in Africa.[1] This means abysmal access to education, healthcare, and some of the lowest standards of living in the world. Infrastructure deficits exacerbate the already dire challenges of trade, mobility, and regional integration. They limit Africa's ability to harness its full potential. An often-cited statistic is that over 600 million Africans, representing about 43% of the population, lack access to electricity, compared to near universal access in Europe and North America. All fifty-four countries together produce less than half of the energy India alone uses. Africa's annual per capita electricity consumption is only about 450 kWh, a mere fraction of the more than 6,800 kWh consumed per capita in the European Union, and the 12,000 kWh per capita in the United States.

Further, Africa's road infrastructure is notoriously underdeveloped. There are only 204 kilometers of road per 1,000 square kilometers of African land, significantly below the global average of roughly 950 kilometers. Just 25% of these roads are paved compared to 100% in China, France, and Germany, and 73% in the United States.[2] As paltry as they are, these numbers mask further significant disparities between urban and rural Africa, where the availability of roads varies drastically, from as little as 0.5 kilometers per 1,000 people in Malawian villages to 35.5 kilometers in Namibian hamlets, with many still unpaved.

The continent's rail network, likewise, is severely subpar. Although Africa is so large that it could comfortably contain the entirety of the United States, China,

India, and most of Europe combined, it has less than 75,000 kilometers of operational rail lines, most of which are concentrated in a few countries, notably, Egypt, Morocco, and South Africa. This compares unfavorably with Europe, which has over 202,000 kilometers of railway, and the United States with 260,000 kilometers. As there is hardly any inter-country rail network in West Africa, neither people nor goods can be transported by train between most cities in the region. People and goods are rather harassed at multiple border checkpoints on roads riddled with potholes.

Africa's ports lag significantly behind those of other regions. With only a few ports capable of handling the largest container ships, Africa's maritime infrastructure is also less efficient, have longer turnaround times, and more goods are damaged, often resulting in substantially higher costs. For example, while it takes on average twenty days for goods to clear through African ports, in Europe and Asia, just three to five days are required on average for goods to clear the ports. Ports in Asia and Europe are also linked with other robust modes of transportation into the hinterlands. Nigerian ports are notoriously among the worst, requiring up to twenty-eight days, or more in some cases. As a consequence of their inadequacies, Africa's ports handle only about 4% of the global container traffic, despite Africa accounting for about 20% of the world's population. This not only hampers the continent's ability to engage in global trade competitively, but it also increases the cost of imports and exports. It stifles the competitiveness of African businesses by limiting access to international markets. For landlocked countries such as Botswana, Ethiopia, and Niger, the challenge is further exacerbated as they face even greater barriers to accessing global trade routes, hindering overall development across the continent.

When it comes to air transportation, only 2.1% of global air traffic passes through Africa's skies, by far the least of any continent, despite Africa being home to almost a fifth of the global population. Perhaps not surprisingly, albeit unacceptably, intra-African routes account for only 21% of the total international traffic on the continent, as the majority of flights either connect to or pass through non-African hubs such as Paris, London, and Dubai. In fact, less than 20% of African airports have the infrastructure to support large, wide-body aircraft, which are essential for long-haul international flights. This has led to a situation where many African airlines, already struggling financially and having limited fleets, cannot compete effectively on the global stage. The lack of modern airport infrastructure not only limits growth, but also discourages investment in the sector, creating a vicious cycle of underdevelopment.

Furthermore, as other parts of the world are rapidly pushing the boundaries of digitalization, Africa's digital divide remains vast. In 2023, internet penetration on the continent was only 40%, limiting access to information, education, and broader socioeconomic opportunities. In other words, millions of lives are unable to tap into the world of opportunities available in the new digital world. The challenge for Africa is not only to close these gaps but to do so in a way that is sustainable and inclusive, ensuring that the continent's abundant resources translate into tangible improvements in the lives of all its people who live within the cradle of civilization and yearn for connection.

Despite Africa's endowments, and spates of socio-economic success, the continent has generally under-performed. First, the optimism that characterized the decolonization in the 1960s insipidly gave way to a bleak outlook as a wave of coup d'états in the 1970s and 1980s cascaded across the continent. In Nigeria's case, October 1, 1960 brought great jubilation, as young leaders promised to establish a stable democratic government and a prosperous economy for a multi-ethnic collection of regions built under the umbrella of the world's newest country. This was brutally interrupted by young military officers on January 15, 1966, in a bloody coup that eventually culminated in the gory three-year civil war that started in July 1967 between the Nigerian government and the secessionist state of Biafra, which had declared independence from Nigeria that May. The war would go on to claim over three million lives, displacing a further three million people, by some estimates.

Growing up

When the war started, I was a two-year-old child living with my parents in Scotland. My father and mother had both been students in Scotland. My mother was a student nurse while my father studied engineering. They had sent my two older sisters to Nigeria to stay with my maternal grandmother, a decision borne out of necessity considering the difficulty of combining studies and raising children in the UK. Therefore, soon after the war started, and having completed their studies, my parents decided to return home to Nigeria. My parents were both born in Item, a town in eastern Nigeria that is the heartland of the nascent Biafra republic. While my mother took care of the wounded and provided maternity services, my father enlisted in the army corps, applying his engineering training in the war efforts.

The war ended in 1970 with the surrender of Biafran forces. On January 15, 1970, Major General Yakubu Gowon, the head of the Nigerian military government, formally accepted the surrender in Lagos. In his famous speech, Gowon declared, "No victor, no vanquished," emphasizing the need for national unity and reconciliation. He announced a policy of "Reconciliation, Reconstruction, and Rehabilitation" aimed at healing the wounds of the war and rebuilding the country.

The Nigerian government took steps to reintegrate the Biafran territories into the Nigerian state. Some efforts were made to rebuild the war-ravaged infrastructure, provide aid to those affected by the conflict, and restore civil administration in the eastern region. Despite these efforts, the aftermath of the war left deep scars, and many challenges remained in terms of social, economic, and political rehabilitation. My parents decided to compete for the expatriate opportunities available in Kano, a historical city almost 1,000 kilometers from eastern Nigeria. My father subsequently served as water engineer in the Kano State Ministry of Works and rose to the position of department head. My mother first served as the matron responsible for the City Hospital, Kano, and subsequently for the Nassarawa Hospital, Kano.

Growing up in the 1970s under military rule showcased a striking contrast with my life in a loving family environment and a delightful multicultural community, yet within a society confronted by socio-political issues in the aftermath of a civil war. Democracy would make a first return a full nineteen years after independence, when President Shehu Shagari was elected to lead the Second Nigerian Republic. This was unfortunately truncated again on December 31, 1983 by another military intervention. This time it was bloodless, but it was nevertheless a setback for the country.

Early career

I graduated from the prestigious University of Nigeria, Nsukka, in 1984 with a first-class honours degree in computer science, and immediately did the one-year mandatory National Youth Service Corps (NYSC). The NYSC is a post-tertiary education scheme established in 1973 by the then Nigerian Head of State, Yakubu Gowon, to "reconstruct, reconcile and rebuild the country after the civil war." After my youth corps, in 1985, I began my career in finance at Centre Point Investments

Limited in Nigeria, a prominent boutique firm, now defunct. It was founded by Chief Dennis Odife, a widely acclaimed leader of the Nigerian capital markets. I was subsequently admitted to Harvard Business School's Master's in Business Administration (MBA) program in 1988, and completed the program in 1990.

Democracy seemed elusive for Nigeria as its successive military regimes continued from the mid-1980s to the late-1990s. From the high hopes of a nation that could become a great example for others, Nigeria had unfortunately become a pariah state. This was because of suppression of free speech, human rights abuses – notably, the Ken Saro-Wiwa execution – and corruption. Thankfully, as the Y2K palaver spread around the world, democratic rule made a comeback to Nigeria, marking the end of nearly sixteen years of successive military dictatorships. In 1999, Olusegun Obasanjo was elected President, after a transition that began with the death of General Sani Abacha in 1998, followed by a series of political reforms initiated by General Abacha's successor, General Abdulsalami Abubakar. The reforms included establishing a new constitution and organizing national elections that were deemed relatively free and fair by international observers. Specifically, on May 29, 1999, Olusegun Obasanjo, a former military ruler himself, was inaugurated, launching Nigeria's fourth republic, restoring civil liberties and reengaging Nigeria with the international community. It also heralded the return of highly skilled Nigerians who were vital to the country's efforts to reform its economy, clean up its tarnished image, and strengthen its institutions. Naturally, this slight reversal of the 'brain drain' phenomenon injected much-needed expertise and dynamism into the country's governance and economic management.

At this point, I was at the African Development Bank (AfDB). The AfDB offered a very fulfilling career that allowed me to live out my two passions: applying finance to make an impact and, importantly, contributing to the development of Africa. The AfDB was founded on November 4, 1964, when ministers from twenty-three newly independent African states convened in Lagos for the inaugural meeting of the Board of Governors. Its dual mandate is the socioeconomic transformation of Africa, and its economic integration.

Today, there are eighty-one shareholders, including fifty-four regional member countries and twenty-seven non-regional member countries. The latter are mostly highly rated members of the Organization for Economic Cooperation and Development (OECD), including the Group of Seven (G7). South Sudan joined as the eightieth member country in April 2015, and the Republic of Ireland became the eighty-first member in May 2020. This diverse group of shareholders is led by Nigeria, which holds approximately 8.5% of the bank's capital. The United States, which holds approximately 6.4% of the bank's capital, is the second largest shareholder, and the largest non-regional shareholder. Contributions from both regional and non-regional members reflect the bank's broad support base, which is crucial for its financial stability and development mandate.

Starting as a financial analyst for public sector projects, my remit covered North Africa and West Africa, delivering on transactions in Egypt and Sudan, Ghana, Nigeria, and Sierra Leone. Projects and lines of credit that I covered ranged from supporting a local vaccine production plant in Jos, Nigeria, to credit lines to agricultural development banks in West and North African countries. My work was deeply satisfying, seeing the tangible impact of my work on the most fundamental needs in society. I believed that each decision I made not only helped to fuel economic growth but also enhanced public health, food security, and access to essential services. My fulfillment was in knowing that my expertise and strategic choices directly contributed to saving lives, empowering farmers, or illuminating rural communities. I subsequently joined the treasury department and worked in corporate finance and the trading room. These roles were equally fulfilling as I raised funds in fixed-income markets globally for the bank's lending activities as corporate finance officer, and managed various fixed-income portfolios as an investment and trading room officer.

Following a rigorous selection process, I was promoted to my first management role in 1997. It was to lead the investment and the AfDB trading room as Division Manager. The AfDB's trading room, even in the late 1990s, was a dynamic and highly sophisticated setup, equipped with the state-of-the-art technology that enabled us to monitor real-time data from global financial markets. I led the team of traders, and other staff in the trading room. The trading room served as the nerve center for monitoring, executing, and over-seeing various financial transactions, including currency transactions for our clients and fixed-income transactions for liquidity management. Our primary role was to help protect the incredibly large capital upon which the bank depended to continue achieving its mandate.

Considering public service

In 2001, I was appointed the Group Treasurer of the bank following another rigorous global search process. My expanded responsibilities included raising funds globally for the bank's operations, ensuring liquidity, overseeing investments, administering payments, and managing treasury risks. All was done for the overall fiscal health of the institution and ensuring that funds were available to support the AfDB's mission of promoting sustainable economic growth and reducing poverty in Africa.

After five years as group treasurer, I became the Group Vice President, corporate services of the AfDB, one of the top five positions at the bank. In this role, I ensured the smooth operation and administration of all of the bank's internal functions. Key departments such as human resources, IT, procurement, facilities management, and administrative services reported to me. I had administrative oversight over all of the bank's offices. We essentially provided effective support for the AfDB's mission of fostering sustainable economic development and reducing poverty across Africa.

During my tenure as Group Vice President, I began contemplating the possibility of returning to Nigeria for public service. I fondly recalled my days as a financial analyst at AfDB, where I worked directly on projects and programs in various African countries. I was eager to continue making a meaningful impact, but this time as a government official, ideally in a cabinet level role. I engaged in regular discussions with mentors and trusted advisers, including several individuals close to Nigeria's newly elected President Umaru Musa Yar'Adua. Backed by President Olusegun Obasanjo, Yar'Adua, a reform-oriented leader and former two-term governor of Katsina State, won the 2007 general elections. Despite the imperfections of his rise to power, he was committed to bringing about significant change.

One of the changes President Yar'Adua was considering was to find a way to deal with the controversial issue of accounting for excess crude oil receipts, a hot topic during the 2007 presidential election campaigns. President Obasanjo established the Excess Crude Oil Account (ECA) in 2004 as a mechanism to save surplus oil revenues generated from crude oil sales when prices exceed the budgeted benchmark. Nigeria's federal government uses an oil revenue benchmark in its budgeting process to set a baseline for projected oil earnings. This benchmark, established annually, reflects the expected average price of crude oil and helps in formulating the national budget. By anchoring the budget to this benchmark, the government aims to align expenditure with realistic revenue expectations and to manage the country's oil-dependent economy more effectively. Any oil revenue exceeding this benchmark is typically allocated to the ECA or used for special projects, while shortfalls may necessitate adjustments, including to borrowings.

This initiative aimed to safeguard against volatile oil prices and ensure economic stability by setting aside excess funds for future use. Initially, the ECA was praised for its foresight in managing Nigeria's oil wealth and helping stabilize the economy. However, it had been marked by controversy, including disputes over the transparency of the account's management. Critics alleged that funds were sometimes used to cover budget shortfalls rather than as savings for future generations. Political tensions flared as state governors, who often felt disadvantaged by the federal government's control over the account, called for a more equitable distribution of the funds.

As a consequence, President Yar'Adua sought a more sustainable approach to managing the ECA, and assembled a team to advise him on ways to address the issue. Through his chief economic adviser, I was invited to be part of this team along with a few ministers and other distinguished Nigerians. We worked for a few months, and the main recommendations we proposed to President Yar'Adua were to convert the savings in the ECA into a sovereign wealth fund for Nigeria and to have a tranche that is invested in domestic infrastructure as a way to catalyse much-needed investment in Nigeria's infrastructure. Sovereign wealth funds (SWFs) at the time were already a well-known idea, but with a very limited footprint in Africa. They were known to play a crucial role in advancing a nation's economic development by providing a strategic tool for managing and investing surplus revenues, often derived from natural resources, to foster long-term economic stability and growth.

The concept of sovereign wealth funds originated as a mechanism for managing resource wealth and stabilizing national economies. The idea gained prominence in the 1950s and 1960s with the establishment of the Kuwait Investment Authority in 1953, one of the earliest examples of an SWF aimed at reinvesting surplus oil revenues. Over time, the model has evolved, with numerous countries establishing their own SWFs to achieve various objectives, such as stabilizing fiscal budgets and funding national development projects. Today, the largest SWFs, including the Government Pension Fund Global of Norway, the China Investment Corporation, and the Abu Dhabi Investment Authority, collectively manage trillions of dollars in assets.

Studies by the International Monetary Fund (IMF) and many others highlight how important SWFs can be.[3] By diversifying investments away from erratic commodity prices and guaranteeing that resource wealth is preserved for future generations, SWFs can stabilize economies. One of the most successful examples is the Norwegian Government Pension Fund Global, which was founded in 1990 to invest the excess income from the nation's oil industry. During the raging days of the global financial crisis, it played a significant role in stabilizing the Norwegian economy and was even relied upon by other jurisdictions to reduce volatility through its vast holdings of a diversified portfolio of international stocks, bonds, and real estate. It remains one of the largest and most prosperous SWFs in the world. Similar to this, the Abu Dhabi Investment Authority (ADIA) has made good use of its SWF to promote economic growth across the United Arab Emirates by making investments in a variety of international assets and making Dubai the attractive hub it has become.

We submitted our report to President Yar'Adua, and the idea of setting up a sovereign wealth fund for Nigeria would eventually become a reality when the Nigerian Sovereign Investment Authority (NSIA) was established in 2011 with a mandate to manage Nigeria's surplus oil revenues and promote economic stability through prudent investment strategies. It started with a seed capital of US$1 billion in 2013. Looking back, Nigeria has unfortunately not prioritized saving much into the fund since it was established, even though it is well managed by an excellent team. As of 2023, the fund has still only about US$2.3 billion, reflecting its role in stabilizing the nation's economy and funding key projects. A dedicated portion of the NSIA's investments is allocated specifically for infrastructure projects within Nigeria, including road construction, power generation, and healthcare facilities, aimed at fostering significant national development and improving public services.

For me, the experience of working with others to contribute such an idea for my country was deeply rewarding, and I was privileged that, through my network, I was able to get an opportunity to serve in that capacity. Leveraging one's network is crucial for career growth, as it provides access to opportunities, insights, and mentorship that can significantly advance professional development. Building and nurturing relationships within your network requires patience and a genuine investment in the success of others, rather than a focus on immediate gains. By maintaining and cultivating these connections, you not only create a support system that can offer valuable advice and introductions, but also position yourself favorably for new opportunities. A well-maintained network can open doors to career advancements, collaborations, and industry insights that might otherwise be inaccessible.

Due to the exigences of politics, President Yar'Adua's first cabinet was dominated by high-profile politicians who helped him to victory in the 2007 elections. One year into his tenure, he was keen to reshuffle his cabinet and increase the number of technocrats that could help him deliver on his widely publicized campaign promises. It was through my connections within President Yar'Adua's circle that I had the opportunity to meet with him to explore potential cabinet positions in his administration.

His principal secretary at the time met with me in Tunisia to discuss the possibility of returning home. I subsequently had a series of meetings with President Yar'Adua to discuss some cabinet roles, including Minister of Finance, Minister of Commerce and Industry, and Minister of Power. While I was most intrigued by the position of Minister of Power, President Yar'Adua himself appeared to prefer that I serve as Minister of Finance. After my first meeting with President Yar'Adua, I called Nwannem, the name of endearment by which my sister and I refer to each other, to inform her of the ongoing discussions I was having about the possibility of serving in government. My sister, who loves public service having served over a decade herself as a public official, was vehemently opposed to my taking up any position in government. She was concerned that I could "tarnish an outstanding reputation built over two decades of very hard work." Even worse, would be to take on my preferred choice of Minister of Power and Works, one of the most difficult, futile and politicised cabinet positions. My sister, who was concerned about the ability to succeed in that role, said she would pray fervently against me getting the job. The general feeling was that every Minister of Power was doomed to fail because of years of underperformance and corruption in the sector, as well as some powerful interests that wanted the status quo maintained. Indeed, the Minister of Power is often the subject of millions of curses, as there are frequent power outages in thousands of locations, multiple times a day around the country. The shout of "NEPA!" would often rend the air each time there was a power outage (a situation also known as being "NEPA Struck"), followed by unprintable curses directed at whosoever was in charge. NEPA, which stood for the "National Electric Power Authority" (and mockingly renamed "Never Expect Power Always"), was established in 1972, as the state-owned monopoly responsible for electricity generation, transmission, and distribution across Nigeria.

NEPA's unreliable service, frequent blackouts, and

power shortages became a daily reality for Nigerians, stifling economic growth and development. In an attempt to reform the sector, and as part of a broader privatization effort, NEPA was unbundled into several entities under the Power Holding Company of Nigeria (PHCN) in 2005. Despite these changes, the power situation in Nigeria remains dire, with generation capacity still far below the country's needs.

The chronic energy deficit has held back everything. In 2007, for a population of 150 million people, Nigeria's power grid only delivered about 3,500 megawatts of electricity per day, one-third of peak consumption in New York City during the summer months. To start a barbershop, for example, you must include the cost of acquiring a petrol-powered mini generator set as part of the initial startup costs. Of course, the daily costs of fueling and maintaining it starved other aspects of the business of the funds necessary for growth. A business killer, Nigerian banks were notoriously pressured by bloated operating expenses, driven by massive energy costs from running diesel-powered generators across hundreds of branches for over 90% of the open hours of a business day. These costs are transferred to customers via higher bank charges and other fees. Other sectors, including manufacturing, regardless of their scale of operations, were not exempt from these challenges.

Ahead of meetings with President Yar'Adua, I was engrossed in research, trying to understand the state of Nigeria's power sector. I remember spending many hours looking at countries with successful examples and how those could be replicated in Nigeria. I had a few meetings with President Yar'Adua to discuss some of my ideas and to hear directly from him about his priorities for the power sector. I was eager for an opportunity to take up what I believed was the most challenging cabinet job. Successive administrations in Nigeria since the mid-1980s came to power determined to fix the country's power problems. The Yar'Adua administration had elaborated a "Seven Point Agenda" within its manifesto. The first of these seven priorities concerned power and energy, articulated as "to develop an adequate power supply so as to ensure Nigeria's ability to develop as a modern economy by the year 2015."

The cabinet reshuffle happened without my name on the list. There was a slight uptick in the number of technocrats, but still a preponderance of politicians. The composition of the cabinet also had to comply with the principle of "federal character," a provision of the 1999 constitution aimed at ensuring equitable representation of different ethnic, regional, and religious groups in government appointments and public service positions in Nigeria. This typically meant that a state could only have one, or a maximum of two, ministers in the federal cabinet, depending on its strategic political importance to the appointing president.

While I am from Abia State, the ministerial slot for Abia State was filled by a highly qualified and connected politician, Mr. Ojo Maduekwe, who was national secretary of the ruling political party. He had held two cabinet positions in the prior administration and was also a close associate of President Yar'Adua, who had backed the President strongly during the party primaries and general elections. He was assigned the coveted position of Minister of Foreign Affairs. The President was also able to appoint a number of technocrats such as Dr. Mansur Muhtar, who took up the finance cabinet position. The President, however, decided to keep the power ministerial portfolio to himself, signaling the importance of the sector among his priorities. He continued to lament political realities that prevented him from having more technocrats than politicians in his cabinet.

When the cabinet was announced, my sister called, elated that my name was missing from the list. Her prayers had been answered. Effective leadership often hinges on having a trusted confidant who consistently provides honest, unvarnished feedback. For me, that person has been my sister. Her unwavering candor, delivered with genuine compassion, has been an invaluable asset in navigating both personal and professional challenges. She offers truth with a delicate balance of empathy, ensuring that she shares difficult truths in a manner that fosters growth rather than resentment. She is dependable, not only because of her sincerity, but also for how reliably correct she is. In her, I have a steadfast ally and a crucial sounding board whose perspectives have profoundly shaped my approach to leadership and problem-solving.

Taking on a new challenge

In March 2009, and three months after the last vacant cabinet position was filled, there was an opening at the SEC, following the departure of the then Director General. President Yar'Adua remembered me and asked his team to reach out to "that woman who knows nobody in Nigeria." He was concerned by the weaknesses of the Nigerian capital markets, which were further exacerbated by the global financial crisis. He believed that someone of my profile, with no political connections and with a track record of integrity, should be in charge of cleaning up the market, restoring investor confidence, and leading much-needed reform. I got a call from the team informing me of the opportunity and urging me to take it. I was initially uninterested as I was concerned about my capacity to have impact in a non-cabinet position. I asked for some time to think about it.

While thinking this through, I sought advice from some friends, especially those who were already leading major institutions in Nigeria. They all saw the SEC DG position as fitting for me, arguing it would be a platform for far-reaching impact, not just within the capital market but in respect of the Nigerian economy. Everyone I talked to highlighted the dire need for leadership and reform within the Nigerian capital market, the kind of which the banking sector was undergoing. Indeed, I ended up considering it an ideal position given its capacity to lead the capital markets reform and the independence of the SEC, including its legal backing. I was excited to accept the opportunity. From this point onwards, it was a race against the clock to get myself ready for the challenge ahead. I love to be prepared for any task and would normally not take on any assignment without diligent preparation. First, I had to plan a smooth exit from AfDB after a seventeen-year career. I had to manage all my responsibilities as Vice President Corporate Services while articulating a vision and studiously planning for the next big task of leading the regulation and development of the Nigerian capital market.

I do not remember how exactly I found it, but I read Michael D. Watkins' *The First 90 Days*, a book I grew to love and still give out as a gift to this day. In this book, Watkins gives many practical tips to enable leaders to successfully navigate the critical transition period when assuming a new role and to avoid common pitfalls, build credibility, and lay a strong foundation for long-term success. I liked the emphasis he placed on the importance of understanding the organization, building key relationships, and securing early wins. For me, this meant reading everything I could find on the SEC, its history, current structure, functions, and strengths. I also looked for any documents that had diagnosed the prevailing situation in the Nigerian capital markets while thinking about how to create coalitions that would support the new initiatives I was planning to implement. Also taking Watkins' advice, I was on a quest to build key relationships ahead of my return to Nigeria.

During my summer vacation in 2009, I visited the

United States Securities and Exchange Commission (US SEC). I saw the US SEC as a benchmark institution for capital market regulation and wanted to make some connections that could help me in my upcoming assignment. I was pleased to be warmly received at the US SEC, especially by the Office of International Affairs team. I shared with them my vision for reforming the Nigerian capital market, and I remember their rapt attention and their enthusiasm and desire to support the Nigerian SEC. I sought their help to conduct a peer review of the Nigerian SEC, which would mean sending a team of experts to visit the SEC in Abuja.

Despite the enthusiasm they expressed, the US SEC team saw some impediments to accepting my request. Firstly, since the US SEC administers the United States Foreign Corrupt Practices Act, they were at the time investigating some cases involving some very high-profile Nigerians and were advised against visiting the country. There were, consequently, concerns about the physical safety of US SEC personnel in Nigeria.

Meanwhile, back home, President Yar'Adua's team was handling the complicated task of finalising my appointment as Director General, SEC Nigeria (SEC). Under enabling legislation, the process begins with the President of Nigeria nominating a candidate for the position of DG SEC. Before his nomination, thorough background checks are conducted by the Nigerian State Security Service. The background checks include verifying the nominee's character and personal background, educational qualifications, professional history, and any past controversies or outstanding legal issues. The checks at that time were indeed thorough. For example, I learnt that a Nigerian security service agent had discreetly approached my neighbor in Tunis, Tunisia, and asked questions about my background and behavior.

Once the president nominates a candidate, the nomination is formally submitted to the Nigerian Senate for consideration. This step involves the president sending a letter to the senate president, notifying the legislative body of the nomination, and providing relevant details about the nominee's qualifications and background. My appointment letter was sent to the Nigerian Senate on July 29, 2009, on the last day of their session, as they were heading for recess.

The nomination is then referred to the Senate Committee on Capital Markets, which is responsible for conducting a thorough review of the candidate. The committee examines the nominee's credentials, professional experience, and overall suitability for the role. The senate committee also conducts interviews with the nominee to assess their vision for the SEC, understanding of capital markets, and strategies for regulatory enforcement and market development. In my time, the senate committee held a televised hearing to enable stakeholders from the capital market, civil society organizations, and the general public to provide input on the nomination. This step is intended to ensure transparency and gather diverse perspectives on the candidate's suitability. After completing its review and holding any necessary hearings, the senate committee prepares a report with its findings and recommendations. The committee may recommend that the senate confirm the nominee, reject the nomination, or request additional information or clarifications from the candidate. The full senate then considers the committee's report and conducts a confirmation vote. During a plenary session, senators debate the nomination and cast their votes. A simple majority is typically required to confirm the nominee. If the nominee is confirmed, the senate sends an official notification to the president, and the candidate is deemed approved to assume office.

By September 2009, all was ready for my confirmation hearing. I was set for my long-awaited trip home, and the Senate had fixed a date for the hearing. Then, the evening before my flight, while making a quick dash down the polished marble stairs of my home in Tunis, my foot slipped on an unnoticed patch of moisture. Time seemed to slow as I tumbled forward, my arms flailing in a desperate attempt to regain balance. The sharp pain of impact shot through my body as I landed heavily on my right arm. As my arm required surgery, I was unable to attend the senate confirmation hearing until December 2009. As the plane descended from the skies of bustling Abuja, the flurry of thoughts crisscrossing my mind intensified. Notwithstanding the discomfort in my arm, which was still in a sling, the two-leg flight between two prominent African capital cities was still irking.

Africa boasts an extraordinary demographic resource, characterized by a young and growing population that is set to be the driving force behind the continent's future. With over 1.4 billion people, more than 60% under the age of twenty-five, Africa will remain the world's youngest continent all through this century. This youthful demographic presents a vast reservoir of energy, creativity, and potential, poised to shape the continent's economic future and lead the quest to tackle humanity's greatest challenges. I asked myself, "How can we harness this burgeoning labor force and expanding market to create opportunities for innovation, entrepreneurship, and sustainable development, to position the continent as a critical player in the global economy of the twenty-first century?" I continued to contemplate where the resources would come from to invest in education, healthcare, and social services that would improve the quality of life for all Africans.

What would it take to leverage our continent's incredible, still untapped, natural resources that are crucial for our ongoing transition towards sustainability? These resources include over 90% of the world's known reserves of the platinum group metals, 75% of the world's diamonds by value, 80% of manganese, 70% of phosphates, 80% of coltan, 40% of gold, 60% of cobalt, 40% of chromium, and vast deposits of uranium, bauxite, copper, iron ore, lithium, zinc, and lead. How can we sustainably exploit these mineral resources, adopting policies that prioritize environmental stewardship, equitable distribution of wealth, and long-term economic diversification? What would it take to ensure the entire value chain remains on the continent, from mining through to local processing and manufacturing, and consequently creating jobs, boosting local economies, and reducing dependency on raw material exports? I also thought that Africa could lead the world in renewable energy, positioning the continent as a leader in the global transition to sustainability.

I reminded myself that the reason I had accepted this new challenge was because I strongly believed that I could help build the foundation for long-term capital for Africa, an important missing link in Africa's socioeconomic transformation. It was clear to me that capital is what can solve this African paradox of extreme poverty in the midst of plentiful resources. World class capital markets are the mechanism by which this capital can be unlocked and unleashed to accelerate investments in infrastructure, wealth creation, and socioeconomic transformation. My job was daunting but simple to understand: lay the foundations for the emergence of world class capital markets capable of catalyzing the transformation of Africa's largest nation.

Africa's transformation from a continent struggling with poverty and inadequate infrastructure to a thriving, prosperous society, hinges on two critical factors: visionary leadership and the development of world class capital markets. Effective leadership is essential for creating and implementing ambitious policies that enable the emergence of world class capital markets. These robust capital markets would provide the necessary financial infrastructure to attract investment, mobilize domestic savings, and support entrepreneurship, driving economic growth and wealth creation. With the right leadership to guide these efforts and a financial system capable of fueling innovation and infrastructure development, Africa could unlock its full potential, lifting millions out of poverty and fostering a future of shared prosperity for all its people.

2
Money

"Know what you own, and know why you own it."
— Peter Lynch, an American investor

I would take long bicycle rides to school as an eight-year-old girl. This was unusual, particularly in 1970s Kano, a conservative city with a deep cultural heritage dating back to the ninth century. As with many other aspects of my upbringing, this was a result of the contrasting personalities and parenting styles of my mother and father. A little girl riding all by herself to school? This was my beloved father's idea, of course against the ultimately futile protestations of my amiable mother. Those daily rides, with the sense of independence and mobility they inspired in me, were also my first memories of money.

Lunch for the day was neatly packed, alongside my

books and school supplies, into my school bag, resting on my back. As I rode through the bumpy streets, I would have a few *kobo* coins in my bag, a small part of what I was saving from the occasional gifts visitors to our home gave me. Most of these precious coins would be safely kept in the handcrafted piggy bank, carefully hidden within the lowest shelf of my bedroom drawer. To this day, I still cherish the tradition of dropping coins into a small ceramic pig. There is something grounding about the tactile experience of saving money this way, an act that connects me to childhood innocence and the true weight of financial responsibility. I even pass along this tradition by gifting piggy banks to young children, though it is harder for them to fill with coins now that digital payments dominate. In a world where money often feels like invisible data in bank apps, the piggy bank is a tangible reminder of patience, discipline, and the joy of watching savings grow – one coin at a time. Even as we transition to cashless transactions, the values tied to these humble acts of saving remain relevant, teaching children about the importance of building habits that nurture their future financial health.

As a little girl, I knew the coins in my bag could easily be lost or exchanged for sweets and various other tasty treats from the corner kiosk, which would quickly dissolve in my mouth and be gone. Or they could be safely kept unspent, as they become more and more through the magic of "addition," a fascinating concept I was learning about in class. Later in the day at the dinner table, I would get a new idea from my father that multiplication is more potent than addition when it comes to money. It is good to save, but even better to invest. My parents were both in public service and only earned modest salaries. These, in addition to the small but profitable side businesses they ran – a block molding firm, a piggery, and a small poultry farm – afforded us a middle-class lifestyle. I knew my parents were not wealthy, but I felt we lacked nothing. My sister and I often helped with customer service and cashier duties in the afterschool hours or on weekends.

Early on, I learned to count money and determine the appropriate balance to give a customer – a thoroughly fulfilling assignment for a little girl in love with arithmetic. The support we provided was unremunerated but taught us early values about the dignity of work. I strongly believe that teaching kids to work from a young age instills valuable life skills and a work ethic that can significantly benefit them throughout their lives. Early exposure to work helps children develop a sense of responsibility and the ability to manage tasks efficiently. It fosters discipline, perseverance, time management, and independence, which are crucial traits for both academic and personal success. By learning the value of hard work, children become more appreciative of the effort required to achieve goals, cultivating a mindset that values persistence and effort over instant gratification. Additionally, engaging in work-related activities, whether through chores, part-time jobs, or community service, helps children build self-esteem and confidence as they see the tangible results of their efforts. Despite my parents' personality differences, on these principles, they were in complete agreement.

Making and managing one's own money is profoundly empowering. It provides the autonomy to make decisions that directly impact one's life. For me, this meant I could finally leave home and live independently of my parents. Of course, my dear father's strict approach to discipline partly contributed to this feeling. The desire to earn my own money and determine the course of the subsequent chapters of my life was in fact the reason why, after I graduated from university, I decided to work instead of continuing with any of the several master's degree options I had. With financial independence, one gains the ability to pursue personal goals, secure basic needs, and even contribute to one's family and community. In my early twenties, with total control over my own money, I felt an even stronger responsibility. I had finally broken free from dependency and could assert my own agency, an empowering feeling in a world that often marginalizes those without financial means. The simple act of earning, saving, and investing one's own money cultivates confidence and self-worth, as it reaffirms the individual's capability to navigate life's challenges and opportunities on their own terms.

I was starting to see the dignity financial independence bestows, not being subject to the whims of others. I had the means to support causes I believe in and invest in furthering my education. This ability to influence one's destiny is a cornerstone of human dignity; it affirms the individual's role as a full participant in the economic and social life of their community and not only elevates the individual but also strengthens the fabric of society, as empowered individuals are better equipped to uplift those around them and propel others to equally succeed.

Having their own income and an admirable level of financial literacy, my parents always put aside some money, which was mostly invested in stocks. Although neither of my parents had any academic or experiential background in finance, they understood the basics of investing in the stock market. Perhaps aware of the limitations of their understanding of risk or driven by their innately conservative risk appetites, they only invested in blue-chip companies. Cadbury Nigeria Plc, Nestle, Unilever, United Africa Company of Nigeria, and a few others – all household names. These companies were known for their consistent dividend payments, a fact that no doubt appealed to retail investors such as my parents. But my parents were also aware of the possibility of capital appreciation; my father would daily track the share price movements published in the newspapers.

Long before I turned ten, my father would give me the bulky annual reports of these companies, which he received as a shareholder, to read aloud, perhaps for his entertainment. This routine sharpened my reading skills, not only turning me later into a voracious reader but also introducing me to concepts that would spark a lifelong affinity for finance. When my piggy bank was finally full, it was an exciting ritual to open it with my mother and count the coins together. Each coin felt like a token of time and effort, and the total, while modest, was a symbol of my budding understanding of saving and responsibility. Once we had counted the sum, I entrusted the money to her for safekeeping, knowing it would be cared for until the end of the year. When the time came, we sat down together and reviewed how much I had saved, and she decided – this would be my contribution toward purchasing shares that my parents had planned to buy for me. This felt significant, knowing that my small effort was helping to plant the seeds for something that could grow and multiply, much like the money I had diligently saved. This early experience not only taught me about the value of saving but also introduced me to the world of investing, where even the smallest contributions can grow into something meaningful over time through the power of compounding.

The magic of compounding

Wealth creation through the theory of compounding demonstrates the exponential growth potential of investments over time. It is such a fascinating, simple enough, yet perplexing concept that Albert Einstein, with a brain that could articulate the theory of relativity from thought experiments, reportedly referred to compound interest as the "eighth wonder of the world."[4] Compounding occurs when the returns on an investment generate additional earnings, which are then reinvested to produce further returns. This cycle of getting returns on both the original principal and the interest that has been added up creates a snowball effect, in which the investment grows at an increasingly rapid rate.

Savvy investors view the geometric mean as a more precise indicator of portfolio performance compared to the arithmetic mean, as it effectively incorporates the effects of compounding over time. Compounding is inherently geometric rather than arithmetic because it reflects the multiplicative nature of growth. In compounding, each period's return is applied to the previous period's accumulated value, creating a growth pattern that multiplies rather than simply adds returns. This means that compounding captures the exponential effect of earning returns on both the initial investment and on previously earned returns, which aligns with the geometric mean calculation. The geometric mean accurately represents this growth by averaging returns in a way that accounts for the cumulative impact of compounding, unlike the arithmetic mean, which simply sums returns and divides by the number of periods without considering the effects of compounding.

The power of compounding is best realized over long periods, making it a powerful means for building wealth or saving for retirement. Because of compounding, if you start saving for retirement at the age of twenty-five by investing US$200 monthly into a retirement account with an average annual return of 7%, by the time you reach sixty-five, your savings will grow to approximately US$525,000. If, however, you waited until thirty-five to start saving, the total would be around US$244,000 at age sixty-five, less than half of the amount you would have had you started just ten years earlier.

In the investment world, a famous example is the story of Warren Buffett, one of the world's wealthiest individuals, who attributes much of his success to the power of compounding. Buffett began investing at age eleven and allowed his investments to grow over decades. His wealth did not skyrocket overnight; rather, it accumulated gradually and then exponentially, particularly in his later years. Buffett's strategy of reinvesting the profits from his investments and patiently allowing them to grow highlights the transformative potential of compounding for long-term wealth creation. His multinational conglomerate holding company, Berkshire Hathaway, reached US$1 trillion in market capitalization in August 2024, the first nontechnology corporation to reach this milestone.[5]

Interestingly, the concept of compounding extends well beyond investing and can be observed in other areas of life where incremental growth leads to significant outcomes. Consistent, small efforts in any area of life can lead to substantial results when allowed to accumulate. In education and learning, compounding occurs when small, consistent efforts to acquire knowledge or skills accumulate and build upon each other. For example, dedicating just an hour a day to studying a new language can lead to fluency. Each day's learning builds on the previous day's knowledge, creating a cumulative effect that accelerates progress. This is what Gautam Baid calls "intellectual compounding" in his book *The Joys of Compounding: The passionate pursuit of lifelong learning* (2019), in which he demonstrates how continuous learning, curiosity, and the consistent application of acquired knowledge lead to exponential growth in wisdom and insight.[6]

Furthermore, in relationships, the concept of compounding can be seen in the way small, positive interactions – such as acts of kindness, words of affirmation, or shared experiences – gradually strengthen bonds. These repeated, positive exchanges build trust and deepen emotional connections, resulting in a stronger relationship. Stephen Covey, in his influential book *The 7 Habits of Highly Effective People* (1989), described the idea of "emotional bank accounts," where consistent deposits of positive interactions build trust and goodwill, akin to how financial investments compound over time.[7]

In health and fitness, compounding is visible in the long-term effects of regular exercise and a good diet. Small, daily actions, such as taking the stairs instead of the elevator or choosing a healthy meal, can lead to significant improvements in physical well-being. These habits have a cumulative effect, resulting in improved health, higher energy, and greater resilience. Sir Dave Brailsford, the former performance director of British Cycling, popularized the concept of "marginal gains," which states that making modest, incremental improvements to many areas of an athlete's routine will collectively lead to significant performance enhancements.

Similarly, in personal development, habits and routines combine to produce considerable personal progress. For example, consistent mindfulness or journaling regularly can lead to a greater sense of clarity, reduced stress, and improved emotional well-being. Each small effort to reflect or meditate adds up, leading to a more balanced and centered life. James Clear, author of *Atomic Habits* (2018), has equally emphasized the power of small, consistent actions in achieving significant lifestyle changes.[8]

Time value of money

Meanwhile, as I moved into secondary school, my saving prowess had seen my second piggy bank almost filled to capacity, and I was thinking of a third. Intuitively, I began to understand the concept of the time value of money. All these years, since I was eight, I had been saving money, but now my savings could buy fewer items each year as the value of each coin in my piggy bank eroded over time. If I had invested the money, as my mother did, using the collections from my first piggy bank, or even just put it in the bank, I might have accumulated more by now. The concept of the time value of money (TVM) is foundational in finance, encapsulating the principle that a naira today holds more value than a naira in the future due to its potential earning capacity.

This principle is deeply rooted in the idea that money has the ability to earn interest over time, making it worth more now than later. For instance, if you invest 1,000 naira today at an annual interest rate of 5%, it will grow to 1,050 naira in a year. This growth illustrates how immediate capital has the potential to generate returns, emphasizing why investors prefer to receive money sooner rather than later. In his influential 1937 paper in the *Journal of Political Economy,* American economist Paul Samuelson demonstrated how discounting future cash flows accurately reflects the TVM, making it crucial for valuing investments and making financial decisions.[9]

Beyond finance, the time value of money also applies to everyday life decisions. For example, consider a decision between receiving US$10,000 now or US$10,500 a year from now. While US$10,500 is a larger amount, the present value of receiving US$10,000 is higher because it can be invested immediately to earn interest or generate returns. This principle extends to personal finance, where it influences decisions, such as saving for retirement or buying a home. A 2018 report by the National Endowment for Financial Education highlights how understanding the TVM helps individuals make informed decisions about saving, investing, and managing debt, illustrating its practical impact beyond professional finance.[10]

In broader societal contexts, the TVM also plays a role in public policy and infrastructure planning. Consider the decision to invest in a new transportation system. Governments must weigh the immediate costs against long-term benefits, such as increased economic productivity and improved quality of life. A 2020 study by the OECD on infrastructure investment illustrates how public projects must account for the TVM to ensure that the benefits of infrastructure investments outweigh future costs.[11]

Inflation, exchange rates and macroeconomic stability

It was also during the time I was in primary school that the inflation rate creeped into double digits for the first time in Nigeria's history, with very visible effects felt even by schoolgirls. It was 1974, at the height of the first oil boom (1973–1974), when Nigeria's inflation rate reached 12%.[12] The oil boom of the 1970s was a period marked by dramatic increases in oil prices, driven primarily by the actions of the Organization of the Petroleum Exporting Countries (OPEC), of which Nigeria was a member. This surge in oil prices, which peaked in the wake of the Yom Kippur War in Israel and the subsequent oil embargo, led to significant economic disruptions worldwide.

The boom resulted in unprecedented wealth for oil-exporting countries, while importing nations faced inflation, recession, and shifts in economic policies. For Nigeria, this was a double-edged sword. On the one hand, we experienced unprecedented government revenues and foreign exchange inflows, and on the other hand, we felt the effect of significant imported inflation due to a rising dependence on imports, a trend that continues to this day.

Inflation is the rate at which the general level of prices for goods and services rises, eroding purchasing power over time. It reflects a decrease in the value of money, where each unit buys fewer goods and services than it did previously. The dual effect of inflation is intriguing; on the positive side, moderate inflation can stimulate spending and investment, as people and businesses are incentivized to spend rather than hoard cash.[13] However, high or unpredictable inflation can lead to economic instability, reducing consumer purchasing power, distorting spending and investment decisions, and potentially leading to increased costs of living and wage demands.[14] Additionally, inflation can erode savings and fixed incomes, creating challenges for those on a fixed budget and potentially leading to greater economic inequality.

The 1970s was also the period when I learned about exchange rates, with the realization of the sheer number of currencies other than the naira. Exchange rates, the value at which one currency can be exchanged for another, are pivotal in the global financial landscape. They fluctuate based on a myriad of factors, including interest rates, economic policies, political stability, and market speculation. These rates are fundamental to international trade as they influence the cost of importing and exporting goods and services. When a country's currency strengthens, its exports become more expensive and imports become cheaper, potentially leading to a trade deficit. Conversely, a weaker currency makes exports cheaper and imports more costly, which can help reduce trade deficits but may also lead to inflationary pressures within the domestic economy.

Research highlights the profound economic implications of exchange rates. For instance, a 1989 article in the *Journal of International Economics* demonstrates that fluctuations in exchange rates can significantly impact global trade balances and economic growth.[15] High volatility in exchange rates often undermines macroeconomic stability by creating uncertainty for businesses and investors, leading to reduced investment and economic instability. Furthermore, large swings in currency values can exacerbate foreign indebtedness, as debts denominated in foreign currencies become more costly to service when a country's own currency depreciates.[16] This dynamic underscores the crucial role of exchange rate stability in fostering sustainable economic growth and maintaining macroeconomic balance.

Evolution of money

Over the years, as I reflected on the evolution of money since my early days as a cashier at the age of eight, I became increasingly aware of its transformative power. I witnessed firsthand how money shapes both personal opportunities and the broader societal landscape. The progression from simple barter systems to the intricate financial networks that underpin today's modern economies mirrors the growth and sophistication of society. The invention of money stands as one of civilization's most significant advancements. Moving beyond the limitations of barter, humanity discovered a more effective way to facilitate trade. From the ancient Mesopotamians using commodities such as barley, spices, textiles, and precious metals as mediums of exchange, to the minting of the first coins around 600 BC, trade was revolutionized. These early coins, stamped with the king's emblem, were not only portable and durable but also carried intrinsic value. The royal stamp assured their weight and purity, thereby instilling trust in their use.

The Romans further refined the concept of money. They established a complex system of coinage with various denominations. This facilitated trade over long distances, encouraged specialization of labor, and allowed for the accumulation of wealth. Roman coins, such as the *denarius* and *sestertius*, became widely accepted throughout the empire, symbolizing stability and prosperity. Temples and palaces amassed great wealth, and merchants grew prosperous, driving economic growth and the expansion of empires. The use of money also led to the development of banking systems, where people could deposit their savings or wealth for safekeeping and borrow money to invest in new ventures. This was crucial to the emergence of markets, the industrial revolution, and the overall modern economy.

In the 1970s, when cash and checks were the primary means of payment, transactions involved physically exchanging money and waiting days for checks to clear. The late twentieth century heralded a shift toward electronic payments with the introduction of credit and debit cards, which brought enhanced convenience and speed. The 1990s further transformed the payment landscape with the rise of the internet, facilitating online banking and e-commerce and enabling transactions with just a few clicks. More recently, the advent of digital wallets, mobile payment apps, and cryptocurrencies has pushed financial innovation to new heights, allowing for instantaneous, secure, and borderless transactions. Today, the integration of advanced technologies such as blockchain and artificial intelligence continues to refine the payment ecosystem, enhancing its efficiency, accessibility, and user-friendliness, while physical cash increasingly fades from prominence.

How people relate to money

The question of how one relates to money is increasingly important. One of my favorite books on this topic is Morgan Housel's book *The Psychology of Money*, in which he explores the intricate relationship between people and money, emphasizing that financial success is not solely about knowledge but also about behavior.[17] He highlights that people's relationship with money is deeply personal and influenced by a variety of factors, including emotions, upbringing, societal norms, and personal experiences. Understanding these diverse perspectives can lead to better financial decision-making and a healthier relationship with money.

The knowledge side of the ledger is foundational and critical. The process of attaining financial literacy, much like other forms of learning in life, is never-ending. It is about constantly seeking to improve one's knowledge, skills, and understanding in managing their financial resources. It can be as basic as a house-wife in Aba budgeting for the food and other necessities for her family while deciding how much can be saved, to more complex concepts such as a young professional in Port Harcourt investing in government savings bonds, or a middle-aged civil servant in Kaduna preparing for her retirement by weighing different annuity options.

No matter your current stage of life, there is always something new to learn about managing your money. Some of the questions that come to mind in the process of planning, organizing, controlling, and monitoring your financial resources to achieve your personal financial goals include: Why do I own what I have? How much comes in? How frequently? How much has to go out? When exactly? How much can be put aside? What can I do with what is put aside? Where should I keep it? For how long? To what end?

On the other side of the ledger, behavior toward money is shaped by a combination of psychological factors, personal experiences, and societal influences. Individuals often develop distinct money habits based on their upbringing, cultural background, and level of financial literacy. For instance, someone who grew up in a household that emphasized saving and frugality might exhibit cautious spending habits and prioritize building an emergency fund. This has been my experience, as with so many with an African upbringing, similar of course to Asian cultures, with their famed high propensity to save. In this case, future security is an ever-present thought, as long periods of historical economic uncertainties and limited social safety nets practically force frugality.

Conversely, those raised in environments where money was freely spent might have a more relaxed attitude toward saving and be more prone to impulsive purchases. Psychological aspects such as risk tolerance, emotional responses to financial stress, and the perceived value of material possessions may cause relative degrees of this approach to emerge. Many Western (particularly American) societies are, rightly or wrongly, associated with this behavioral manifestation. Social norms and media typically promote a consumer culture where success and happiness are equated with material wealth and consumption, sometimes leading individuals to prioritize spending on luxury items, even at the expense of financial stability.

I will not argue in favor of either approach, as it has not been determinative of a society's relative standard of living. I have, however, noted how in a very religious society like Nigeria, money often gets a bad name, which affects how people relate to it. Many Nigerians of the Christian faith have grown familiar with 1 Timothy 6:10, which states, "For the love of money is the root of all evil." This passage has significantly shaped how people perceive money, often casting it in a negative light when pursued excessively. This verse suggests that an inordinate desire for wealth can lead individuals down a path of moral compromise and spiritual destruction.

Throughout history, this idea has influenced societal attitudes, with many viewing money as a potential source of corruption and unethical behavior. Others in secular circles have viewed it as a critique of capitalism and the relentless pursuit of financial gain. The verse has been frequently cited in religious and philosophical discussions to emphasize the dangers of greed and highlight the potential ethical pitfalls associated with the pursuit of wealth.

However, Ecclesiastes 7:12 offers a contrasting yet complementary perspective: "Wisdom is a defense as money is a defense, but the advantage of knowledge is this: Wisdom preserves those who have it." This verse acknowledges the practical value of money, likening it to wisdom as a protective force in life. It suggests that money, when used wisely, can provide security and stability, much like wisdom itself. Rather than condemning money outright, Ecclesiastes 7:12 therefore encourages a balanced view, recognizing money's potential to be a positive force when coupled with wisdom and ethical consideration.

My view is that money, in itself, is neither inherently good nor evil. The good book does not condemn money itself but rather the love of money – the excessive desire or obsession with it – as the root of evil. Money is a tool that can be used for various purposes depending on the intentions behind it. One should hold a more balanced approach to wealth, valuing contentment and generosity rather than the accumulation of riches at any cost. While 1 Timothy 6:10 rightly warns against the dangers of loving money to the point of moral decay, Ecclesiastes 7:12 reminds us that money can also be a valuable resource for an individual or a society when managed with wisdom. People should approach wealth with a sense of responsibility, using it to create shelter and stability in their lives while ensuring that their pursuit of money is guided by wisdom and ethical principles.

The value of capital markets

In societies where money is more readily available, numerous advantages emerge, fostering both individual prosperity and collective well-being. Greater access to financial resources enables people to invest in education, healthcare, and entrepreneurship, driving personal growth and economic development. These societies often experience higher levels of innovation and productivity, as people are empowered to pursue new ideas and ventures without the constraints of financial insecurity. Additionally, the availability of money facilitates a more vibrant and dynamic economy, where businesses can flourish, jobs are created, and consumer demand stimulates growth. Socially, the ease of financial transactions promotes inclusivity and equity, as more people can participate fully in the economy, reducing disparities and enhancing the quality of life for all. Ultimately, when money is accessible, it acts as a catalyst for a thriving society, where both individuals and communities have the means to achieve their full potential.

But what makes money more readily available both to individuals and businesses? How is a newly married couple in Oxford able to access a thirty-year mortgage for their first home, but a similarly young couple in Osogbo cannot get a home loan beyond five years? Assuming the aforementioned couple in Oxford borrows £500,000 over thirty years at a 6% fixed rate, they will pay just double the amount borrowed in total (including interest and principal) over the term of the mortgage. Contrast this with what the Osogbo household would face. If, by some miracle, they somehow get a ten-year mortgage, say, a tenth of what the Oxford couple borrowed – the naira equivalent of £50,000 – at prevailing interest rates around 35%, they would pay almost four times the amount borrowed (including interest and principal) in just ten years!

What enables Alstom SA to raise a very affordable €700 million seven-year bond to modernize the rail network in the Netherlands?[18] Alstom often accesses long-term money to implement its projects across the Netherlands, including supplying high-speed trains and tram systems, and the implementation of sustainable, innovative rail technologies that enhance the efficiency and connectivity of the Dutch transportation network. This not only supports economic growth by improving logistics and commuting options, but it also raises the quality of life for people in the country. Why is it not even an option for the government of South Sudan to access long-term capital to finance critical infrastructure?

Over the course of my career, I have become

convinced by empirical evidence that the great differentiator between societies that work and those that do not, between countries with high standards of living and those in desperate want, are well-functioning capital markets. Especially world class capital markets, which, if properly regulated, support businesses to grow, accelerate wealth creation, enhance people's living standards, engender good governance, and ultimately catalyze national transformation.

Individuals in countries with advanced capital markets, such as the United States or the United Kingdom, enjoy access to a wide range of investment opportunities. They can invest in a variety of financial instruments, including stocks, bonds, mutual funds, and exchange-traded funds (ETFs). These markets also offer access to global investments, allowing individuals to diversify their portfolios and mitigate risk. For example, an American can easily invest in international stocks or bonds through platforms such as Vanguard or Charles Schwab, benefiting from diversified global economic growth and reducing reliance on domestic markets.

In contrast, individuals in countries with underdeveloped capital markets, such as many in Africa, often have limited investment options. They might only have access to local stocks and government bonds, with fewer opportunities for diversification. The lack of sophisticated financial products and platforms means these investors are more exposed to local economic fluctuations and less able to take advantage of global growth opportunities. For example, a Cameroonian might struggle to invest in foreign markets due to regulatory barriers and a lack of accessible investment platforms.

Undoubtedly, individuals in countries with deep, world class capital markets enjoy significant advantages over those in countries with less sophisticated markets. They have access to a broad range of investment opportunities, which allows for better diversification and risk management. Their wealth accumulation and retirement planning are more robust due to a variety of financial products and tax-advantaged accounts. Moreover, they benefit from greater financial stability and economic resilience, supported by advanced market mechanisms and regulatory frameworks. These contrasts highlight the critical role that well-developed capital markets play in enhancing individual financial well-being and economic security. The leadership required to help such disadvantaged countries build robust capital markets is the gist of this book.

3
Capital Markets Within The Financial Ecosystem

"Capital is that part of wealth which is devoted to
obtaining further wealth."
— Alfred Marshall

A strong financial ecosystem is crucial for a prosperous nation. When people have access to reliable
and innovative financial services, including opportunities for investment and the resources needed to innovate and grow, they contribute to their nation's growing
prosperity. This, in turn, creates a virtuous cycle where
the economy grows, social mobility increases, and the
quality of life improves for the vast majority. A prosperous nation is often characterized by more than just
wealth or high gross domestic product (GDP) figures. It
is a place where the average person feels secure in their
ability to meet daily needs – such as access to nutritious

food, decent shelter, and reliable healthcare – while also having an environment that fosters opportunities to grow and improve their quality of life. In prosperous nations, citizens not only survive, but thrive, supported by peace, stability, and the assurance that they can aspire to more: better education, rewarding careers, and the chance to provide a higher standard of living for their families. Prosperity is intertwined with societal well-being, where people feel empowered, free from extreme poverty, and confident in their future.

Studies show that these attributes of a prosperous nation – peace, security, and macroeconomic stability – are essential in creating an environment conducive to individual well-being. Research from the Legatum Prosperity Index highlights how countries with strong safety and security metrics, such as Norway or New Zealand, consistently rank high in terms of prosperity.[19] This stability allows people to focus on long-term goals, such as education or entrepreneurship, rather than just surviving the day-to-day, as is often the case in countries experiencing high rates of physical insecurity. When citizens can invest time and resources in improving themselves and their surroundings, the nation as a whole benefits from their contributions to innovation, productivity, and social cohesion.

In prosperous nations, daily life often revolves around opportunities for personal and professional growth. On a typical day in Denmark, one of the world's most prosperous countries, a professional might start their morning by cycling to work, knowing that their healthcare needs are covered, regardless of their financial situation. After a productive day in a work environment that prioritizes work-life balance, they may spend their evening in a well-maintained public park or at a cultural event, accessible to all due to inclusive public policies. This routine reflects a key aspect of prosperous societies – accessible and equitable systems that empower people to live fulfilling lives. Denmark's robust social welfare system and strong financial ecosystem are fundamental to making this everyday prosperity possible.

Undergirding this prosperity is a robust, well-regulated financial ecosystem that nurtures both individuals and businesses. Bank regulation, typically overseen by the central bank, tends to involve fewer players and is primarily focused on ensuring that banks meet strict quantitative requirements related to capital adequacy, liquidity, and risk management. These measures aim to maintain the stability of the financial system by safeguarding depositors' funds and preventing bank failures. On the other hand, regulation of capital markets is more diversified and oriented toward market conduct. With a wide range of participants – including investment firms, traders, as well as retail and institutional investors – capital market regulation focuses on transparency, fairness, and ethical behavior to ensure the smooth functioning of these markets. Unlike the more centralized control over banking institutions, capital market regulation involves multiple bodies and is designed to protect investors and maintain the integrity of trading activities in an open and competitive environment.

A strong banking system providing predominantly short-term funds, for instance, ensures that citizens have access to credit, savings, and financial services, allowing them to plan and invest in their future. Banking transactions are typically conducted in a bilateral manner, where banks engage directly with their customers to offer personalized, over-the-counter services that cater to individual financial needs, such as tailored loan options, savings plans, and investment advice, fostering a relationship that blends convenience with customized financial solutions.

In turn, capital markets play a critical role in allocating resources efficiently across the economy, providing businesses with the longer-term funds needed to grow, innovate, and hire more workers. In nations with well-functioning capital markets, such as the United States or the United Kingdom, individuals and firms can rely on a transparent and competitive system that supports long-term growth and stability. Unlike the banks, capital markets are inherently multilateral, involving the buying and selling of tradable securities such as stocks and bonds between multiple parties, including investors, financial institutions, and intermediaries, all functioning within a complex, transparent system that facilitates the efficient allocation of capital and resources across the economy.

Venture capital (VC) and angel investors further contribute to the prosperity of advanced economies. These forms of financing enable entrepreneurs to turn innovative ideas into thriving businesses. According to the National Venture Capital Association, venture-backed companies have historically been responsible for significant job creation and innovation in the United States, for example.[20]

In addition to fostering innovation, a strong financial ecosystem supports macroeconomic stability, which is critical for long-term prosperity. A well-regulated banking system mitigates financial risks, reducing the likelihood of economic crises that can throw millions of people into hardship. The International Monetary Fund (IMF) notes that countries with resilient banking systems are better equipped to withstand shocks, such as the 2008 global financial crisis.[21] In prosperous nations, financial institutions operate within a framework that promotes transparency, trust, and accountability, helping to protect both the economy and the people from systemic risks.

Capital markets also play a pivotal role in attracting foreign investment, which can further boost national prosperity. For instance, Singapore has become a global financial hub partly due to its well-regulated capital markets. Investors from around the world are drawn to Singapore's stable economy and transparent financial systems, bringing in capital that supports infrastructure projects, innovation, and overall economic development. As a result, Singapore's citizens benefit from high living standards, world class healthcare, and an educational system that prepares them for the future. In short, by democratizing access to capital and finance, a strong financial ecosystem ensures that this prosperity is inclusive, ensuring that opportunities are widely available as people and organizations interact freely.

Understanding capital

The free enterprise system is often called "capitalism," a word sometimes used pejoratively. Yet, regardless of one's view of the merits or demerits of a market-led economy, it is hard to argue against the central role of capital within that system. In classical economics, capital is only one of the four factors of production – alongside land, labor, and entrepreneurship – used to produce goods and services. The concept of the factors of production has evolved significantly throughout the history of economic thought, reflecting the changing priorities and understanding of what drives economic growth.

In classical economics, the factors of production did not include entrepreneurship, and were traditionally defined as land, labor, and capital. These were seen as the primary resources necessary for producing goods and services, with land representing natural resources, labor embodying human effort, and capital encompassing tools, machinery, and buildings. Classical economists including Adam Smith, often considered the father of modern economics, and David Ricardo emphasized the role of these factors in determining a nation's wealth, with particular focus on land and labor as the foundations of economic activity.

As economic theory advanced into the nineteenth and early twentieth centuries, understanding of the factors of production expanded with the rise of neoclassical economics. Scholars such as French classical economist Jean-Baptiste Say and English neoclassical economist Alfred Marshall introduced the concept of "enterprise" or "entrepreneurship" as a fourth factor of production, highlighting the role of entrepreneurs in organizing land, labor, and capital to create value.[22] This shift acknowledged the importance of innovation, risk-taking, and decision-making in driving economic progress, moving beyond the more static view of production held by earlier classical economists.

Alfred Marshall succinctly describes capital as a portion of existing wealth that is invested to further grow wealth.[23] Naturally, this encompasses much more than just money. Capital has also been broadly defined as "anything that confers value or benefit to its owners, such as a factory and its machinery, intellectual property like patents, or the financial assets of a business or an individual."[24] I simply view capital as long-term money.

The evolution of the concept of capital in economic thought reflects the changing priorities and understandings of different eras. Adam Smith viewed capital primarily as a stock of wealth used in the production of goods and services. In his seminal work *The Wealth of Nations* (1776), he emphasized the importance of capital accumulation as a driver of economic growth, arguing that the division of labor and increased productivity depended on the availability of capital to finance these activities.[25] Smith's focus was on capital as a critical ingredient in the wealth creation process, laying the foundation for classical economic thought.

Karl Marx, writing in the nineteenth century, took a more critical view of capital, seeing it not just as a resource for production but as a social relation embedded in the capitalist system. In *Das Kapital* (1867), Marx argued that capital was the product of labor exploitation, where the capitalist class appropriated the surplus value generated by workers.[26] For Marx, capital was not merely a physical stock of goods or money, but a dynamic force that perpetuated inequality and alienation within society. His analysis highlighted the conflicts inherent in capitalism, where the accumulation of capital by the bourgeoisie came at the expense of the proletariat. Marx's view marked a significant departure from classical economics, emphasizing the social and political implications of capital.

In the twentieth century and beyond, economists continued to refine and expand upon the concept of capital. John Maynard Keynes, for instance, emphasized the role of capital in determining aggregate demand and its impact on economic cycles, focusing on the importance of investment in driving economic activity.[27] More recently, economists such as Thomas Piketty have revisited the issue of capital in the context of inequality. In his influential work *Capital in the Twenty-First Century* (2013), Piketty argues that the concentration of wealth and capital in the hands of a few is leading to increased inequality, echoing some of Marx's concerns but with a modern empirical approach.[28] Piketty's work underscores the enduring relevance of capital as a central concept in economics, with its implications for both growth and equity continuing to be a subject of intense debate among economists today.

Capital is far from a mere theoretical construct in

economics; it is a tangible and powerful force that shapes the realities of businesses, governments, and individuals alike. For businesses, capital represents the lifeblood that fuels operations, enabling investment in innovation, expansion, job creation, and the day-to-day functioning necessary to compete in the marketplace. Governments rely on capital to fund infrastructure projects, provide critical public services, stimulate economic growth, and sustain the prosperity and stability of a nation. For individuals, capital is a source of security and opportunity, allowing for the accumulation of wealth, investment in education, and the pursuit of entrepreneurial ventures. Whether through the financing of a new business, the construction of public works, or the savings that safeguard a family's future, capital is a fundamental reality that drives economic activity, underpins social stability, and enables the pursuit of human aspirations.

Capital market definitions

Capital can originate from a variety of sources, including personal savings, contributions from friends and family, angel investors, venture capital, corporations, government entities, financial institutions, business operations, and both private and public investors. Capital markets serve as a sophisticated mechanism that integrates these diverse sources and participants, effectively linking those in need of capital with those possessing surplus funds to invest through various financial instruments.

The complexity of capital markets makes them difficult to define precisely, and even more challenging to fully understand in their entirety. Despite my extensive experience – ranging from an analyst role on the buy side, to serving as the head of a major regulatory body and as Group Treasurer for leading multilateral development institutions – I still find it challenging to adhere to a singular definition of capital markets.

Some limit the definition to the venues and platforms commonly associated with the most visible form of capital markets – the stock market. For example, the Corporate Finance Institute defines capital markets as "the exchange system platform that transfers capital from investors who want to employ their excess capital to businesses that require the capital to finance various projects or investments."[29] Similarly, Investopedia describes capital markets as:

> "... the in-person and digital spaces in which various entities trade different types of financial instruments. These venues may include the stock market, the bond market, and the currency and foreign exchange (forex) markets. Most markets are concentrated in major financial centers such as New York, London, Singapore, and Hong Kong."[30]

Others define capital markets around the types of instruments they offer. The Federal Reserve Bank of St. Louis defines capital markets as "financial markets that bring buyers and sellers together to trade stocks, bonds, currencies, and other financial assets. Capital markets include the stock market and the bond market. They help people with ideas become entrepreneurs and help small businesses grow into big companies."[31],[32] I particularly like the definition given by New York-based data analytics company LexisNexis, which puts it simply as "the market for medium- and long-term securities."[33] This definition clearly delineates capital markets from other parts of the financial market that facilitate trade in short-term securities (maturing in less than one year), such as foreign exchange and money market products.

Stocks

Stocks are financial instruments that represent ownership shares in a company, traded within the capital markets. In fact, in much of the world, stocks are simply called "shares." Investopedia defines stocks as a security that represents the ownership of a fraction of the issuing corporation. When an individual or institution purchases a stock, they acquire a portion of the company's equity, entitling them to a share of its profits and, potentially, voting rights in corporate decisions. They become shareholders, or stockholders. Stocks are pivotal products in the capital market, facilitating the raising of capital by companies and providing investors with opportunities to benefit from the company's growth and performance. The value of stocks fluctuates based on market conditions, company performance, and broader economic factors. This makes stocks a key component of investment portfolios and a critical element of financial markets.

Stocks capture the public's imagination more than any other element of the capital markets, largely because stock exchanges are highly visible symbols of economic vitality, frequently featured in news cycles and popular media. They represent a dynamic and accessible way for individuals to participate in the growth of the economy, often seen as a reliable vehicle for long-term wealth creation. This perception is particularly compelling in high-growth developing countries, where stock markets offer a pathway to capitalize on rapid economic expansion. Research underscores this connection, with a study published in the *Journal of Finance* demonstrating that, over extended periods, stock market returns closely align with the growth of a country's economy, validating the notion that investing in equities mirrors broader economic progress.[34] For investors in emerging markets, where economies can grow at accelerated rates, stocks not only provide an opportunity to capture substantial returns but also enable them to participate directly in the transformative growth of their nations. This alignment between equity returns and economic expansion highlights why stocks are a powerful tool for wealth creation, especially in regions poised for significant economic development.

Data from SIFMA and World Federation of Exchanges (WFE) show that global equity market capitalization was over US$115 trillion at the end of 2023, with the U.S. stock markets accounting for 42.6%. While China represented 9.5% of 2023 global equity market capitalization, and emerging markets, excluding China, make up only 7.3%.

Global Equity Market Capitalization in 2023
(Source: SIFMA, World Federation of Exchanges)

	US$ billion	Percentage of total
United States	48,979.4	42.6%
European Union	12,621.9	11.0%
China	10,935.8	9.5%
Emerging Markets	8,390.8	7.3%
Japan	6,149.2	5.3%
UK	3,096.0	2.7%
Australia	1,788.7	1.6%
Others	23,062.9	10.40%
Total	**115,024.8**	**90.3%**

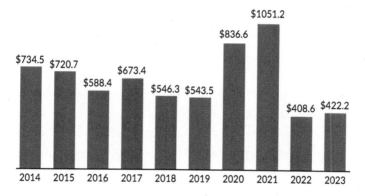

Global Equity Issuance (US$ billion) (Source: SIFMA)

The data also showed new issuances on the global equity markets have slowed down substantially to the lowest levels seen in the last ten years. In 2023, total global equity issuance was US$422 billion, slightly above the US$409 billion raised in 2022, well below half of the issuance high of US$1.05 trillion in 2021.

Bonds

Bonds are long-term fixed income instruments that represent a loan made by an investor to a borrower, typically a corporation or government, according to Investopedia.[35] The bond includes details such as the interest rate (coupon), the repayment date (maturity), and the principal amount to be repaid at maturity. Essentially, when an investor purchases a bond, they are lending money to the issuer in exchange for periodic interest payments and the return of the bond's face value at maturity. Bonds are a crucial part of the capital markets as they provide a predictable stream of income and are often used to diversify investment portfolios.

The global bond market, often used interchangeably with the global fixed income market, is pivotal to the financial system, with its immense size and impact on global financial flows. As of 2023, the global bond market was valued at approximately US$141 trillion, surpassing the equity market in scale and highlighting its importance in facilitating capital flow and investments worldwide (SIFMA, 2023).

Each year, the funds raised by governments and corporations from the fixed-income market dwarf the amounts raised from the stock market. In 2023, for example, more than US$20.4 trillion was raised from the fixed-income markets, over forty times the amount raised from the equity markets globally that year.

Global Fixed-Income Outstanding (2023)
(Source: SIFMA, Bank of International Settlements)

	US$ billion	Percentage of total
United States	55,298.8	39.3%
European Union	25,829.7	18.4%
China	22,913.5	16.3%
Emerging Markets	7,035.2	5.0%
Japan	11,495.7	8.2%
UK	5,841.0	4.2%
Australia	2,258.6	1.6%
Others	10,027.5	7.1%

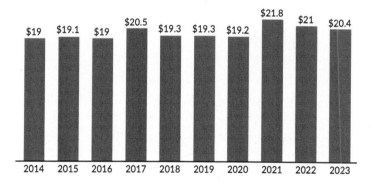

Global Long-Term Fixed-Income Issuance (US$ Trillion)
(Source: SIFMA, Bank for International Settlements)

In developing countries, local stock markets often show greater sophistication and liquidity than their bond markets, a trend well documented in empirical research. For instance, a World Bank study highlights that in many emerging economies, stock markets are more established and vibrant than bond markets due to historical underdevelopment and a narrower investor base for bonds.[36] Several factors contribute to this disparity: stock markets typically offer more accessible investment opportunities for a diverse range of investors, including retail participants, whereas bond markets are often limited by specialized requirements in these developing countries. Furthermore, challenges such as inadequate domestic savings, limited institutional involvement, and underdeveloped credit rating agencies impede the growth of bond markets in these regions.[37]

In contrast, developed markets tend to feature more advanced and liquid bond markets. In mature economies, such as the United States and the Eurozone, the bond markets are not only deeper but also more liquid than stock markets, reflecting a robust infrastructure and extensive regulatory frameworks that support bond issuance and trading. Research by the Bank for International Settlements (BIS) indicates that in these developed regions, bond markets are pivotal for financing, with institutional investors playing a significant role and a broader spectrum of bonds available for trading.[38] This comparative depth and liquidity in bond markets of developed economies underscore the stark difference in market maturity between developed and developing nations, as, historically, these advanced countries first developed bond markets before stock markets emerged.

History of capital markets

Early forms of capital markets can be traced back to ancient Mesopotamia and Greece, where agricultural loans and rudimentary forms of credit were in use. During the Roman Empire, the concept of "*societates*" allowed for public funding of large projects, resembling joint-stock companies. In many cases, that was how the impressive network of roads, amphitheaters, and water and sewer systems were accomplished. During the medieval period, the Italian city-states of Venice, Genoa, and Florence allowed merchant bankers to trade in government securities issued by the city-states to finance wars and public works, the earliest forms of fixed-income instruments. Additionally, medieval fairs, such as those in Champagne, France, served as important centers for trade and finance, laying the groundwork for more formalized exchanges.

The birth of modern capital markets can be traced to the establishment of the Amsterdam stock exchange in 1602 by the Dutch East India Company.[39] It was the first company to issue stocks and bonds to the public and allowed for the trading of these securities. It introduced many practices that are still in use today, such as market making and short selling. Almost a century later, the London Stock Exchange (LSE) would begin listing prices of a few commodities, such as salt, coal, paper, and exchange rates in 1698.[40] From its humble beginnings in the 1500s in coffee houses, the LSE started allowing merchants to trade stocks in 1773, already becoming the world's leading and first regulated exchange building. It benefited from the growth of the British Empire and its global trade networks. Meanwhile, on the other side of the Atlantic, a burgeoning exchange was emerging during the last decade of the 1700s with the signing of the famous Buttonwood Agreement by twenty-four stockbrokers. The New York Stock Exchange (NYSE) would quickly become a key player in global finance, especially with the rise of the American economy.[41] Progressively, the twentieth century saw the expansion of the NYSE and other regional exchanges, capturing the industrial growth of the United States.

Capital markets involve a complex system of primary and secondary markets, a variety of financial instruments, numerous participants (investors, issuers, intermediaries), regulatory bodies, and technology. These all combine to facilitate the efficient allocation of capital, liquidity, and investment opportunities, driving economic growth and development. The primary market is where new securities are issued and sold for the first time, offering companies and governments the platform to raise new capital. In this segment of the market, equity capital can be raised, for example, through initial public offerings, popularly known as IPOs. Likewise, debt capital, such as government bonds and corporate bonds, can be issued in this segment. Participants include issuers, which are typically companies and governmental entities; intermediaries, such as investment banks as underwriters or issuing houses; and investors, including institutional and retail investors. Issuers work with investment banks to underwrite and price the new securities. The securities are then sold to investors through initial offerings.

The secondary market is the venue where previously issued securities are bought and sold among investors. Unlike the primary market, where securities are initially issued and sold by companies or governments to raise capital, the secondary market facilitates the trading of these securities after they have been issued. This market provides liquidity, enabling investors to buy and sell securities after their initial issuance. Products traded in the secondary market include equities, exchange-traded funds, real estate investment trusts, fixed-income instruments, derivatives, and more. Participants in this market are diverse, ranging from individual investors and institutional investors, such as pension funds and mutual funds, to financial intermediaries such as brokers and dealers who facilitate transactions. Stock exchanges such as the New York Stock Exchange (NYSE) and Euronext are prominent examples of secondary markets.

Capital market products and participants

Exchange-Traded Funds (ETFs)

ETFs are investment funds that trade on stock exchanges, much like individual stocks, providing investors with a way to buy a diversified portfolio of assets in a single transaction. Unlike traditional mutual funds, which are only traded at the end of the trading day at a set price, ETFs offer real-time trading flexibility and are priced throughout the trading day based on market demand. The concept of ETFs was first introduced in the early 1990s, with the launch of the S&P 500 Index Trust (SPDR) in 1993, which was designed to track the performance of the S&P 500 Index.[42] This innovation revolutionized the investment landscape by combining the diversification benefits of mutual funds with the liquidity and trading convenience of individual stocks. Since then, the ETF market has expanded rapidly, with thousands of ETFs now available globally, covering a broad array of asset classes, sectors, and geographical regions. This growth reflects the increasing popularity of ETFs as a flexible, cost-effective tool for both individual and institutional investors seeking to implement various investment strategies.

Real Estate Investment Trusts (REITs)

REITs are companies that own, operate, or finance income-producing real estate across a range of property sectors, including residential, commercial, and industrial spaces. REITs provide investors with a way to invest in large-scale, diversified real estate portfolios without having to directly buy or manage properties. The concept of REITs was established by the U.S. Congress in 1960 with the passage of the REIT Act, designed to allow individual investors to benefit from real estate investments similarly to how mutual funds offer diversified stock portfolios.[43] This legislation created a framework for REITs to operate and required them to distribute at least 90% of their taxable income to shareholders in the form of dividends, thus offering a regular income stream to investors. Over time, the REIT model has evolved and expanded globally, with variations emerging in different countries. The structure has become increasingly sophisticated, incorporating diverse property types and investment strategies, and REITs have grown into a major asset class in the global financial markets, providing liquidity, transparency, and accessibility to real estate investments.

Derivatives

Derivatives are financial instruments whose value is derived from the performance of underlying assets, such as stocks, bonds, commodities, interest rates, or market indexes. The main types of derivatives include futures, options, swaps, and forwards. **Futures** are standardized contracts obligating the buyer to purchase, or the seller to sell, an asset at a predetermined price at a specified future date. **Options** give the holder the right, but not the obligation, to buy or sell an asset at a set price before a specific date. **Swaps** involve the exchange of cash flows or other financial instruments between parties, typically to manage interest rate or currency risk. **Forwards** are customized contracts between two parties to buy or sell an asset at a specified price on a future date, similar to futures but not traded on exchanges.

Derivatives are used for various purposes, including hedging risk, speculating on price movements, and enhancing investment returns. They are crucial for businesses and individuals to manage risk by providing a way to hedge against potential losses due to price fluctuations. American wheat farmers concerned about the possibility of wheat prices dropping by the time of harvest have ways to protect against this risk, for example by entering into a futures contract, a type of derivative, which locks in a price at which they will sell their wheat in the future. This ensures that, even if the market price falls, the farmer will still receive the agreed-upon price, thereby safeguarding their income. A corn farmer in Nigeria does not readily have this possibility.

Derivatives are most commonly traded in over-the-counter (OTC) markets, which are decentralized markets where financial instruments are traded directly between two parties without the supervision of an exchange. Unlike in exchanges, OTC transactions occur through a network of dealers and brokers who negotiate terms privately. This setup provides greater flexibility in terms of contract customization and the ability to trade a wider variety of assets. However, OTC markets often come with higher counterparty risk due to the lack of a central clearinghouse.[44] These markets are crucial for trading less-standardized financial products and for providing liquidity in markets that might not have enough volume to justify exchange trading.

Participants in the capital markets include retail and institutional investors, brokers and dealers, market makers, custodians, and the exchange platforms themselves, including their clearing and settlement systems.

Retail investors

Retail investors are individual investors who buy and sell securities for their personal accounts rather than for institutional purposes. Unlike institutional investors, who manage large sums of money on behalf of clients or organizations, retail investors typically invest small amounts of their own money. They participate in the capital markets to achieve personal financial goals, such as saving for retirement, education, or other long-term objectives. In advanced capital markets, retail investors have access to a wide range of financial products and trading platforms, allowing them to manage their investments directly or through financial advisers. As of 2023, retail investors accounted for approximately 25% of the equity trading volumes in the United States, a significant increase that began with a frenzy during the COVID-19 pandemic.[45] This surge has also been driven in part by the rise of online trading platforms, low-cost brokerage accounts, and increased access to financial information. Retail investors collectively control a substantial portion of the market, with some estimates suggesting they hold over US$23 trillion in assets, demonstrating their considerable influence on market dynamics and price movements.[46]

Recently, the impact of retail investors is particularly evident in the rise of "meme stocks" and other market phenomena, where coordinated buying by individual investors has led to significant price fluctuations in certain stocks. For example, in early 2021, retail investors were largely responsible for the dramatic price increase of GameStop, which saw its stock price surge by over 1,700% in a matter of weeks.[47] This event highlighted the power of retail investors to move markets, often in ways that differ from traditional institutional trading patterns.

Retail investors wield considerably more influence in the United States markets compared to their counterparts in Europe. European markets are more dominated by institutional investors, and retail investors have historically played a smaller role in equity trading. Cultural factors, less widespread adoption of online trading platforms, and differing financial market structures contribute to this difference. Consequently, while retail investors in Europe do participate in the markets, their influence on overall market dynamics is generally less pronounced than in the United States.

In Nigeria, retail investors ruled the market before the 2008 financial crisis. In 2007, retail investor participation on the Nigerian Stock Exchange (NSE, currently, Nigerian Exchange Group, NGX) was significantly higher, ranging between 60–70% of the total market transactions.[48] This period marked a boom in the Nigerian stock market, driven by high levels of enthusiasm among individual investors, fueled by a strong economic environment and high returns on investments. However, this high level of retail participation was dramatically reduced after the 2008 global financial crisis, which led to a market crash and a subsequent loss of confidence among retail investors. Current levels of participation hover around 35% in 2023, even higher than in the United States.[49]

Overall, the growing importance of retail investors underscores their role as a vital force in the markets, contributing to both market liquidity and the democratization of investment opportunities. Positively, their participation encourages financial innovation, leading to the development of new investment products and platforms, and they collectively influence corporate governance through shareholder voting rights. By actively buying and selling securities, retail investors help ensure the smooth functioning of markets and facilitate the capital-raising process for companies, ultimately supporting economic growth and development. Most regulators consider retail investors as key stakeholders in the market that must be protected because they often lack the sophisticated knowledge and resources of institutional investors.

Institutional investors

Institutional investors are large organizations that pool together substantial sums of money to invest in various financial markets and instruments. These entities include pension funds, mutual funds, insurance companies, hedge funds, endowment funds, and sovereign wealth funds. Institutional investors typically have significant resources, expertise, and access to detailed market information, allowing them to make large-scale investments and influence market trends. Their investment activities can span a wide range of asset classes, including stocks, bonds, real estate, and private equity. Due to their size and influence, institutional investors play a crucial role in the stability and efficiency of financial markets, often serving as key drivers of market liquidity and price discovery.

According to research by Boston Consulting Group, total assets under management (AUM) of institutional investors was over US$98 trillion in 2022, down by about US$10 trillion year-over-year.[50] These are led by BlackRock, with about US$10.5 trillion in AUM as of mid-2024, making it the world's largest asset manager.[51] Vanguard Group follows closely with around US$8.7 trillion in AUM, renowned for its dominance in index funds and ETFs.[52] Charles Schwab rounds out the top three, managing approximately US$7.3 trillion in assets.[53] In Nigeria, AUM is dominated by pension funds, which account for over 75% of the 24 trillion naira (approximately US$15 billion) under management.[54]

During the global financial crisis of 2008, large institutional investors such as Norway's Government Pension Fund Global (often referred to as the Norwegian Oil Fund) helped stabilize financial markets by continuing to invest in equities and bonds when many other investors were fleeing the markets. The fund's long-term investment horizon allowed it to weather the market volatility and contribute to market stabilization, demonstrating how institutional investors can provide a steadying influence in times of economic turmoil. In a separate area, the Canada Pension Plan Investment Board (CPPIB) has invested billions in infrastructure projects around the world, including toll roads, airports, and renewable energy facilities. These investments not only provide stable, long-term returns for the pension fund's beneficiaries, but also contribute to the development of critical infrastructure that supports economic activity and job creation in the regions where the projects are located.

Qualified investors

Qualified investors, also known as accredited or sophisticated investors, are individuals or entities that meet certain financial criteria, such as a high-net-worth, significant annual income, or substantial professional experience in financial markets. These investors are deemed by regulatory bodies to have the expertise, knowledge, and financial capacity to engage in more complex and higher-risk investment opportunities. In the United States, a qualified investor is defined by the U.S. SEC as an individual or entity having a net worth of over US$1 million (excluding the value of their primary residence), or an annual income exceeding US$200,000 (US$300,000 if combined with a spouse) for the past two years, with the expectation of maintaining the same income level.[55] Alternatively, entities such as banks, insurance companies, or trusts with assets exceeding US$5 million also qualify. In Europe, the concept is similarly defined under the Markets in Financial Instruments Directive (MiFID II), where qualified investors or professional clients are entities or individuals who possess the experience, knowledge, and expertise to make informed investment decisions and properly assess the risks involved.[56] These clients include large companies meeting specific size criteria, institutional investors, and individuals who opt to be treated as professionals, provided they meet certain conditions, such as having significant financial assets or a long history of active market participation.

Because of their financial sophistication, qualified investors have access to a wider range of investment products, including private equity, hedge funds, venture capital, and other unregistered securities that are not available to the general public. Their participation in these markets is critical, as they provide the capital and risk tolerance needed to fuel innovation, growth, and liquidity in various sectors of the economy. The importance of qualified investors to the global economy and financial markets cannot be overstated. These investors provide essential funding for startups, infrastructure projects, and other ventures that drive economic development. By taking on higher levels of risk, qualified investors enable the launch and expansion of businesses that might not receive traditional financing, promoting innovation and job creation. Additionally, their involvement in complex financial instruments and markets contributes to market efficiency and liquidity, helping to stabilize financial systems and promote economic growth.

Brokers and dealers

Brokers are intermediaries who facilitate transactions between buyers and sellers in financial markets. They act on behalf of clients to execute trades and earn a commission or fee for their services. Brokers can also provide advice, market analysis, and trade execution services. They help their clients (who can be retail or institutional) access various markets, including stocks, bonds, commodities, and derivatives. Dealers are individuals or firms that buy and sell financial instruments for their own accounts, acting as principals in transactions. They earn profit through the spread between the buying and selling prices (bid-ask spread). Dealers provide liquidity to the markets by being ready to buy and sell securities at any time. They often hold an inventory of securities and can facilitate large transactions. Some of the largest broker-dealers in the world are also among the biggest institutional investors, including JP Morgan, which serves 82 million customers,[57] including its banking clients; Vanguard, with more than 50 million active accounts;[58] Fidelity, also with 50 million;[59] and Charles Schwab, with more than 35.6 million active brokerage accounts.[60]

Market makers

Market makers are firms or individuals that actively quote two-sided markets in a particular security, providing both bid (buy) and ask (sell) prices, and standing ready to buy or sell at those publicly quoted prices. By being ready to buy and sell securities at any time, market makers ensure there is always a counterparty for traders, thus guaranteeing liquidity. Their continuous activity helps narrow bid-ask spreads and reduces price volatility, contributing to more stable and predictable markets. They also fulfill the orders of other market participants, enabling quicker execution of trades and reducing the time it takes to complete a transaction. Market makers earn profits primarily through the bid-ask spread, which is the difference between the price at which they buy a security (bid price) and the price at which they sell it (ask price). Large investment banks, specialized trading firms, and financial institutions often act as market makers on major stock exchanges and other trading platforms. Citadel Securities, one of the largest market makers globally, handles approximately 40% of all US-listed retail volume and more than 1.4 billion shares traded per day across equities, options, and fixed-income markets.[61] Some regulators have expressed concerns about the impact on pricing such a level of control by one market maker could have.[62] As with most things, competition almost always makes things better.

Custodians

Custodians are financial institutions that hold and protect securities and other assets on behalf of investors, ensuring their safety and proper management. Custodians store physical securities (such as stock certificates) and maintain electronic records of ownership, protecting assets from theft, loss, or damage. They facilitate the efficient transfer of securities and cash during trade settlements, ensuring transactions are completed accurately and on time. Importantly, they maintain detailed records of asset ownership, transaction histories, and account balances, providing transparency and accountability. They manage corporate actions such as dividend payments, interest payments, stock splits, and proxy voting on behalf of the asset owners. Custodians provide regular statements and reports to investors, ensuring compliance with regulatory requirements and providing valuable information for financial planning and tax purposes.

For international investors, custodians often offer services related to foreign exchange transactions, local market access, and compliance with local regulations. Prominent custodian banks include BNY Mellon with US$44 trillion assets under custody (AUC), Euroclear with US$31 trillion AUC, JPMorgan Chase with US$29 trillion AUC, State Street with US$37 trillion AUC, and Citibank with US$26 trillion AUC.[63] In the custody business, the separation of the safekeeping of assets from trading or dealing activities is crucial to mitigate potential conflicts of interest and ensure the security of client assets. Custodians are responsible for holding and safeguarding financial assets on behalf of their clients, which requires a high level of trust and impartiality. If a custodian were also involved in trading or dealing in the same securities they hold, it could create a conflict of interest. For instance, the custodian might have access to sensitive information about the securities they are holding, which could be improperly used to influence trading decisions or to benefit one client over another.

This separation of duties ensures that the custodian focuses solely on the safekeeping and administration of assets without any conflict that could arise from trading activities. It protects the integrity of the markets by ensuring that those who hold and manage assets do not have the ability to influence the market for their own gain. Moreover, it provides clients with confidence that their assets are held securely and are not at risk of being used for unauthorized transactions or subject to inappropriate trading practices. This clear delineation of responsibilities is a fundamental aspect of the trust placed in custodians by investors, and it helps maintain stability and transparency in the capital markets.

Fund/portfolio managers

Fund/portfolio managers oversee the investment activities of mutual funds, pension funds, hedge funds, and individual investment portfolios. Their primary responsibility is to manage and allocate assets in a way that aligns with the investment objectives and risk tolerance of their clients or fund mandates. This involves conducting thorough market research, analyzing financial statements, assessing economic trends, and using various financial models to make informed investment decisions. By diversifying investments across different asset classes, sectors, and geographies, fund and portfolio managers aim to optimize returns while minimizing risks. Their expertise and strategic insights are essential in navigating the complexities of the financial markets, making them vital to the success of the funds they manage. The importance of fund and portfolio managers extends beyond individual portfolios to the broader capital markets. They contribute to market efficiency by actively trading securities, which helps in price discovery and liquidity provision. Their investment activities can also influence corporate governance, as they often hold significant stakes in companies and can advocate for better management practices and strategic decisions. Additionally, fund and portfolio managers play a key role in capital formation by directing funds to various sectors, thus facilitating economic growth and development. Through their actions, they help maintain market stability and investor confidence, ensuring that capital markets function effectively and sustainably. Their decisions impact not only their clients' financial well-being but also the overall health of the financial ecosystem.

Rating agencies

Rating agencies provide independent assessments of the creditworthiness of issuers and their financial instruments, such as bonds and other debt securities. These agencies evaluate the financial health, business risks, and economic conditions of entities ranging from corporations to governments, assigning ratings that reflect their ability to meet financial obligations. The ratings range from high grades, indicating low risk of default, to low grades, signifying higher risk. For example, Moody's Investors Service uses a scale that ranges from Aaa, the highest rating indicating minimal credit risk, to C, the lowest rating indicating a high likelihood of default. The ratings are further divided into categories: investment grade (Aaa to Baa3) and speculative grade (Ba1 to C). Each major rating category (except for Aaa) has three sublevels (eg, Aa1, Aa2, Aa3) to provide more granularity in credit assessments.

These ratings help investors evaluate the relative risk of different investments and make informed decisions. Investors and other market participants rely on these ratings to make informed decisions about the risk and return profile of their investments, thereby influencing the cost of borrowing for issuers and the flow of capital within the markets. The importance of rating agencies extends to enhancing market transparency and stability. By providing standardized and widely recognized ratings, these agencies help reduce information asymmetry between issuers and investors, contributing to more efficient pricing of securities and better risk management. Their assessments facilitate the comparison of credit risk across different entities and instruments, aiding investors in diversifying their portfolios and managing risk effectively. Additionally, rating agencies play a crucial role in regulatory frameworks, as many financial regulations and investment guidelines are tied to credit ratings.

Auditors and accounting firms

Auditors and accounting firms play a pivotal role in the proper functioning of capital markets by ensuring the accuracy, transparency, and reliability of financial information. Their primary responsibility is to conduct independent assessments of companies' financial statements, verifying that they are presented fairly and in accordance with established accounting standards – Generally Accepted Accounting Principles (GAAP) in the United States, and International Financial Reporting Standards (IFRS) used by companies in more than 140 jurisdictions.[64] Financial statements are the cornerstone of transparency and comparability in the capital markets. These statements – comprising the balance sheet, income statement, and cash-flow statement – provide investors, analysts, and regulators with a consistent framework to evaluate a company's profitability, liquidity, and solvency. When reliably audited, they provide investors, regulators, and other stakeholders with confidence that the financial information disclosed by companies reflects their true financial position. Without the oversight provided by auditors, markets would be more susceptible to misinformation, fraud, and financial misstatements, all of which could undermine investor confidence and market stability.

Moreover, auditors serve as an essential check and balance within the corporate governance framework, helping to maintain trust in the system. By scrutinizing the internal controls and financial reporting processes of companies, auditors help to detect and prevent irregularities that could lead to financial scandals or significant losses for investors. This role is particularly crucial in complex markets, where the sheer volume of transactions and the complexity of financial instruments require a high level of oversight to ensure integrity and transparency. Auditors thus act as guardians of market fairness, ensuring that all participants have access to accurate and reliable financial information, which is the bedrock of informed decision-making in the capital markets.

Furthermore, accounting firms contribute to the health of capital markets by providing a range of advisory services that enhance the quality of financial reporting and corporate governance. These firms help companies adopt best practices in accounting, risk management, and compliance, ensuring that they meet regulatory requirements and maintain investor confidence. The expertise and guidance provided by accounting firms enable companies to navigate the increasingly complex financial landscape and reporting standards.

One of the unique features in Nigeria is that auditors and accounting firms operate under the regulatory oversight of the SEC, which plays a crucial role in ensuring the integrity and transparency of financial reporting in the capital markets. The SEC mandates that all public companies and entities seeking to raise capital in the Nigerian market adhere to stringent financial reporting standards, which must be audited by qualified and independent auditors. These auditors are required to be registered with the Financial Reporting Council of Nigeria (FRCN), and their activities are further registered as market participants in the capital market. The SEC's oversight is designed to safeguard the interests of investors and maintain confidence in the financial disclosures of publicly traded companies. Its regulatory purview extends to ensuring that auditors and accounting firms maintain high levels of professional competence and ethical standards, including the authority to enforce sanctions on auditors and accounting firms found to be in violation of regulatory requirements, such as engaging in unethical practices or failing to detect significant financial misstatements.

Underwriters

Underwriters facilitate the issuance of new securities, such as stocks and bonds, to investors. They assess the financial health and market potential of the issuing entity, determine the appropriate pricing of the securities, and commit to purchasing any unsold shares during the initial offering. This guarantees that the issuer will raise the desired amount of capital. Underwriters typically form syndicates to spread the risk associated with underwriting large issues.

By providing this assurance and expertise, underwriters help companies and governments efficiently access the capital needed for growth, expansion, or public projects. Underwriters help to maintain the stability and integrity of the capital markets by conducting thorough due diligence, ensuring that all disclosures in the offering documents are accurate and comply with regulatory requirements, thereby protecting investors from potential fraud and misinformation. Additionally, by setting fair and market-driven prices for new issues, underwriters facilitate liquidity and market confidence. Their role in vetting and supporting issuers contributes to investor trust, as underwriters' reputations are often built on the success and reliability of the offerings they manage.

Solicitors

Solicitors provide essential legal services that facilitate various capital market transactions and ensure regulatory compliance. Their responsibilities include drafting, reviewing, and negotiating a wide range of legal documents such as prospectuses, underwriting agreements, and regulatory filings. Solicitors work closely with issuers, underwriters, and regulatory bodies to ensure that all transactions, including IPOs, mergers and acquisitions, and bond issuances adhere to relevant laws and regulations. Their expertise helps navigate the complex legal landscape of the capital markets, mitigating legal risks and ensuring that all parties fulfill their legal obligations. This legal oversight is crucial in maintaining the integrity and smooth operation of financial transactions. The importance of solicitors in the capital markets cannot be overstated, as they contribute significantly to market stability and investor confidence. By ensuring legal compliance and protecting the interests of their clients, solicitors can help reduce legal disputes and financial misconduct. Their involvement in due-diligence processes ensures transparency and accuracy in the information disclosed to investors, which is vital for making informed investment decisions. Additionally, solicitors' advisory roles in corporate governance and regulatory changes support the implementation of best practices, fostering a fair and efficient market environment. Overall, solicitors' legal acumen and diligence are essential for the functioning and development of robust and trustworthy capital markets.

Exchanges and clearing houses

Exchanges are centralized platforms where securities, such as stocks, bonds, and other financial instruments, are bought and sold. They facilitate the trading process by providing a regulated and transparent environment that ensures fair pricing through the forces of supply and demand. Exchanges also play a crucial role in maintaining market integrity and investor confidence by enforcing rules and standards, offering price-discovery mechanisms, and ensuring liquidity by matching buyers and sellers efficiently. Additionally, they support the broader financial ecosystem by enabling companies to raise capital through the issuance of new securities and providing investors with opportunities to buy and sell assets. Examples of prominent exchanges include the NYSE, NASDAQ, LSE, Shanghai Stock Exchange (SSE), Euronext – a pan-European exchange with locations in Amsterdam, Brussels, Dublin, Lisbon, Milan, Oslo, and Paris – Japan Exchange Group (JPX), Hong Kong Stock Exchange (HKEX), Bombay Stock Exchange (BSE), and the Johannesburg Stock Exchange (JSE). Clearing and settlement houses serve as intermediaries that ensure the smooth and secure completion of trades between buyers and sellers. Their primary function is to manage the post-trade process, which includes confirming trade details, netting transactions to minimize the amount of cash and securities that need to be exchanged, and transferring the ownership of securities from the seller to the buyer. They mitigate counterparty risk by guaranteeing the performance of trades, meaning that even if one party defaults, the clearing house ensures that the transaction is completed. This process enhances market efficiency, reduces the risk of default, and maintains the integrity and stability of the financial system. Examples of prominent clearing and settlement houses include the Depository Trust & Clearing Corporation (DTCC) in the United States and Euroclear in Europe.

Issuing houses

Issuing houses play a crucial role in the capital market by acting as intermediaries between companies seeking to raise capital and potential investors. Their primary function is to assist companies in the issuance of new securities, whether through IPOs, secondary offerings, or private placements. This involves a wide range of activities, including advising on the timing and structure of the offering, preparing the necessary documentation, and ensuring compliance with regulatory requirements. Issuing houses also help determine the appropriate pricing of securities, conduct due diligence to verify the financial health and operational integrity of the issuing company, and market the securities to potential investors to generate sufficient interest and demand. Beyond these core functions, issuing houses also provide ongoing support to issuing companies post-issuance. This includes facilitating the listing of the securities on stock exchanges, managing investor relations, and assisting with any subsequent capital-raising activities. They may also offer strategic advice on mergers and acquisitions, restructuring, and other corporate finance matters. By performing these functions, issuing houses help to ensure that the process of raising capital is efficient, transparent, and successful, contributing to the overall stability and development of the capital market.

Atop both segments of the market are regulatory bodies, commonly starting with the platforms themselves serving as self-regulatory bodies, with all participants operating under the watchful oversight of an apex regulator such as the Securities and Exchange Commission (SEC) in Nigeria and the United States, the Financial Conduct Authority (FCA) in the United Kingdom, the Japan Financial Markets Council, or the European Securities and Markets Authority (ESMA) in the European Union. The function of these regulatory bodies is to ensure transparency, fairness, and investor protection by enforcing securities law, regulating market participants and exchanges, ensuring accurate and timely disclosure of information, and protecting investors from fraud or market manipulation.

Modern capital markets are interconnected, with securities traded across various international exchanges. Enabled by the adoption of increasingly sophisticated technology, global capital flows allow for cross-border investment and diversification, necessitating coordination among different regulatory regimes. As electronic trading becomes more widespread, algorithmic trading continues to expand, and blockchain and other forms of cryptocurrencies proliferate, regulators are more and more vigilant, aiming to maintain market integrity while fostering innovation.

4

Other Segments Of The Financial Ecosystem

"Credit is not only the reflection of a society's trust in its individuals, but also the cornerstone of a country's prosperity."
— John Stuart Mill, philosopher and economist

Banks serve as the primary conduit for the flow of money and credit in an economy. They accept deposits, provide loans, and offer payment services, facilitating everyday transactions and enabling businesses to expand by providing the necessary credit facilities. Banks serve as intermediaries between savers and borrowers, ensuring that funds are efficiently allocated to productive uses, fueling economic growth. By offering credit, banks enable businesses to invest in new projects, hire employees, and develop new products, all of which contribute to economic growth. For individuals, banks provide access to financial services, from savings accounts to mortgages, allowing them to manage their personal finances and plan for the future. On a global scale, the banking system is integral to the functioning of international trade and investment. Banks facilitate cross-border transactions, manage currency exchanges, and provide the financial infrastructure that supports global commerce.

When a bank provides a business with a line of credit, it allows the company to manage its cash flow more effectively, particularly during periods of uneven revenue or unexpected expenses. This access to revolving credit ensures that the business can meet its short-term obligations, such as payroll or supplier payments, without disruption. Additionally, banks offer term loans to finance major capital expenditures, such as purchasing new equipment, expanding operations, or acquiring another business. These loans are typically structured with fixed or variable interest rates and repayment terms that align with the business's cash flow, making it easier to invest in growth opportunities without compromising financial stability.

A bank facilitates trade by issuing letters of credit (LCs), which act as a financial guarantee to exporters that they will receive payment once they meet the terms outlined in the contract, such as delivering goods or services. The buyer's bank issues the LC, promising to pay the seller upon presentation of specific documents that prove the transaction's fulfillment, such as a bill of lading or an invoice. This process mitigates the risk for both the buyer and the seller, as the seller is assured of payment even if the buyer defaults, while the buyer knows payment will only be made once the agreed conditions are met. Letters of credit are particularly crucial in international trade, where trust and the enforcement of contracts can be challenging due to different legal systems and geographical distances.

Similarly, another banking product, bank guarantees, enhances trust and confidence in commercial transactions, particularly in situations where parties may be unfamiliar with each other. By providing a bank guarantee, the bank assures one party that the other will fulfill their contractual obligations, whether it be payment, delivery of goods, or completion of a project. This assurance reduces the risk of default, enabling businesses to engage in larger and more complex transactions, thus fostering economic growth. Additionally, bank guarantees support the financing of large infrastructure projects, encourage foreign investment by mitigating perceived risks, and facilitate smoother trade, all of which contribute to a more robust and dynamic economy.

Beyond traditional lending, banks also support businesses by offering a range of advisory services and financial products designed to enhance operational efficiency. For instance, banks can assist a company in managing foreign exchange risks through the use of hedging instruments, particularly if the business engages in international trade. By locking in exchange rates, the company can protect itself from adverse currency fluctuations that could impact profitability. Furthermore, banks provide businesses with merchant services, enabling them to accept credit and debit card payments, which is crucial in today's increasingly cashless economy. Additionally, banks offer payroll-processing and cash-management services, helping businesses streamline their financial operations and focus on their core activities. Through these services, banks not only provide the necessary capital but also act as strategic partners in a business's long-term success.

In the United States, businesses have traditionally relied more heavily on capital markets for their financing needs, particularly through the issuance of stocks and bonds, because their capital markets are among the largest, deepest, and most sophisticated in the world. By contrast, bank loans remain the predominant source of funding for firms in the European Union (EU). European banks often have close relationships with their corporate clients, offering not only loans but also advisory services and other financial products tailored to the specific needs of businesses. Equity market capitalization is only 81% of GDP in the EU compared with 227% in the United States, and the euro-area bond markets are three times smaller than in the United States. At the end of 2023, total banking assets in the United States nearly topped US$24 trillion, while it was well over US$37 trillion in the EU.[65],[66]

The reliance on capital markets is partly due to the well-established equity culture in the United States, where both institutional and retail investors actively participate in the stock market. Additionally, the regulatory environment, under the oversight of the U.S. SEC and other bodies, supports a transparent and efficient capital market system that drives down the cost of capital and encourages companies to raise capital through public offerings and other market-based instruments. As a result, businesses in the United States often favor issuing equity or debt securities to fund growth, expansion, and innovation.

European businesses, on the other hand, have traditionally been more reliant on bank financing as access to capital markets is more difficult, especially for small and medium-sized enterprises (SMEs), where capital markets are generally less developed and less liquid than those in the United States. However, recent trends, including efforts to develop a Capital Markets Union in the European Union, aim to shift some of this reliance toward capital markets, enabling more companies to tap into diverse sources of funding and reducing the economy's dependence on banks.

The interconnectedness of national banking systems means that they play a vital role in the stability of the global economy, as disruptions in one country can quickly ripple across borders. The 2008 global financial crisis demonstrated how vulnerabilities in the banking sector can have profound and far-reaching effects on the global economy.

Startup funding

There are various funding sources, each catering to different stages of a startup's growth. In the earliest stages, entrepreneurs often rely on personal savings, funds from family and friends, or angel investors. Angel investors are typically high-net-worth individuals who provide seed capital in exchange for equity, helping startups take their first steps without the constraints of traditional financing methods. This initial capital is essential for developing a prototype, conducting market research, building early traction, and laying the groundwork for future growth.

Beyond financial support, angel investors frequently bring valuable industry experience, mentorship, and networks to the startups they back, helping founders navigate the complexities of launching and growing a new business. Angel investors' willingness to take on the high risks associated with early-stage investments enables innovative ideas to flourish that might otherwise struggle to secure funding through traditional channels. This support is vital for fostering entrepreneurship, driving innovation, and contributing to the broader economy. According to data from Crunchbase, in 2023, angel investors supported startups with over US$30 billion in seed stage funding, down significantly from US$44 billion in 2022.[67]

As startups begin to gain traction and require more substantial funding to scale, venture capital (VC) firms become a vital component of the financial ecosystem. Venture capitalists invest in high-growth potential startups in exchange for equity, bringing not only financial resources but also valuable expertise, industry connections, and strategic guidance. VC funding often occurs in multiple rounds, such as Series A, B, and C, with each round designed to help the startup achieve specific milestones, whether it's expanding the team, entering new markets, or developing new products.

Series A funding is the first significant round of venture capital investment and is typically used to scale a startup's product or service after it has demonstrated some initial success. At this stage, the startup has usually established a user base and a revenue model, and the funds are often used to optimize the product, expand the team, and enter new markets. Series A rounds typically raise between US$2 million and US$15 million in the United States, but can be as small as US$25,000.[68] Series B funding is the next stage, focused on scaling the business further. This round is generally used to expand the company's market reach, enhance technology, and increase operational capacities. The startup at this point is likely generating significant revenue but needs additional resources to grow. In the United States, Series B rounds typically raise between US$10 million and US$50 million or more, and involve more established venture capital firms.[69] But again, in other parts of the world, these numbers are typically much smaller. Series C funding is aimed at scaling a company to new heights, such as entering new markets, acquiring other companies, or preparing for an IPO. Startups in this stage are usually well established, with strong revenue streams and proven business models. Series C rounds can raise tens to hundreds of millions of dollars, often involving not just venture capital firms but also hedge funds, private equity firms, and investment banks, reflecting the company's maturity and reduced investment risk.[70]

The involvement of reputable VC firms also lends credibility to startups, attracting further investment and facilitating partnerships that can accelerate growth. Another report from Crunchbase revealed that global startup investment in 2023 declined 38% to US$285 billion, down from the US$462 billion invested in 2022 – most of these raised by VCs.[71] Venture capital in the United States remains significantly more advanced than in Europe and other parts of the world, typically accounting for more than half of global amounts raised.

By allocating capital to innovative enterprises, venture capital facilitates technological advancements and economic productivity, creating massive amounts of wealth across the economy. As these startups mature, capital markets provide them with the access to further capital needed to sustain growth through IPOs. An IPO is a pivotal milestone for a company capable of launching a little-known startup into a globally known publicly traded powerhouse. This transition not only provides a company with substantial capital to fuel growth and innovation but also significantly enhances its visibility and credibility. By listing on a major stock exchange, a company gains access to a broader investor base and gains exposure to the global market, often elevating it from a relatively unknown startup to a recognized global brand.

Apple Inc had incredibly humble beginnings in 1976, when two friends, Steve Jobs and Steve Wozniak, came together with a shared passion for technology and innovation. Working out of Jobs' family garage, they built the first Apple computer – Apple I – using Wozniak's engineering prowess and Jobs' vision for bringing personal computing to the masses. With a modest capital of just US$1,300, mostly raised by Jobs selling his Volkswagen van and Wozniak parting with his beloved HP calculator, they launched what would become one of the most influential companies in the world. Their limited resources forced them to be resourceful, hand-assembling each circuit board and personally persuading local electronics stores to stock their creation. What started as a small venture with minimal capital quickly evolved into a revolution that would transform the technology landscape. Apple's IPO, just four years after its founding in 1980, raised US$110 million, valuing the company at US$1.8 billion.[72] These were unimaginably huge sums at the time, even if they seem trivial by today's standards.

In 2011, Apple became the most valuable company in the world with a market capitalization of US$340 billion.[73] It became the first company ever to reach a US$1 trillion valuation in mid-2018, followed by US$2 trillion in August 2020, becoming the first U.S. company to achieve this milestone.[74,75] As of August 2024, Apple's market capitalization was US$3.44 trillion, surpassing the combined GDP of the entire African continent.[76] Amazingly, Apple is only one of a number of American companies to have attained trillion-dollar valuations, alongside other tech giants such as Alphabet Inc, Amazon.com Inc, Microsoft Corp, Meta Platforms Inc, Tesla Inc, and Nvidia Corp, all of which were at some point lowly startups. A study by the National Venture Capital Association (NVCA) reveals that VC-backed companies have a substantial presence in major stock indices. Notably, as of 2021, over 60% of the companies in the NASDAQ-100 Index and a significant number in the S&P 500 were initially funded by venture capital.[77]

In addition to venture capital, other players, such as crowdfunding platforms, government grants, and corporate venture arms, contribute to the diversity of startup funding. Crowdfunding platforms, including Kickstarter and Indiegogo, allow startups to raise small amounts of capital from a large number of individuals, often in exchange for early access to products or other rewards. This approach not only provides funding but also helps validate the market demand for a startup's offering.

Within well-known ecosystems that foster startup growth, such as Silicon Valley in the United States, we have seen the emergence of incubators and accelerators providing startups with office space, resources, mentorship, and networking opportunities. They also help startups refine their business models, develop products, and connect with potential investors. We have also seen broader innovation hubs and technology parks that foster a collaborative environment where startups can interact with peers, potential customers, and investors. These hubs often have strong links to capital markets, facilitating easier access to funding. And as expected, capital markets connect startups with international investors, providing access to a global pool of capital. This can be particularly beneficial for startups with scalable business models that aim to expand internationally.

Government grants and subsidies, on the other hand, often target specific sectors such as technology or clean energy, providing nondilutive funding to startups that align with national economic or innovation goals. In France, Banque publique d'investissement (Bpifrance) is the French public investment bank that offers a range of subsidies, loans, and equity investments to startups.[78] One of its key programs is the French Tech Grant, which provides up to €30,000 for the development of innovative technology startups. Bpifrance also offers larger amounts of funding through co-investment with private investors and venture capital firms. For instance, the French startup Algolia, which specializes in search-as-a-service technology, received significant backing from Bpifrance, contributing to its global expansion and success.

Also, the Singaporean government, through its Startup SG initiative, provides substantial support to startups in the form of grants, equity financing, and mentorship. One of the flagship programs, Startup SG Founder, offers grants of up to SGD 50,000 to first-time entrepreneurs with innovative business ideas, matched with 1:3 by the founders, meaning that for every dollar the grant provides, the founders must contribute three dollars of their own funds or resources.[79] Additionally, the Startup SG Equity scheme co-invests with private sector investors in high-growth startups, particularly in deep-tech sectors. For example, the biotech startup Engine Biosciences received funding from Startup SG Equity, allowing it to advance its AI-driven drug discovery platform. In the United States, the Small Business Innovation Research (SBIR) program is a highly competitive initiative that provides early-stage funding to small businesses engaged in research and development (R&D) with the potential for commercialization. The program offers grants in phases, with initial phase I awards typically up to US$150,000 for feasibility studies, followed by phase II awards of up to US$1 million to support further development. A notable success story was Qualcomm, which received early SBIR funding in the 1980s, helping it become a global leader in telecommunications technology.

Similarly, corporate venture arms, which are investment branches of large companies, offer strategic investments that can lead to partnerships, acquisitions, or co-development opportunities. Among the most prominent is Google Ventures, which has made significant investments in companies including Uber, Slack, and Flatiron Health, helping to propel these startups into global leaders in their respective fields.[80] Another key player is Intel Capital, which has invested in over 1,500 companies, including prominent names such as VMware and DocuSign, driving innovation in cloud computing and digital transactions.[81] Salesforce Ventures, the venture arm of Salesforce, has been instrumental in advancing the software-as-a-service (SaaS) ecosystem with investments in companies such as Zoom and Twilio, both of which have become essential tools in the modern digital workplace.[82] These corporate venture arms not only provide capital but also offer strategic guidance, industry connections, and access to vast resources, making them vital partners in the startup ecosystem.

The ecosystem for startup funding is equally supported by a network of incubators, accelerators, and financial advisers who guide startups through the complex process of raising capital. Incubators and accelerators provide mentorship, office space, and early-stage funding in exchange for equity or fees, helping startups refine their business models, connect with investors, and prepare for scale. Financial advisers and consultants offer expertise in structuring deals, managing equity, and navigating legal and regulatory requirements, ensuring that startups are well-positioned for long-term success. Together, these elements create a robust ecosystem that nurtures innovation, drives economic growth, and enables startups to move from concept to market with the necessary financial support.

Interplay between segments of the financial ecosystem

When capital markets, banking, angel investors, VCs, government initiatives, and crowdfunding work in concert, they create the robust financial ecosystem that drives economic growth, wealth creation, and the overall prosperity of a society. Banks, insurance companies, and other institutional investors leverage capital markets to avoid asset-liability mismatch, which can occur when a financial institution's assets and liabilities have differing maturities and interest rate sensitivities, leading to potential liquidity and solvency risks. For example, if a bank uses short-term deposits (liabilities) to fund long-term loans (assets), it risks facing a scenario where it must repay depositors before it receives payments from its long-term loans. This mismatch can create liquidity issues if the bank cannot renew its short-term liabilities or if interest rates fluctuate, affecting the cost of liabilities more rapidly than the returns on assets.

Similarly, pension funds have long-term obligations to pay out benefits to retirees, which means their liabilities are generally predictable and extend over many years. Ideally, the assets that the pension fund holds should be chosen to match the timing, risk profile, and amount of these future liabilities. An asset-liability mismatch can occur if, for example, a pension fund invests heavily in short-term, volatile assets such as equities, which may not perform consistently or generate sufficient returns when liabilities come due. If the market value of these assets declines or if the timing of returns does not match the timing of liabilities, the fund may face a shortfall. This can result in the pension fund being unable to meet its obligations to retirees, potentially requiring additional contributions from the sponsoring employer or reducing the benefits paid to retirees.

Effective asset-liability management is crucial to mitigate these risks and ensure the institution's financial stability and operational efficiency, and capital markets offer the right type of long-term instruments to achieve this objective. This might involve investing in long-term bonds that match the duration of liabilities or using derivatives to hedge against interest rate fluctuations.

For companies and government institutions, capital markets can offer some advantages that a bank or even a syndicated loan among multiple banks cannot match. For example, bonds provide issuers with access to a broader pool of investors, potentially resulting in lower interest rates due to competition among investors.[83] They also allow for greater flexibility in structuring terms, such as fixed or variable interest rates and various maturities, tailored to the issuer's needs. Additionally, issuing bonds can enhance an issuer's public profile and credit rating, demonstrating financial stability and market confidence. Bond terms are often more favorable and less restrictive, with fewer covenants and requirements, allowing issuers more freedom in managing their operations and finances. Furthermore, bonds can be traded in secondary markets, providing liquidity for investors and potentially attracting a wider range of buyers.

In addition, VCs rely on both capital markets and banks to ensure the successful scaling and eventual exit of their investments. Capital markets are crucial for providing liquidity through IPOs, which allow VCs to exit their investments profitably by selling their equity stakes when the companies go public. Capital markets offer ongoing valuation benchmarks that help start-ups attract further funding and strategic partnerships. Banks play a complementary role by providing essential financial services such as loans, credit lines, and cash management, which help startups manage their working capital needs and fund day-to-day operations. Moreover, banks can offer bridge financing during periods of transition, such as when a startup is preparing for an IPO or other significant financial events. Together, capital markets and banks provide the financial infrastructure that supports the growth, stability, and ultimate success of venture-backed companies, thereby catalyzing wealth creation.

For wealth creation to be sustained, macroeconomic stability is crucial. Macroeconomic stability refers to a state in which a nation's economy operates without excessive volatility, characterized by steady growth, low inflation, manageable levels of unemployment, and a sustainable balance of payments. This stability is critical for creating a predictable economic environment, which fosters investor confidence and supports long-term planning by businesses and consumers. Research consistently highlights the importance of macroeconomic stability in driving economic growth and wealth creation. For instance, a study by the IMF demonstrates that stable macroeconomic conditions contribute significantly to sustained economic growth by reducing uncertainty and fostering a favorable investment climate.[84] In contrast, economies plagued by high inflation, volatile exchange rates, or fiscal imbalances often experience slower growth and reduced wealth accumulation, as instability undermines both consumer confidence and investor interest.

In his seminal paper published in 1970 on efficient capital markets, Eugene Fama reviewed various empirical studies to assess the validity of the Efficient Market Hypothesis, which posits that financial markets are "informationally efficient."[85] Beyond the subtleties of "weak form," "semi-strong form," and "strong form" efficiency, there is no debating the fact that no market within an economy aggregates and integrates as much information about the economy as do capital markets. This is why, for example, the stock market is sometimes termed "the barometer of the economy." This concept reflects the belief that the stock market's performance is indicative of the overall health and direction of the economy.

For example, rising stock prices may signal that businesses are expected to be profitable, consumer confidence is high, and economic growth is strong. Conversely, when the stock market is declining, it may indicate economic troubles, such as reduced business profits, lower consumer confidence, or an impending recession. This is certainly not a foolproof "barometer," as prominent American economist and Nobel laureate Paul Samuelson famously quipped, "The stock market has predicted nine of the last five recessions," highlighting the market's tendency to sometimes give false signals about the economy.[86] All things considered, capital markets influence consumer and investor sentiment because of the information they compile, both historical and prospective.

Capital markets enable the efficient pricing of securities based on supply and demand through the price-discovery process. Price discovery in capital markets is the process by which the market determines the

fair value of financial instruments through the interaction of supply and demand. In the context of bond
issuances, price discovery occurs during the underwriting process, where initial pricing is established based
on bids from institutional investors and market conditions. The final bond price reflects the consensus of
these bids, which incorporates factors such as interest
rates, credit risk, and the issuer's financial health. As
trading begins, the bond's market price may fluctuate based on new information and changes in market
sentiment, continuously adjusting to reflect the bond's
perceived value.

For stocks, price discovery happens through IPOs
and secondary market trading. During an IPO, the issuing company and underwriters set an initial price range
based on market research, investor demand, and financial metrics. This range is refined through a book-building process where institutional investors place orders,
influencing the final offering price. Once listed, stock
prices are determined by ongoing trading activities,
where buy and sell orders reflect investors' views
on the company's performance and market conditions. Empirical research supports the efficiency of this
process. For instance, a study by Roll, Schwartz, and
Subrahmanyam (2009) in the *Journal of Finance* demonstrates that price discovery in equity markets is highly
efficient, with prices rapidly incorporating available
information and aligning with fundamental values.[87]
Similarly, research by Jones, Lamont, and Lumsdaine
(1998) in the *Review of Financial Studies* shows that bond
prices adjust quickly to new information, highlighting

the effectiveness of the price-discovery mechanism in both equities and fixed-income markets.[88]

The interplay between monetary policy and macroeconomic stability is crucial for fostering economic growth and resilience, making central banks, who are typically in charge of monetary policy, important actors in the modern economy. Effective monetary policy aims to stabilize inflation, manage employment levels, and ensure sustainable economic growth, which in turn supports overall macroeconomic stability. According to research by the IMF, prudent monetary policy reduces economic uncertainty and enhances the investment climate, leading to a more stable macroeconomic environment.[89] Central banks depend on capital markets for the effectiveness of their monetary policy. Well-developed capital markets enable efficient pricing of financial assets and provide diverse funding sources for businesses and governments, contributing to economic resilience. For instance, a report by the Bank for International Settlements (BIS) underscores that mature capital markets enhance the effectiveness of monetary policy by providing a robust platform for interest rate transmission and liquidity management.[90] This mechanism ensures that monetary policy changes are rapidly reflected in market conditions, which helps stabilize inflation and support economic growth.

Furthermore, the sophistication of capital markets also supports macroeconomic stability by offering avenues for risk management and capital mobilization. Research by the World Bank indicates that countries with deeper and more sophisticated capital markets experience greater stability in times of economic stress, as these markets provide mechanisms for diversifying and managing risk, thus mitigating the impact of economic shocks.[91] The development of financial instruments such as government bonds, corporate securities, and derivatives allows for effective hedging and resource allocation, which contributes to a more stable economic environment. Undoubtedly, a well-developed financial ecosystem is an indispensable vehicle for sustainable economic growth that supports inclusive wealth creation.

5
The State Of The Nigerian Capital Market In 2010

"The greatest enemy of progress is not stagnation, but false progress."
— Sydney J. Harris

Nigeria had a budding capital market well before independence. The colonial government issued its first bond of about £300,000 in 1946 as part of a ten-year local loan plan, following which more was issued to finance public infrastructure projects, including an impressive network of narrow-gauge rail tracks linking the northern and southern protectorates.

As the then-young nation was gearing up for independence, the Broadcasting Corporation of Nigeria became the first Nigerian company to raise long-term money from the domestic bond market in 1960. A year later, an organized stock exchange was set up as the

Lagos Stock Exchange, which later became the Nigerian Stock Exchange (currently referred to as NGX) in 1977, as the need for a structured capital market became more pronounced to mobilize domestic savings and channel them into productive investments. The Lagos Stock Exchange began operations in 1961 with just nineteen securities listed.[92] During the 1960s, almost all of the country's savings were housed as deposits in the banking system with very limited capital market institutions. Wealthy households and knowledgeable Nigerians at this time would invest mostly on the London Stock Exchange, typically through London-based stockbrokers.

As the Lagos Stock Exchange gained popularity, more and more Nigerian retail investors began to invest some of their savings in the opportunities it availed them. Noticing that trend, the Lagos bourse savvily opened trading floors further south in the oil-rich city of Port Harcourt, and up inland in the fast-growing northwestern city of Kaduna. The domestic debt capital market did not fare as favorably as businesses relied heavily on banks and government rather focused on short-term treasury bills to fund budget shortfalls.

In the following decade, the Nigerian Enterprises Promotion Decree (also known as the Indigenization Decree) of 1972 and 1977 was introduced.[93] This policy required foreign companies to divest a portion of their holdings to Nigerians. This protectionist policy increased local participation in the stock market. The decree aimed to increase indigenous ownership of businesses and spur capital market activities by mandating listings on the stock exchange.

The 1980s and 1990s saw some modest growth and diversification of Nigeria's capital markets. Key developments during this era included the establishment of additional regulatory frameworks and institutions to support market operations. The Securities and Exchange Commission (SEC) was established in 1979 and restructured in 1988 to regulate the capital markets and protect investors.

The structural adjustment program (SAP), initiated in 1986 by the Nigerian government under the guidance of the International Monetary Fund (IMF) and World Bank, aimed at liberalizing and diversifying the economy.[94] The SAP encouraged the privatization of state-owned enterprises, many of which were subsequently listed on the stock exchange, increasing market capitalization and activity.

The turn of the millennium brought about appreciable technological advancements and reforms to further modernize Nigeria's capital markets. In 2000, the stock exchange introduced its automated trading system (ATS), replacing the traditional open outcry system and enhancing the efficiency and transparency of trade executions. Eight years prior, it had incorporated the Central Securities Clearing System (CSCS) as a subsidiary of the stock exchange with a mandate to provide automated clearing and settlement as well as act as the market's central depository. Apart from clearing, settlement, and delivery, the CSCS also provided custodial services. On commencement of operations in 1997, the CSCS settled and cleared trades on a T+5 settlement cycle. This was later improved to T+3 in March 2000.

In the early 2000s, the federal government declared plans for a restructured FGN bond issuance program, issuing 150 billion naira in 2003 alone, a first in over fourteen years.[95] In the four years that followed, the federal government would go on to raise more than 750 billion naira from the local bond market using papers of varying tenors ranging from three to ten years. This movement on the government bond side, however, did not trigger an expected burst of activity on the corporate bond market. In fact, there were only seven corporate bonds issued between 2000 and 2008.

Within a few years before I took the helm of affairs at the SEC, the Central Bank of Nigeria (CBN) had led banks through a series of recapitalization exercises. The banking sector recapitalization involved clear and stringent guidelines that mandated banks to increase their minimum capital base from 2 billion naira (only US$14 million at the time) to 25 billion naira (US$175 million). This drastic increase in capital requirements was strictly enforced and broadly considered successful, resulting in mergers and acquisitions that reduced the number of banks from eighty-nine to twenty-five.[96] The recapitalization effort was intended to create a more robust and resilient banking sector capable of withstanding financial shocks, advancing Nigeria's economic growth, and becoming global players.

Several banks successfully met the new requirements through mergers and strategic partnerships. For example, Access Bank acquired Marina International Bank and Capital Bank International, while United Bank for Africa (UBA) merged with Standard Trust Bank. Another prominent example was the consolidation of nine banks, including Afribank, Mainstreet Bank, and Omega Bank, into what became Skye Bank. These strategic moves allowed the banks to pool resources and expand their capital base and enhance their competitiveness both domestically and internationally. It is impressive how the Nigerian banking industry embraced this challenge in 2004, transforming themselves into globally relevant financial services institutions. Before the 2004 recapitalization exercise, no Nigerian bank made the top 1,000 banks in the world list compiled annually by *The Banker Magazine*. Shortly after the recapitalization, five Nigerian banks were consistently featured in the top 500 banks in the world list.[97] As of the first quarter of 2024, Nigerian banks are again gearing up to undergo another round of recapitalization, with minimum capital for some categories of banks expected to increase by as much as ten-fold.

As the banking sector recapitalization came to a close, the Nigerian capital market looked extremely promising. Standard & Poor's said the Nigerian equity market was the fastest growing among emerging markets in 2007.[98] That year, the stock exchange's all-share index increased a whopping 141%, market capitalization crossed the 8 trillion naira (US$ 65 billion) mark for the first time ever in July, and daily trading volumes increased fifty-fold.[99] On the primary market side, activities were ramping up. Between 2002 and 2007, the value of new equity issued increased at a compound annual growth rate of 87%.

Much of this was driven by the 2005 banking sector recapitalization. As banks rushed to meet the new minimum capital requirement, many opted to raise capital through equity offerings, especially IPOs and rights issues, leading to a sharp increase in the number of banking stocks listed on the stock exchange. Consequently, the banking sector's representation on the exchange became disproportionately large, with financial institutions making up a significant portion of the market capitalization. This heavy weighting meant that the performance of the Nigerian capital market became closely tied to the health and performance of the banking sector, increasing the overall market's vulnerability to sector-specific risks.

Moreover, the consolidation process resulted in fewer but larger banking entities dominating the stock exchange. This consolidation intensified concentration risk as the fortunes of the entire market were increasingly influenced by a handful of large banks. At a point, fifteen of the twenty most capitalized companies were banks, together accounting for almost 60% of total market capitalization. This meant that any adverse developments within these major banks, such as financial instability or operational challenges, could trigger substantial market volatility and impact investor sentiment broadly.

Already, several regulatory and risk-management failures were emerging, undermining the initial successes of the recapitalization effort. One of the key failures was the lack of robust regulatory oversight to ensure that the newly capitalized banks maintained prudent risk-management practices. Many banks, buoyed by their increased capital base, embarked on aggressive expansion and risky lending practices without adequate risk assessment. This included extensive exposure to the capital markets, where banks engaged in speculative trading and extended large, unsecured loans to stock market investors, inflating asset prices and stirring market bubbles.

To make matters worse, the regulatory framework at the time was insufficiently equipped to detect and mitigate these emerging risks. The CBN and other regulatory bodies did not implement effective supervision and enforcement mechanisms to monitor the banks' activities closely. Within the banks, emphasis on risk management and corporate governance did not evolve commensurately to support the fast growth. Invariably, the additional capital raised by the banks went into speculative lending to the oil and gas sector and unregulated margin finance to brokers and individual investors, which fueled an asset bubble. In some instances, banks engineered overvaluation of their stocks on the stock exchange before accessing the market for capital. Some were even financing the purchase of their own stock in the primary market to create a semblance of huge investor appetite for such stock through shell companies.

Other types of wrongdoing that were rife at the time include insider lending and deliberate flouting of internal controls. Additionally, there was a lack of comprehensive stress testing and risk-management protocols within the banks themselves, which meant they were ill-prepared to handle adverse economic conditions or market shocks. These vulnerabilities would soon be exposed, leading to significant levels of non-performing loans and liquidity crises among Nigerian banks. The aftermath saw several banks needing government intervention and bailouts, underscoring the critical need for stronger regulatory oversight and risk-management frameworks to ensure the long-term stability of the banking sector.

The global financial crisis

By March 2008, total market capitalization of listed companies in Nigeria had peaked at 12.65 trillion naira (US$85 billion). That same month in the United States, Bear Stearns, one of the leading investment banks in the country, collapsed, sending jitters around global financial markets. Almost exactly six months later, Lehman Brothers, another major investment bank, filed for bankruptcy due to its severe exposure to subprime mortgages and inability to secure fresh financing.[100] This event is often considered the tipping point of what would become the 2008 financial crisis. The Lehman Brothers affair on September 15, 2008, caused the biggest single-day sell-off on the U.S. stock markets since the September 11 attacks with a 4.5% one-day drop in the Dow Jones Industrial Average.[101]

Lehman Brothers, founded in 1847, was one of the

oldest and most respected financial institutions on Wall Street, with a storied history that spanned over 160 years. The firm began as a humble cotton-trading business in Montgomery, Alabama, before evolving into a global financial powerhouse, specializing in investment banking, equity, and fixed-income sales, trading, research, and investment management. Over the decades, Lehman Brothers became synonymous with stability, weathering numerous economic downturns and expanding its influence across international markets. By the early 2000s, the firm was considered one of the leading investment banks in the world, deeply entrenched in the fabric of the global financial system.

The sudden collapse of Lehman Brothers in September 2008 sent shockwaves throughout the financial world, as it was widely believed that the firm was "too big to fail." The bankruptcy filing, the largest in U.S. history at the time, was precipitated by Lehman's heavy exposure to the subprime mortgage market, which had turned toxic as the housing bubble burst. The firm's failure to secure a government bailout or a buyer in the final days before its collapse highlighted the severity of the financial crisis and marked a turning point that deepened the global recession. The downfall of such a venerable institution, seemingly overnight, shattered confidence in the financial system, leading to a cascade of market turmoil and economic instability that underscored the interconnectedness of modern global finance.

In the United States, subprime mortgages are home loans offered to borrowers with poor credit histories or limited financial resources, often at higher interest rates due to their inherently higher risk of default. During the early 2000s, these loans became widely available as part of a trend in the financial industry to extend credit to a broader range of consumers. Lenders, motivated by the booming housing market and the potential for high returns, increasingly issued subprime mortgages with adjustable rates that often started low but could skyrocket after a few years. These mortgages were then bundled into mortgage-backed securities (MBS) and sold to investors, including major financial institutions such as Lehman Brothers. The widespread issuance of subprime mortgages, coupled with the complex financial products derived from them, created a ticking time bomb within the global financial system.

Lehman Brothers played a significant role in this ecosystem, heavily investing in MBS and other financial products linked to subprime mortgages.[102] As housing prices began to plummet in 2007, the underlying value of these subprime mortgages collapsed, leading to massive defaults. The financial products that Lehman and others had created and traded so extensively became toxic, rapidly losing value and causing severe losses. Lehman Brothers found itself unable to cover the mounting losses, and its massive exposure to these high-risk assets precipitated its downfall. The firm's collapse underscored the dangers of excessive risk-taking and the profound vulnerabilities in the financial system, where the failure of a single institution could trigger a global economic crisis due to contagion risk. This risk is heightened in today's financial system, where markets are deeply integrated through cross-border investments, complex financial products, and multinational institutions, necessitating constant vigilance and cross-border cooperation by regulators.

Back in Nigeria, the stock market was in turmoil, experiencing a painful, unprecedented crash where it lost about 70% of its value by the end of that year, seeing US$50 billion of market capitalization wiped off.[103] This was overwhelmingly driven by foreign portfolio outflows as investors, spooked by the global uncertainty, sought to flee to safer assets. Data from the Nigerian Stock Exchange showed foreign portfolio outflows estimated at over US$15 billion by the end of 2008, further exacerbating the market correction and weighing on the CBN's reserves, compromising its capacity to defend the local currency. The flight of foreign investors, coupled with domestic panic-selling, created a vicious cycle of declining asset prices and reduced investor confidence, leading to the worst market crash in Nigerian history. Because retail investors in Nigeria make the bulk of their investments directly, unlike in the developed markets where investors invest through collective investment schemes, mutual funds, or other organized investment vehicles, investor confidence was decimated. It also precipitated other crises across the financial system, most prominently the banking crisis of 2008 that gave my colleagues at the CBN many a sleepless night.

Around the same time I was preparing for my transition to public service in Nigeria, the appointment of

Sanusi Lamido Sanusi as the Governor of the CBN was announced in June 2009. It came at a critical juncture during the global financial crisis, which had severely impacted Nigeria's banking sector. Sanusi, known for his reformist stance and deep understanding of banking risk management, was tasked with stabilizing the fragile system. He took quick actions aimed at enhancing transparency, strengthening regulatory oversight, and addressing the systemic risks that had been exposed. His decisive actions included the audit and recapitalization of troubled banks, the removal of their top executives, and the establishment of the Asset Management Corporation of Nigeria (AMCON) to manage nonperforming loans. Sanusi's leadership was pivotal in restoring confidence in the banking sector, promoting financial stability, and laying the groundwork for sustainable recovery.

I saw some of those early actions taken by the CBN and was preparing to complement these efforts with similarly decisive reforms in the capital market. Capital market development is often defined by the actions taken during or following a major crisis. The only example I can think of where significant reforms did not follow a major crisis is the 1636 Tulip Mania in the Dutch Republic. Tulip bulbs became highly sought after, with prices skyrocketing to extraordinary levels. As prices collapsed in February 1637, many investors suffered massive financial losses, demonstrating the dangers of speculative bubbles even within the relatively rudimentary financial systems of the time.

Perhaps with lessons learned from that experience, no major financial crisis thereafter was left without far-reaching reforms.

Indeed, less than a century after the Tulip Mania in Amsterdam, the South Sea Company, a British joint-stock company, saw its stock price soar based on inflated expectations of profits from trade in South America. The bubble would burst in late 1720, causing widespread financial ruin among investors. In response, the British government introduced the Bubble Act of 1720, which sought to regulate joint-stock companies and prevent speculative bubbles.[104] A further example, perhaps one of the most consequential, is the Great Crash of 1929 – the precursor of the Great Depression. In the United States, the stock market boom of the 1920s culminated in a speculative bubble fueled by margin trading and rampant speculation. On the orig-inal "Black Tuesday," on October 29, 1929, the mar-ket crashed, wiping out thousands of investors who lost billions of dollars. What reform followed? The Securities Act of 1933 and the Securities Exchange Act of 1934 established the U.S. SEC to oversee securities markets and protect investors.

Another example, and one to which I have a per-sonal and professional connection, is the already men-tioned 2008 global financial crisis. Many jurisdictions implemented reforms to address the weaknesses iden-tified during that crisis. In the United States, the Dodd-Frank Wall Street Reform and Consumer Protection Act of 2010 was introduced as a comprehensive financial regulation package aimed at reducing systemic risk, increasing transparency, and protecting consumers. Key provisions included the Volcker Rule, which restricted proprietary trading by banks, and the creation of the Consumer Financial Protection Bureau (CFPB).

6
Preparation

"The will to succeed is important, but what's more important is the will to prepare."
— Bobby Knight

As the crisis raged in Nigeria, some reforms were being considered. Unlike in the United States, such efforts were not led by parliament. It was left to the respective regulatory bodies of the financial system to determine the right course of action. At the SEC, a fifteen-person committee of capital market experts was established to conduct a review of the Nigerian capital market, assess its weaknesses, and recommend a five-year plan for addressing those weaknesses. The technical committee's work would later be articulated in a document titled "Making World Class a Reality," containing thirty-two recommendations linked to specific strategic initiatives covering six aspects of the market. I studied this document thoroughly before my return home to take up the challenge of leading the capital market community to implement these recommendations.

The recommendations mostly covered three prominent areas: strengthening market integrity to restore investor confidence, introducing products and unlocking domestic savings to enhance market depth, breadth, and liquidity, and lastly, reviewing the legal and regulatory framework, technology, and strengthening institutions with a view to increasing market sophistication. After studying this document, I was convinced that the committee of experts had rightly diagnosed the key challenges facing the Nigerian capital markets. I therefore felt it would be valuable to use the report as a basis for galvanizing alignment around actions that need to be taken.

Enabling the articulation of a shared vision is one of the most critical responsibilities of a leader. This vision must be a clear, compelling vision capable of serving as the foundation upon which all strategic initiatives are built and around which the whole team must align. By clearly defining the desired future state, leaders can inspire and motivate the team to move as one toward actualizing that shared objective. Once the vision is articulated, the next crucial step is to galvanize support for its execution. This involves not only gaining buy-in from key stakeholders but also actively engaging the entire team in the journey toward achieving the vision. I knew that to do this I would need to communicate consistently and transparently, reinforcing the vision and demonstrating how the contributions of each individual or group are essential to its realization. Perhaps it also did help that many people, rich and poor, had lost significant savings and welcomed a "Messiah," as someone described me, to rescue the market from the bottomless pit into which it was descending.

I admire Chinese philosophy for its often-rich insights in many areas of life, one of which is the wisdom in the Mandarin word for "crisis," *Wei Ji*, where *"Wei"* signifies crisis and *"Ji"* means opportunity. In the midst of a crisis within Nigeria's capital markets, I was determined for us to see it as an opportunity to transform the devastation into a foundation for world class capital markets. Challenges should be seen as catalysts for growth. Rather than succumbing to the instability that threatened the market, I saw the potential to innovate, reform, and strengthen the market. My challenge would be to use this volatile period to introduce reforms that not only restored confidence but also paved the way for long-term resilience and global competitiveness. By harnessing the opportunity hidden within the crisis, we would lay the groundwork for a capital market in Nigeria that could thrive even in the face of future challenges, creating a blueprint for sustainable growth and leadership in the global financial landscape.

By the time I assumed duty at the SEC in January 2010, this was the state of the Nigerian capital market I was coming home to lead. It was often described as rather unsophisticated, shallow, lacking breadth and highly concentrated. It had limited product offerings and less than impressive liquidity metrics. Transaction costs were too high and not competitive compared to other emerging markets. There was structural opacity as existing market infrastructure did not appear to support the real-time transmission of trading prices to international investors. In addition, there were significant limitations to the research on listed securities, industries, and markets, as well as frequent delays in the release of financial information to the market. Market institutions were weak and fragmented. There were significant deficits in the governing rules and regulations. Investor confidence was lost. And perhaps most worrisome, the market was under a dark cloud of uncertainty worsened by high-profile cases of manipulation and wrongdoing. It was a market operating far below its potential and incapable of unlocking the incredible benefits of world class capital markets.

Regulatory Framework as at December 31, 2009

Thankfully, I met a strong regulatory framework to work with, robust enough to enable the kind of reforms we were envisioning. A significant milestone in the building of that regulatory foundation was the Securities and Exchange Commission Decree No. 71 of 1979, which superseded the Capital Issues Commission in 1979, creating the SEC to oversee and regulate the Nigerian capital markets. The SEC's mandate included the regulation of securities issuance, market intermediaries, and trading practices.

The enactment of the Investment and Securities Act (ISA) in 1999 marked a pivotal moment in the history of capital markets regulation in Nigeria. The ISA provided a robust legal framework for the regulation of the Nigerian capital markets, addressing the shortcomings of previous regulatory regimes. It empowered the SEC with extensive authority to oversee all aspects of the securities industry as the apex regulator. It was to approve the issuance and trading of securities, the conduct of market participants, and the enforcement of compliance. The ISA also introduced stringent disclosure requirements, investor protection measures, and mechanisms for dispute resolution. Subsequent amendments to the ISA, particularly the Investment and Securities Act of 2007, further strengthened the regulatory framework, aligning it with international best practices.

Investor protection was a cardinal objective for the SEC under the enabling legislation. As part of its investor protection efforts, the SEC established the Investor Protection Fund (IPF) as a mechanism designed to safeguard investor interest and promote confidence in the Nigerian capital market. The fund was envisioned under the Investment and Securities Act (ISA) 2007 but it was in 2012 that we finally incorporated the fund with a starting size of 5 billion naira (US$32 million). The IPF aims to compensate investors who suffer financial losses due to the insolvency, bankruptcy, or negligence of capital market operators. The fund is

financed through contributions from market operators, fines, and penalties imposed by the SEC, ensuring
a robust pool of resources to address investor claims.
The IPF provides a safety net, encouraging greater participation in the capital markets by mitigating potential risks associated with investment activities. Payouts
from the IPF have been instrumental in compensating
investors for various losses, with notable cases including compensation for fraud, operational failures, and
other malpractices by licensed operators.

We simultaneously encouraged and supported
the stock exchange to set up its own investor protection fund designed to compensate investors for losses
arising from any negligence of its dealing members.
Around the world, other jurisdictions have established
similar investor protection funds to compensate investors for losses arising from the failure of regulated institutions, particularly in cases of fraud or insolvency.
Like our IPF, these funds are designed to maintain
investor confidence and stability in financial markets
by providing a safety net for retail investors. For example, in the United States, the Securities Investor Protection Corporation (SIPC) is one of the most well-known.
Starting from a size of US$150 million in 1970, the U.S.
SEC's SIPC has a current target size of US$5 billion. The
SIPC protects investors for up to US$500,000 in secu-
rities, including a US$250,000 limit for cash claims, in
the event a brokerage firm fails.[105]

In Europe, many countries have similar mechanisms
in place. The United Kingdom's Financial Services
Compensation Scheme (FSCS) is a prominent example,

offering protection for up to £85,000 per investor per firm.[106] The FSCS fund size is substantial, backed by levies on the financial services industry, and serves as a critical component of the UK's financial safety net. In Asia, Hong Kong's Investor Compensation Fund (ICF) provides up to HKD 150,000 per investor, with the fund managed by the Securities and Futures Commission (SFC).[107] These funds vary in size and scope depending on the jurisdiction, but all serve the vital role of protecting investors and maintaining trust in financial markets globally.

The legislation in Nigeria also provided for innovative dispute resolution mechanisms, one of which is the Administrative Proceedings Committee (APC) of the SEC. It is a vital component of the regulatory framework, established to handle violations of securities laws and regulations. The APC functions as a quasi-judicial body within the SEC, tasked with conducting hearings and making determinations on cases involving misconduct, noncompliance, and other infractions by market participants. The committee comprises SEC officials and legal experts who possess the necessary expertise to evaluate complex securities issues. During proceedings, the APC reviews evidence, hears testimonies from both the SEC and the accused parties, and ensures that the process adheres to principles of fairness and due process.

The APC employs a structured process designed to ensure transparency and accountability. Once a case is brought before the APC, a notice of hearing is issued to the concerned parties, outlining the allegations and scheduling the hearing date. During the hearings, both parties present their cases, including any relevant documents and witness testimonies. The APC then deliberates on the evidence presented, applies the relevant securities laws and regulations, and makes a determination. If a violation is established, the APC has the authority to impose sanctions, which can include fines, suspensions, or revocations of licenses, and other corrective measures.

As a Committee of the Board of SEC, APC recommendations are ratified by the full Board, who generally tend to accept the recommendations made. The decisions are binding, but aggrieved parties have the right to appeal to the Investment and Securities Tribunal (IST) if they are dissatisfied with the outcome. As head of the apex regulator, I presided over several APC proceedings, which I considered among my most solemn duties. I would ask probing questions of both the SEC, which was making the accusations, and the market participant, usually the defendant, aiming to establish the truth. As I conducted these proceedings in all seriousness, unknown to me, some of my staff had apparently nicknamed me "Judge Judy," in reference to Judith Sheindlin, the retired American family court judge and television personality best known for her long-running reality courtroom show of the same title. I was bemused to hear that, despite my obvious lack of formal legal training, I could be deemed to conduct quasi-judicial hearings as "masterfully as the famed American television judge."

Above the APC, the Investment and Securities

Tribunal, IST, is the most important dispute resolution body in the Nigerian capital market, serving as a specialized judicial body dedicated to resolving disputes arising from investments and securities transactions. The IST has jurisdiction over a wide range of issues, including disputes between capital market operators, investors, and regulatory authorities. It is required under law to promote the swift dispensation of justice, given a maximum of ninety days from the date of first filing to reach resolution on a case. Cases from the IST go straight to the appellate divisions of federal courts in Nigeria, bypassing the often-slow proceedings of the high courts. Judges of the IST are knowledgeable on investment and securities matters, and they are therefore able to conduct a more focused and expedited resolution process compared to conventional courts.

Additionally, the ISA also encourages the use of other alternative dispute resolution (ADR) methods, such as mediation and arbitration, to settle conflicts amicably. The SEC plays a crucial role in facilitating ADR by providing guidelines and support for the mediation and arbitration processes. This approach not only helps to decongest the tribunal and court systems but also offers a more flexible, cost-effective, and less adversarial means of resolving disputes.

The ISA strengthens the independence of the SEC by ensuring its operational and financial autonomy. In a way, this gives the Nigerian SEC even more financial autonomy than the U.S. SEC, which must go through the federal appropriations process for its annual operating budget, even though it also collects registration fees that exceed its appropriations. The U.S. SEC must remit these fees to the treasury and will rely on disbursements to fund its budget. In the SEC's case, the ISA requires the SEC to collect and keep these fees to fund its operations. Surpluses at the end of a fiscal year can then be paid into the treasury. The financial independence provided by the ISA empowers the SEC to make decisions based on regulatory priorities rather than financial constraints, fostering a regulatory environment that is both robust and credible. This autonomy is crucial for the SEC to effectively monitor, regulate, and develop Nigeria's capital markets, ensuring they operate transparently, efficiently, and in the best interests of investors.

Strengthening the enforcement powers of SEC

It is when it comes to enforcement capacity that the ISA falls slightly short. In the United States, the U.S. SEC has the authority to prosecute civil offenses associated with the securities laws. For civil enforcement, the U.S. SEC can bring actions in federal court or through administrative proceedings, seeking remedies such as injunctions, disgorgement of ill-gotten gains, monetary penalties, and bans. The U.S. SEC does not have criminal prosecutorial power, so it structurally works with the Department of Justice to seamlessly refer cases that involve willful violations of securities laws for criminal prosecution. This collaboration allows for offenders to face criminal charges, which can result in imprisonment and substantial fines, thereby providing a strong deterrent against securities fraud and misconduct.

In Nigeria, that level of collaboration did not exist for criminally prosecuting securities market offenses. I knew that, in order to give teeth to our enforcement actions, we needed to establish close collaboration with the law enforcement, particularly the Nigeria Police Force and the department of public prosecutions of the Federal Ministry of Justice.

We negotiated directly with the Inspector-General of Police to send some of his brightest officers to the SEC to staff a resident police desk at our offices. In April 2010, he sent us eighteen of his best men and women, who were very eager to help us respond to enforcement matters speedily and promptly. We immediately referred 437 cases with criminal elements to the police desk for further investigation and enforcement action. We also put together an interagency committee on "wonder banks," a menace at the time of fraudulent schemes masquerading as legitimate financial institutions, promising unusually high returns on investments. The committee comprised the CBN, SEC, Nigeria Deposit Insurance Corporation (NDIC), Corporate Affairs Commission (CAC), Economic and Financial Crimes Commission (EFCC), and the Nigeria Police Force. We created a budget for the committee to launch a nationwide media campaign to sensitize the public to the dangers posed by illegal fund managers/ wonder banks.

Afterwards, with the help of the police, we took

several enforcement actions against wonder banks. One notable example was the case against the investment scheme operated by the company, Wealth Solution Investment Services Limited, in 2013. The SEC intervened after numerous complaints from investors who had been promised extraordinary returns that were unsustainable and indicative of a Ponzi scheme. Backed by the police, the SEC shut down the operations of Wealth Solution Investment Services, froze its accounts, and pursued legal action against its operators to recover investors' funds. Between 2011 and the end of my tenure, we took similar enforcement actions against dozens of similar "wonder banks," most of the time relying on tips from the public to launch investigations. I was always attentive to investor complaints reporting Ponzi schemes because I knew about the Bernie Madoff case in the U.S., during which the U.S. SEC missed multiple red flags, including public warnings. The Bernie Madoff case is one of the most infamous financial frauds in history, involving a massive Ponzi scheme that defrauded thousands of investors out of approximately US$65 billion. Madoff, a one-time chairman of the NASDAQ stock exchange and a respected figure on Wall Street, promised consistent, high returns to his clients through what he claimed were sophisticated investment strategies. In reality, Madoff was using new investments to pay returns to earlier investors, rather than generating legitimate profits, a classic Ponzi scheme. His scheme unraveled in December 2008, when he was unable to meet US$7 billion in redemption requests, leading to his arrest and subsequent sentencing to 150 years in prison.[108]

As the Madoff scheme was ongoing, the U.S. SEC received credible tips and reports, including from financial analyst Harry Markopolos, who had been sounding alarms for nearly a decade.[109] The oversight lapses allowed Madoff's Ponzi scheme to continue unchecked, ultimately resulting in devastating financial losses for countless investors and a significant blow to the credibility of financial regulators. The scandal stands as a stark reminder that even the best and most esteemed regulators, such as the U.S. SEC, are not impervious to lapses in vigilance. It is also a reminder to build and maintain sophisticated oversight and unyielding diligence.

The collaboration between the Nigeria Police Force and the SEC turned out to be crucially effective, combining the SEC's expertise in securities laws with the investigative and enforcement capabilities of the police. When the SEC identifies potential criminal violations of securities laws, such as fraud, insider trading, or market manipulation, it works closely with the Nigeria Police Force to conduct thorough investigations. The SEC provides detailed information, evidence, and technical assistance to the police. We formalized this collaboration through a memorandum of understanding facilitating coordinated efforts and resource sharing between the two agencies.

We sought further collaboration to ensure that our enforcement actions are a powerful deterrent against securities fraud and misconduct. We negotiated to have officials from the office of the Director of Public Prosecution from Nigeria's Federal Ministry of Justice seconded to the SEC to assist the Commission in the prosecution of criminal cases. The officials were expected to work with our lawyers and the police desk to increase the level of convictions. A closer partnership with the Ministry of Justice should remain a goal pursued by the SEC to eventually replicate the sort of collaboration we see every day between the U.S. SEC and the DOJ.

Ensuring compliance with international best practice

In 1985, Nigeria took the first steps toward imbibing global best practices in our capital market by joining the International Organization of Securities Commissions (IOSCO), which was established two years prior, in 1983, to serve as a global cooperative body for securities regulators. The formation of IOSCO represented the consolidation of efforts by existing regional organizations, including the Inter-American Conference of Securities Commissions and the European Regional Committee of Securities Commissions. The primary goal was to create an international forum where securities regulators could collaborate, share information, and develop standards to enhance market integrity and investor protection. Since its inception, IOSCO has grown to include over 130 members who together regulate more than 95% of the world's securities markets.[110] The 130 members include two each from the United States and Canada – the U.S. SEC and the U.S. Commodity Futures Trading Commission (CFTC); and the Ontario Securities Commission and the Autorité des Marchés Financiers in Quebec are Ordinary, respectively.

In a world where crime and its ill-gotten gains traverse borders with alarming ease, and markets are increasingly interconnected, international cooperation is indispensable. The IOSCO was borne out of that necessity and has become an important feature of market conduct regulation, harmonizing the diverse regulatory landscapes of its member nations to foster collaboration and set global standards. As a standard-setter, IOSCO has doubtless been more impactful on securities regulation than other trade bodies have been on their respective industries.

In 2002, members established the Multilateral Memorandum of Understanding (MMOU), which set the framework to facilitate information sharing among jurisdictions and collaboration in the enforcement of securities laws and the regulation of securities markets. It addresses critical issues such as insider trading, market manipulation, and other forms of securities fraud. By providing a structured mechanism for cooperation, the MMOU helps to ensure that regulators can effectively oversee and investigate market activities across different jurisdictions, thus enhancing the global effort to maintain fair, efficient, and transparent markets. The MMOU is considered a benchmark for international regulatory cooperation and has been endorsed by numerous jurisdictions worldwide, including Nigeria.

Complementing the MMOU, IOSCO's thirty-eight Principles serve as the foundation for robust securities regulation and are categorized into eight groups, covering the regulator's responsibilities, self-regulation, enforcement of securities regulation, cooperation in regulation, issuer regulation, auditor oversight, credit rating agencies, and collective investment schemes. These principles provide a comprehensive framework for securities market regulation, emphasizing the need for regulatory independence, clear and consistent legal frameworks, effective enforcement, and cooperation among regulators. They also stress the importance of transparency, investor protection, and the integrity of financial reporting. By adhering to these principles, IOSCO members commit to maintaining high standards of regulatory practice, to promote the stability and integrity of global securities markets. The principles are periodically reviewed and updated to reflect evolving market conditions and regulatory challenges, ensuring their continued relevance and effectiveness.

Furthermore, apart from facilitating the convergence of regulatory practices across jurisdictions, IOSCO provides a forum for international cooperation and conducts research and analysis on emerging market trends and risks. IOSCO issues a wide range of reports and guidelines aimed at improving market surveillance, enhancing enforcement capabilities and protecting investors. It also plays a pivotal role in crisis management by coordinating responses to global financial crises and ensuring that securities markets can continue to function effectively under stress. Additionally, IOSCO offers training and technical assistance to member jurisdictions, helping to build regulatory capacity and foster the implementation of best practices worldwide. Through these activities, IOSCO supports the creation of resilient, transparent, and well-regulated securities markets, which are essential for sustainable economic growth on a global level.

As a member of IOSCO since 1985, the Nigerian SEC has actively participated in various IOSCO committees and working groups, contributing to the development of international regulatory standards and best practices. By engaging in these activities, the Nigerian SEC has helped to shape policies on critical issues such as market integrity, investor protection, and cross-border cooperation. This involvement has also had the beneficial effect of enhancing Nigeria's regulatory framework, as our enabling legislation and the rules and regulations are designed within standards outlined in IOSCO's thirty-eight principles. I consider it a badge of honor that our enabling legislation in Nigeria aligns with, and in many instances exceeds, the global leading standards within IOSCO principles.

Moreover, the Nigerian SEC's leadership in IOSCO extends to its role in promoting regional cooperation and integration among African securities regulators. Through initiatives such as the African and Middle East Regional Committee (AMERC) of IOSCO, the Nigerian SEC has been instrumental in fostering dialogue and collaboration among regulators in the region. This leadership has facilitated knowledge sharing, capacity building, and the move toward harmonizing regulatory standards across African markets. For practically all of my time as the DG of SEC, I also led the Africa/ Middle East Regional Committee (AMERC). At the twenty-fifth annual meeting in Montréal, during the thirty-fifth IOSCO annual conference, I was elected Chair of AMERC. The group included players such as Algeria, South Africa, Dubai Financial, Saudi Arabia, and Israel (before it moved to the Europe region). I found immense value in this role, facilitating platforms for cross-border learning and collaboration among our members. I consider one of my notable achievements on the IOSCO Board as enabling more rights for the regulators from Africa and the Middle East. I also enhanced the understanding of Islamic finance and the unique regulatory issues of this region.

In May 2010, during the AMERC annual meetings held in Mombasa, Kenya, the Capital Markets Authority graciously hosted our delegation. I urged my team to seize this opportunity to observe the process of demutualizing the Nairobi stock exchange, as we were similarly embarking on the demutualization of the Nigerian Stock Exchange. That same week, the Capital Markets Authority of Uganda celebrated its anniversary and invited me to deliver a keynote address, which provided me with a platform to advocate for the adoption of global best practices and the development of world class capital markets across our continent.

Peer review of SEC Nigeria by U.S. SEC

When I decided to take up the responsibility of leading the regulation and development of Nigeria's capital market, the U.S. SEC was my first port of call. I wanted to get their help carrying out a peer review of the Nigerian SEC: an honest, independent assessment of the suitability of the institution to coordinate and successfully implement the market-wide reforms needed to reposition the Nigerian capital markets. It was important to me that we benchmark ourselves against the best, and this peer review would be a good first step.

Before I assumed office, I met with the staff of the U.S. SEC Office of International Affairs to ask them to assist me with a peer review of SEC Nigeria. The team were encouraged that I had proactively reached out to them and were willing to undertake the peer review. However, three weeks after I assumed office, in early January 2010, I met Ethiopis Tafara, the then Director of the U.S. SEC Office of International Affairs, in Madrid, at my first IOSCO meeting. I was delighted to see him during the first session and immediately approached him during our first coffee break to follow up on my meeting with his team, a few months prior. He explained that his team would not be able to visit Nigeria for the peer review because of security concerns, more so since the U.S. SEC was responsible for prosecuting some corruption cases that could indict some very well placed Nigerians. I assured him that I would take the necessary steps to ensure the safety and security of his team during any visits to Nigeria. He was initially unconvinced. I did not however give up, and eventually, the leadership of U.S. SEC had enough comfort to sanction the team's trip to Nigeria.

Tenacity is an important quality in a leader. You must show resilience, determination, and unwavering commitment to achieving goals despite challenges and setbacks. This episode with the U.S. SEC was one of the earliest setbacks I needed to manage and figure out how to solve. We leveraged connections with the national security adviser to get experienced protection detail for the U.S. SEC team who arrived in Nigeria in March 2010. We also ensured that the U.S. SEC team got all of the cooperation and information they needed to conduct a thorough peer review.

Their review included interviews with relevant Nigerian SEC staff at our Abuja and Lagos offices. They likewise visited and interviewed officials of the Investment and Securities Tribunal (IST), the Economic and Financial Crimes Commission (EFCC), the stock exchange (including demonstrations of their surveillance systems, trading floor, and clearing and settlement offices), outside counsel, broker-dealers, securities trade organizations, CBN, and academics. In all, the U.S. SEC team interviewed over 100 people and was provided with what they described as "extraordinary access to nearly all documents and persons that were requested."

In April 2010, the peer review was completed, and the report was on my desk. The executive summary begins with this:

"The NSEC [Nigerian SEC] suffers from a number of fundamental problems in its oversight of the Nigerian capital market that if not remedied will prevent it from developing into a world class market. The NSEC has not been an effective regulator and has not provided effective oversight of the market or vigilant enforcement of violations of securities laws."

Wow! But I asked for it. That was the kind of frank assessment we needed.

The report goes on to describe the SEC's enforcement program as "dysfunctional in large part because the core functions of investigating and prosecuting violations are disaggregated." It added:

"The enforcement program has not brought any recent insider trading, market manipulation, or financial fraud cases, yet market participants informed us of a number of apparent such frauds that have gone unanswered. The few larger cases that have been recently initiated are characterized by deficient investigations. There are reported 440 identified Ponzi schemes (called 'wonderbanks') that have been identified but not satisfactorily resolved. Many of the problems undermining the Nigerian capital market exist in large part because there is little perceived leverage or deterrence due to an ineffective NSEC enforcement program over capital market operators."

The peer review alleged that "60–75 percent of the Nigerian broker-dealers are insolvent" and that "many broker-dealers are reportedly commingling customer assets."

The U.S. SEC team recommended reorganizing our enforcement and inspection programs, creating an independent ethics office, and launching an effort to reassert ourselves as the apex regulator to rein in the stock exchange, which the report stated had "no effective surveillance program for detecting insider trading and market manipulation" as it suffered from "complicated and entrenched governance problems." They concluded the recommendations with the need to fix capacity issues in terms of IT systems and to attract a new talent pool to help Nigeria develop world class capital markets.

Looking back, I feel very grateful for this support from the U.S. SEC. Their peer review confirmed a lot of the deficiencies I was already aware of. Importantly, though, their clear recommendations helped a great deal in guiding our early initiatives, particularly on the enforcement side. The U.S. SEC has set the gold standard for effective enforcement in the securities markets since its founding in the aftermath of the Great Depression. This was a period marked by severe economic turmoil and a dramatic loss of public confidence in the financial markets. The stock market crash of 1929 exposed widespread fraud, insider trading, and other unethical practices, prompting the need for substantial reforms. In response, President Franklin D. Roosevelt and Congress enacted the Securities Act of 1933 and the Securities Exchange Act of 1934. These landmark laws aimed to restore investor confidence by promoting transparency, honesty, and accountability in the securities markets. The U.S. SEC was officially established in 1934 as a federal agency responsible for enforcing these laws and regulating the securities industry.

The U.S. SEC's enforcement role is crucial to creating fair and efficient capital markets. By rigorously monitoring market activities and investigating potential violations, the SEC ensures that all participants adhere to the rules and regulations designed to protect investors. The commission has the authority to bring civil enforcement actions against individuals and companies that violate securities laws, including cases of insider trading, accounting fraud, and market manipulation. These enforcement actions serve as a powerful deterrent against misconduct, fostering a level playing field where all investors have access to accurate and complete information. The SEC's ability to impose penalties, secure disgorgement of ill-gotten gains, and seek injunctions against wrongdoers underscores its pivotal role in maintaining market integrity.

The importance of the SEC's enforcement activities extends beyond punishing wrongdoers; it also plays a vital role in preventing future violations and promoting investor confidence. By holding violators accountable, the SEC sends a clear message that fraudulent and manipulative behavior will not be tolerated. This helps to build trust among investors, encouraging greater participation in the capital markets.

The U.S. SEC has imposed some of the largest fines and sanctions in history on major financial institutions and corporations for various violations of securities laws. Notably, in 2013, JPMorgan Chase agreed to pay US$13 billion to settle allegations related to its mortgage-backed securities practices leading up to the financial crisis.[111] Another significant case involved Bank of America, which paid US$16.65 billion in 2014 to settle similar charges of misleading investors about the quality of their mortgage-backed securities.[112] In 2003, WorldCom faced a US$750 million fine for accounting fraud, one of the largest penalties for corporate misconduct at the time.[113] More recently, in 2020, Goldman Sachs was fined US$2.9 billion for its role in the 1MDB scandal, involving the misappropriation of billions of dollars from a Malaysian sovereign wealth fund.[114] These substantial fines underscore the SEC's commitment to holding major entities accountable and maintaining the integrity of the financial markets.

These strong enforcement actions contribute to lowering the cost of capital, making the U.S. securities markets one of the most affordable venues anywhere in the world to raise capital. In his influential work *Law and the Market: The impact of enforcement*, John C. Coffee Jr delves into the critical role that enforcement plays in maintaining the integrity and efficiency of financial markets.[115] Coffee argues that strong enforcement mechanisms are essential for deterring misconduct and ensuring that market participants adhere to regulatory standards. Through a comparative analysis of different regulatory regimes, he highlights how jurisdictions with robust enforcement policies, such as the United States, tend to have more transparent and efficient markets. Coffee emphasizes that the mere existence of laws and regulations is not sufficient; effective enforcement is necessary to foster investor confidence, reduce fraudulent activities, and promote fair market practices.

One of Coffee's major insights is the significant impact of private litigation in supplementing public enforcement efforts. He posits that private lawsuits, particularly class actions, play a crucial role in holding corporations accountable and compensating investors for losses due to misconduct. Coffee also discusses the deterrent effect of both public enforcement actions and private litigation, noting that the threat of substantial penalties and reputational damage compels firms to adopt better compliance practices. Additionally, he explores the interplay between different enforcement mechanisms, suggesting that a balanced approach, combining rigorous public enforcement with active private litigation, is most effective in achieving optimal market outcomes. This underscores the importance of a multifaceted enforcement strategy in sustaining healthy and vibrant securities markets.

In times of global financial uncertainty, capital consistently flows to the United States, based on its reputation as a bastion of stability and security. This phenomenon, known as "flight to safety," is largely due to the perception of the U.S. capital markets as exceptionally robust and reliable. Research by the International Monetary Fund (IMF) underscores that, during periods of market turbulence, such as the 2008 global financial crisis, U.S. treasury securities experienced substantial inflows, with demand for these "safe haven" assets surging markedly.[116] Further empirical evidence reinforces the notion that investors flock to the United States during crises due to its deep and liquid markets. A study by the Bank for International Settlements (BIS) revealed that, after the 2011 European debt crisis, substantial assets were reallocated into United States government bonds, leading to lower yields, strengthening the U.S. dollar.[117] The strength of the U.S. capital markets, characterized by their unparalleled depth, liquidity, and credibility, along with a strong legal framework and historical resilience during economic downturns, ensures that the U.S. remains the preferred destination for capital during periods of global financial stress.

I have long admired the United States capital markets for their ability to absorb these vast amounts of capital from all over the world with remarkable efficiency and stability, embodying a blend of rigorous regulatory oversight and innovative practices. Its robust framework not only attracts global investors but also sets a benchmark for regulators worldwide. Inspired by these attributes, I was committed to laying the foundations for similarly sophisticated capital markets in Nigeria. My goal was to create a vibrant and resilient ecosystem that mirrors the dynamism and reliability of its American counterpart.

A forewarning of what lay ahead

While I was pondering the best ways to reform the Nigerian capital markets, there was an episode that happened during the AfDB annual meetings of 2009 that gave me sleepless nights. The AfDB annual meetings are pivotal events that bring together finance and economic planning ministers representing member countries (the AfDB shareholders), as well as various stakeholders from all over the world. In addition to the bank's affairs, the annual meetings provided opportunities for participants to discuss the continent's economic and developmental issues. These meetings commenced in 1964, the year the AfDB was established. They typically occur in May or June, rotating among member countries, providing a platform for reviewing the bank's operations and charting the future course of action. They are usually a key highlight in the calendars of many leaders around the world with an interest in Africa. While I was Vice President of Corporate Services, one of my responsibilities was to ensure the annual meetings ran smoothly.

In addition to the main agenda, a range of activities take place on the sidelines of the meetings, creating a vibrant atmosphere for networking, knowledge sharing, and partnership building. These include high-level panel discussions, seminars, and workshops that delve into critical issues such as infrastructure development, climate change, poverty reduction, and regional integration. During the session on capital market developments in Africa, one of the panelists, a senior analyst from one of the major global investment banks, spent several minutes decrying the depths of market abuses that were supposedly ongoing at the Nigerian Stock Exchange. I remember sitting there in the audience, my face tightening with every word from her descriptions of the exchange's leadership's complicity in these alleged abuses. Listening to the analyst publicly denigrate the exchange and clearly articulate the market abuses that were apparently prevalent at that time corroborated many of the prior reports I had received about the Nigerian Stock Exchange. It further clarified to me that I indeed had my work cut out for me.

7

A New Sheriff In Town

"The greatest danger in times of turbulence is not
the turbulence; it is to act with yesterday's logic."
— Peter Drucker

From the very beginning and, indeed, even before I
assumed office, as I transitioned from the corporate
world, I quickly realized that unparalleled resistance
was the modus operandi in the Nigerian public sector.
One of the earliest indicators of this came shortly after
my confirmation by the Nigerian Senate, in December 2009. Despite the presidency's desire that I assume
office earlier in 2009, I faced an unexpected bureaucratic hurdle even when I had been asked to resume
work unfailingly before the end of 2009. This was also
after my confirmation on December 4, 2009. Despite it
being the holiday period, I arranged to commence work

on December 28, 2009. Bizarrely, I was told that morning that I could not start work because my appointment letter that was supposed to be issued to me was supposedly not ready. This was even though the Nigerian President had written to the Senate, six months earlier (in July 2009), indicating that he had appointed me and was seeking their confirmation of my appointment. The appointment had also received wide coverage by the media, on the basis of a press announcement by the government. This was particularly surprising given my understanding that the Senate's confirmation process would have been preceded by all necessary documentation.

I soon discovered that the Nigerian public sector was marred by complex layers of bureaucracy. I pondered about the fact that six months after my appointment by the President of Nigeria had been publicly announced and after I had appealed to be allowed until the end of year to close out things and return to Nigeria, a formal letter from the Office of the Secretary to the Government of the Federation was still not ready. This experience underscored how often government bureaucracy was used as a ploy to stall or even stop appointments, notwithstanding if it was made by the President of the nation and confirmed by the Senate, as was my case.

My resumption at the SEC

While awaiting my appointment letter, I spent time meeting with people in government, regulatory bodies, and operators in the market. A frequent topic that came up during those meetings, unprompted by me, was the continued theme of worrisome market abuse, infractions, and wrongdoing that were rampant within the capital market. I would finally go to the head office building for the first time on January 7, 2010, a sunny harmattan morning in Abuja. We drove through the imposing gate made of metallic bars on the western side of the six-story building. A brief ride up the elevator and a soft chime announced our arrival at the sixth floor. I walked into the office, greeted by two staff in the front office, busy processing incoming paper mail. A short corridor led to the spacious office with a large conference table by the left, and several yards away was a lengthy curved wooden desk at the broad side with a huge glass wall as a backdrop, providing a nice view of the Abuja skyline. In addition to two seats for visitors across from the main wooden desk, there was a sofa set, probably to host visitors in a more relaxed manner. This office would be where I would spend sixteen and, at times, twenty hours a day with my staff working on the many challenging issues facing the capital market.

As I sat in my chair for the first time, a sudden realization of the weight of responsibility came upon me. Here I was, twenty-five years after my first stint in the Nigerian capital market began, now back as the CEO of the apex regulator of this same market. I reminisced about the titans of the market who had occupied the same position, their portraits prominently displayed on the walls of the commission's board room located on the sixth floor, only two dozen steps from my office. I particularly fondly remember the pioneer DG, Mr. George Akamiokhor, a very distinguished finance professional who worked at the CBN from 1960 and helped transition the SEC from a small committee within the central bank to a full-fledged commission. In 1980, he became the acting chief executive of SEC, which had been established by decree a year earlier. By 1984, he became the substantive DG and chief executive, and would go on to serve until 1997, when he retired meritoriously from service.

When I began my career in late 1985 at Centre Point Nigeria, Mr. Akamiokhor was serving as the Director General of the SEC. He was part of a distinguished group of leaders in the Nigerian capital market, renowned for their exceptional competence, integrity, and vision. Among them were Apostle Hayford Alile, CEO of the Nigerian Stock Exchange from 1976 to 2000 and an evangelist for capital markets; Chief Dennis Odife, celebrated as a "capital market guru" for his expertise as a merchant banker; Dr. Gamaliel Onosode, famously known as "the boardroom guru"; and the unparalleled Otunba Michael Balogun, founder of First City Merchant Bank, now FCMB Group, one of Nigeria's most esteemed financial institutions. As a young woman embarking on a career in finance, I greatly admired these leaders, who were dedicated to mentoring the next generation. At that time, both the SEC and market participants were supported by highly skilled professionals, including my sister, Nwannem, who was then employed at the SEC.

While still sitting in the chair, I rolled forward to glance at the pile of documents set upon my desk, and atop the stack was a bulky document boldly titled "Report of the Inspection of the Nigerian Stock Exchange." I thought to myself, "At last, I can verify whether the troubling stories I had heard about the exchange were grounded in reality or mere rumors." I swiftly reviewed the executive summary. It was a forensic audit of the Nigerian Stock Exchange aimed at uncovering any financial irregularities and mismanagement within the institution. This audit was initiated amid allegations of financial impropriety, lack of transparency, and governance issues that had significantly eroded investor confidence.

The forensic audit report proved glaring instances of fraud, embezzlement, and other forms of financial misconduct, operational weaknesses, and gross governance malpractices. Upon completing my review of the executive summary of the report, I went to meet with the Executive Commissioner for Operations, who had acted as DG SEC, prior to my resumption. In our meeting, I prioritized a briefing on the inspection report. I wanted to know if any actions had been taken to address the glaring and urgent matters arising from the damning inspection report. I was concerned that the issues were not being handled with the urgency required. I was also keen to quickly start addressing the recurring topic of market abuses and begin to attempt restoring investor confidence that was decimated during the crisis.

The next day, I assembled the legal, enforcement, and monitoring teams to discuss the immediate steps required. We decided to give the management of the stock exchange an opportunity to respond to the findings in the inspection report, including inviting them to meet us for deliberations on the issues. It was rather shocking that the leadership of the stock exchange either did not appreciate the gravity of the situation or did not respect the SEC enough to make time for the meeting. We graciously gave many other opportunities that were equally rebuffed.

Zero-tolerance posture

In the meantime, we were planning to conduct the most extensive inspection exercise in the history of the commission. The initial step was to carry out a thorough clean up ahead of the inspections. I termed it a "fit and proper test." This was designed to send a clear message to the domestic and international investors that we were determined to build world class capital markets anchored on the highest integrity standards. Our initial review showed that dozens of broker-dealers were missing their mandatory filings with impunity – some had missing records running into years.

Under our rules, broker-dealers were mandated to comply with a set of time-bound regulatory filings with the SEC to ensure transparency, compliance, and the integrity of the capital markets. These filings include periodic financial statements such as quarterly and annual reports, which detail their financial health and operations. They must also submit disclosure statements for any significant events, such as changes in ownership, management, or corporate structure. Additionally, broker-dealers are required to file transaction reports that detail their trading activities, ensuring that all trades are conducted fairly and within regulatory guidelines. Compliance reports, including those related to anti-money laundering measures and adherence to ethical standards, are also essential filings. These documents collectively help the SEC monitor and regulate broker-dealer activities, safeguarding investor interests and maintaining market stability.

It was simply unacceptable that many of the over 300 broker-dealers were allowed to miss long periods of these filings. We wrote stern letters to thirty-five of the most delinquent of these broker-dealers, giving a maximum of two weeks for them to show justifiable cause why those filings were missed. The letter also included an unmistakable clarification of what the consequences of noncompliance with the requests would entail. We were clear that the SEC under my leadership would not allow the bad eggs to taint the good ones.

As those letters went out, we also announced the intention to gradually move our market from a compliance-based to a risk-based supervision framework. A compliance-based approach to market supervision focuses on ensuring that market participants adhere strictly to established rules, regulations, and standards. This method emphasizes checking for adherence to legal and regulatory requirements and often involves routine inspections and audits to verify compliance. Conversely, a risk-based approach to market supervision prioritizes identifying and managing potential risks that could threaten the stability and integrity of the market. This approach involves assessing the likelihood and impact of various risks, allowing regulators to allocate resources more efficiently by focusing on areas with the highest risk. While the compliance-based approach is rule-centric and reactive, the risk-based approach is proactive and strategic, aiming to pre-emptively address issues that could lead to significant market disruptions. We consequently ordered the inspection of market operators, focusing on identifying areas of risk and weakness.

Knowing what we found out when the stock exchange was under the microscope, I was apprehensive about the sort of malpractice and wrongdoing the inspection of broker-dealers would reveal. This is particularly because I understood the economics of the broker-dealer business model, which operates on relatively low margins, as these firms generate revenue primarily through transaction fees, commissions, and spreads on trades. Due to competition and the commoditization of basic trading services, these margins were getting even thinner.

To stay afloat, broker-dealers often diversify their revenue streams by offering value-added services such as financial advisory, wealth management, and proprietary trading. They may also focus on increasing trading volumes, leveraging technology to reduce operational costs, and managing risk carefully to maintain profitability. Additionally, some broker-dealers engage in securities lending and margin lending to boost revenue, while others could seek economies of scale through mergers and acquisitions. I knew the broker-dealers we were dealing with were not attempting any of these, further exacerbating my concern that many of them may be cutting corners or relying on malpractice to stay afloat. Many of them were extremely small operations with the bare minimum of structure in place to meet regulatory minimums, if at all. At the time, 90% of transactions were done by the top ten brokers. The remaining 300 broker-dealers squabbled over the remaining 10%.

On Friday, February 5, 2010, I flew to Lagos with my team, a month after my assumption of duty. It was time for the first quarter Capital Market Committee meeting. I am not aware of anywhere else in the world where this kind of meeting is held, bringing together a wide range of capital market stakeholders to discuss market developments. The Nigerian SEC had started these meetings about a decade earlier. I saw it as my first opportunity to introduce myself to the market and address the capital market community about the expectations for my time at the helm. My intention was also to restructure these quarterly rendezvous to focus on reviewing market performance, formulating and implementing new policies, and engaging with stakeholders to address their concerns while fostering collaboration. I spent time putting together a presentation titled "A Roadmap for Transforming the Nigerian Capital Markets," outlining the reform agenda that would form the priority of the SEC under my leadership.

During the meeting, I spoke clearly and categorically to the market participants that the SEC under my tenure would adopt a zero-tolerance posture to wrongdoing. I described how effective governance is key to a well-functioning capital market and reviewed some of the governance weaknesses, improper behaviors, and sharp practices that had been allowed to persist, particularly in the previous two years. I told the market that I was determined to stamp out sharp practices, deter malpractice, and change behaviors, by ensuring that there would not only be huge institutional costs that far outweighed the benefits, but also significant personal costs, including prosecution after rigorous and just investigations. I enunciated our intention to ensure high standards in regulatory oversight and enforcement, and that we would not hesitate to name and shame, where necessary.

I could hear groans and murmurs in the room as I warned the market community that we were launching detailed inspections, following which, those found erring would be issued a warning, fined, depending on the gravity and nature of the violation, and have their licenses suspended. For those already thinking of ways to avoid detection, I specified steps we would take to beef up our investigation, enforcement, and prosecution efforts. All these would be done without compromising on fairness.

After the meeting, I explained to the media how well-functioning capital markets are essential to Nigeria's economic development. I emphasized that, to realize her full potential, our country must have a world class capital market that is strong, sustainable, and that plays a central role in the economic development of our nation. It must be a market that improves the well-being of our people and will serve as a benchmark for the continent and the world. This was the vision that I was trying to rally the market and entire country to achieve. I also informed the press that the immediate priority of my reform agenda was to restore investor confidence, as no capital market can flourish without the trust of investors. To restore investor confidence, we would significantly enhance our dual role of effective regulatory oversight and capital market development.

I called on the media to become our partners in the goal of raising the level of financial literacy across our vast country while promising that the SEC would improve communication with the public through the media. I craved their indulgence to ensure that they only report and provide accurate information to the investing public to enable them to make informed investment decisions. I concluded with the many market development plans we had outlined and were planning to roll out in the coming months.

Monday morning the next week, I was initially taken aback as I saw the headlines in the newspapers. I had thought that the media would report on the vision I had articulated about how world class capital markets would help our country's economy to be transformed.

In a nation grappling with poverty in the throes of a crisis that caused widespread losses to retail investors, I thought the media would focus on the many market development initiatives we shared. The most prominent headline was the "zero-tolerance" posture I disclosed during the closed-door meeting but did not underscore at the press conference. I would later learn that the phrase used to describe me by some market participants was that there was indeed "a new sheriff in town."

Early actions to strengthen the stock exchange

As the first few months of my tenure flew by, the market inspections I had ordered were progressing apace. Around July that year, I finally got a clear picture of the depths of rot in the system. The audit revealed several critical issues, including discrepancies in financial statements, unauthorized transactions, and weak internal controls. To back up our word, we instituted legal proceedings against 260 individuals and entities for various forms of market infractions, seeking the disgorgement of any illegally gained profit, sending a clear signal that there were personal costs to market infractions and that the cost of market abuse would be higher than any benefits that could accrue.

We filed mostly civil charges but included criminal charges too, where appropriate. This earned me the moniker "Nigerian Iron Lady" splashed in a BBC headline.[118] By the end of 2010, as part of the fit and proper cleanup, we had suspended the licenses of thirty-four brokers-dealers who failed to comply with the reporting obligations, and we imposed various sanctions on ninety-two other market operators who violated the provisions of our anti-money laundering regulations. We also punished, by imposing fines, about a dozen quoted companies for various market infractions. The dearth of capacity that our inspections revealed shocked me, and I wondered how our market, which boasted amazing talent, integrity, and expertise when I started out my career, could have deteriorated to that level within some twenty-odd years.

I was now laser-focused on the exchange. We had exhausted all opportunities afforded to the management of the exchange to respond to the jarring findings in the forensic audit report. Even the grim descriptions I got from different sources before joining the SEC did not prepare me for the kind of findings in the reports. The findings of the forensic audit revealed substantial evidence of financial misconduct and governance failures within the exchange's leadership including evidence of financial skimming, misappropriation, false accounting, misrepresentation, and questionable transactions. Among the more salacious findings of the report were a yacht bought in 2008 as a gift with no records of the receiver, and 165 Rolex wrist watches were given as prizes, but only seventy-three were actually accounted for. After years of mismanagement, the exchange was on the verge of bankruptcy.

It was clear to me that strong, quick action was needed to address the most egregious of the findings, which included several breaches of the Investment and Securities Act (2007), refusal to file statutory accounts after every fiscal year as required by law, and the latest available accounts were qualified by external auditors who highlighted several financial irregularities. Furthermore, the report was replete with incidents of governance challenges and ineffective board oversight. The needed action had to be meticulously and discreetly planned considering the considerable amount of political clout and influence members of the Nigerian Stock Exchange's management exerted.

The CEO at the time was known to wield considerable political influence in Nigeria, with a record of conducting fundraising for top politicians in the country. One of the most notable instances of her political involvement was the role she played in a controversial fundraising event for Barack Obama's 2008 presidential campaign.[119] This event, held in Lagos, aimed to raise funds and show support for Obama. It attracted considerable attention and scrutiny. The event was attended by several high-profile Nigerian businessmen and politicians. It led to significant backlash, including investigations by Nigerian authorities and criticism from various quarters. The U.S. Embassy in Nigeria distanced itself from the event.

I consulted with the Minister of Finance at the time about our intended actions, and he advised us to ensure that we get political backing from the highest levels before proceeding. He was a very supportive minister, who was also back home from the diaspora to serve our nation.

His Excellency Goodluck Jonathan became the President of Nigeria in May 2010, following the death of President Yar'Adua. In addition to my role as DG SEC, I was invited to subsequently become a member of his Economic Management Team (EMT), which functions as a high-level strategic advisory body that formulates and coordinates the implementation of economic policies targeted at sustainable growth and development of Nigeria. Composed of key government officials and some industry leaders, the team advises the President on a wide range of economic issues, including fiscal policy, monetary policy, investment, trade, and infrastructure development. Its importance lies in its role in addressing economic challenges, promoting stability, and fostering an environment conducive to investment and job creation. By providing informed analysis and policy recommendations, the EMT was designed to enhance economic performance, reduce poverty, and improve the overall standard of living for Nigerians.

President Jonathan, who, though I was hired by his predecessor, gave me great support and made himself accessible throughout my time at the SEC, despite his hectic schedule as leader of the largest black nation on Earth. The then Minister of Finance and I set up an appointment to meet with the President to brief him about our plans regarding the stock exchange. We got a slot to have a discreet meeting in his office at the Aso Rock villa. He sat quietly taking in the information we shared with him, looking focused as we shared the details of our findings with him. We explained to the President the importance of strong action proportional to the gravity of the misconduct discovered, knowing that he was already aware of the low level of investor confidence in the market. We highlighted how this loss of confidence was linked to the long-standing unethical practices that had been tolerated for so long. Commendably, despite knowing it could cost him some sizable political capital, President Jonathan agreed with our assessment and assured us of his full political backing for any actions we deemed necessary.

A leader who places full trust in their team exemplifies true leadership, empowering them with the confidence and freedom to execute their duties effectively. This trait not only fosters a sense of responsibility and ownership among cabinet members or top officials, but also encourages innovation and decisive action. President Jonathan embodied this trait. From feedback I have received from others who worked with him, he always demonstrates a deep commitment to collective governance, understanding that empowering capable leaders within his administration strengthens the overall effectiveness of government.

This episode early on in my public service reiterated to me the importance of meticulous planning, which is what led me to discover the importance of getting political support for our actions. Meticulous planning ensures that every aspect of a strategy is carefully thought through, reducing the likelihood of unforeseen complications. Securing political support is likewise crucial, especially when those actions may be contentious, and particularly in less-advanced democracies or developing countries. We had tried many avenues to take the less dramatic option, all of which were blocked repeatedly. It was now time to take action, as any further delay would undermine the nation's capital markets and economy.

On Wednesday, August 4, 2010, we were ready to move on the exchange. As part of our meticulous planning, we got a team of security agencies and law enforcement to accompany our SEC team, which included my most trusted colleagues. Very early in the morning, the policemen were in tactical formations, having sealed off all entry points into the exchange's towering building. Brokers and other market participants were denied access to the trading floor to forestall the possibility of sabotage in which someone sympathetic to the exchange's management might tamper with the trading systems. By the end of the day, we had met no meaningful resistance to our action.

Trading for the day went on smoothly after we had removed the leadership team of the stock exchange. Thereafter, we named an ex-Deloitte executive to lead an interim leadership team to steer the exchange through a transition period before a substantive CEO could be recruited. The interim team was mandated to secure and ensure a smooth transition and initiate the recruitment of a substantive CEO and executive director. We also established an interim team representing the broker-dealers on the council of the exchange, choosing large institutional investors and credible, well-known business leaders. This was crucial to restoring confidence in the exchange, ensuring that its operations were conducted transparently and in compliance with the highest standards. We empowered the interim administrators and interim council to take steps aimed at strengthening the governance and operational frameworks of the exchange even during the brief transition. These actions sent a clear message across the world that the exchange was committed to maintaining a fair and transparent market. And since an exchange is a visible symbol of any securities market, the market welcomed the decisive steps we took to strengthen Nigeria's.

Testimony before the United States Congress

In November 2010, I was invited by the United States House of Representatives Committee on Financial Services Sub-Committee on International Monetary Policy and Trade to discuss how Nigeria was addressing the financial crisis that was still raging globally at the time. In the testimony before Congress, I elaborated on the impact of the global financial crisis on Nigeria's capital markets and the subsequent reforms undertaken by the SEC. I described how the crisis led to a significant decline in government revenues, weakened the banking sector, and caused a substantial stock market crash, exposing the vulnerabilities in Nigeria's financial system. However, I made sure to emphasize that the crisis also presented an opportunity for substantial reforms aimed at building a world class capital market capable of supporting Nigeria's economic growth and diversification.

I detailed the multifaceted reform agenda we were already implementing to restore confidence and stability. I particularly highlighted our strong enforcement actions, enhanced regulatory oversight, and the introduction of new rules to improve market integrity and transparency. I added that significant efforts were being made to address issues such as inadequate filing of returns by market operators and market abuses including insider trading, pump and dump, and share price manipulation. I highlighted the initiative of the central bank in dealing with the issue of nonperforming loans that threatened the banking sector. Established in the aftermath of the 2008 financial crisis, the Asset Management Corporation of Nigeria (AMCON) was instrumental in purchasing bad debts from banks, thereby restoring liquidity and confidence in the financial system. By managing and restructuring these toxic assets, AMCON helped prevent the collapse of several banks, maintained the overall stability of the system, and fostered recovery.

I ended my testimony before Congress by emphasizing the importance of international cooperation and support from organizations such as the U.S. SEC and multilateral entities such as the World Bank and the International Organization of Securities Commissions (IOSCO). I underscored how these partnerships provided essential technical assistance, capacity building, and financial support, which were crucial for the successful implementation of the SEC's reform initiatives. I assured the congressional committee that by leveraging these collaborations, Nigeria aimed to develop a resilient and strong capital market that could effectively mobilize capital for economic development, reduce poverty, and improve the living standards of its citizens.

8
Building World Class Institutions

"The key to creating a better future lies in building strong, transparent, and accountable institutions."
— Kofi Annan

The market is only as strong as its institutions. But in Nigeria, the capacity deficits among investors, operators, and the regulator itself were glaringly apparent. As apex regulator of the market, the SEC was my first priority, as I reminded myself of the retort, "Physician, heal thyself." One should address their own flaws or issues before attempting to correct or advise others. Anyone with self-awareness and personal integrity, especially those in positions of authority, must first address their own shortcomings before offering guidance or criticism to others. I could not go around telling brokers to invest in IT infrastructure when the apex regulator lacked basic tools. How could I insist that fund managers hire competent risk managers while leading an organization with the massive capacity gaps the whole market could see. I was sure that we would have more credibility with the market if we acknowledged our shortcomings upfront, and even more when they see us clearly taking steps to address them.

Accenture, the Irish American consulting firm, was engaged and had conducted a complete diagnostic of the SEC's capacity to deliver on its mandate, and recommended a plan for transformation and closing the identified gaps. Accenture approached the task relying on IOSCO diagnosis methodology. The findings were frankly depressing. The commission relied on manual processes for monitoring and surveillance, registration of market functions, filing processing, and the logging and tracking of investor complaints. We did not have even the most basic modules of Enterprise Resource Planning (ERP) that are useful in automating processes in finance, human resources, services, procurement, and so on. To begin with, we needed to articulate an IT strategy that would define our IT goals and delineate the enterprise capability architecture. When both were validated, we could begin to plan for IT procurement, deployment, and management of the IT assets.

To regulate an advanced capital market, leveraging technology is especially crucial, so I wanted the SEC to have the latest technology needed to improve productivity, service delivery, investor protection, and effective market oversight. Our benchmark, the U.S. SEC, employs a variety of advanced technologies to regulate the securities markets effectively. One of the key technologies it uses is the Market Information Data Analytics System (MIDAS), which collects and analyzes vast amounts of trading data from multiple sources, including national exchanges and alternative trading systems. MIDAS processes billions of records daily, allowing the SEC to monitor market activity in real-time, detect irregularities, and identify potentially manipulative or fraudulent behavior.[120] By providing a comprehensive view of the market, MIDAS enables the SEC to perform detailed analysis and take timely enforcement actions when necessary.

Another critical tool adopted under Rule 613 of the U.S. SEC is the Consolidated Audit Trail (CAT), which is designed to track all orders, quotes, and trades in the U.S. equities and options markets. CAT provides the regulator with a complete and accurate record of market transactions, enhancing its ability to oversee trading activities and investigate market disruptions or suspicious activities. Additionally, the U.S. SEC uses sophisticated data analytics and machine-learning algorithms to sift through large datasets, uncover patterns, and predict potential market abuses. These technologies, combined with robust cybersecurity measures to protect sensitive information, enable U.S. regulators to maintain market integrity, protect investors, and ensure fair and orderly markets. In Nigeria, we were at, or near, zero. I was determined to significantly increase the IT budget to get the basics. I thought that would set an example for the market to make similar commitments to revamp their IT assets and utilization.

By the time I resumed work in January 2010, the SEC budget for that fiscal year had already been submitted to the national assembly, the parliament. The next budget cycle, we took account of the technology needs identified by Accenture's diagnosis and allocated additional resources for the IT renewal plan. In 2011, we commenced the process of overhauling our IT systems. We invested in modern servers capable of supporting the advanced applications and services we were gearing up to deploy. We simultaneously commenced the development of an application software for electronic registration and returns analysis, and succeeded in building a shared technology system for common services and capabilities. This enabled the head offices and the zonal offices to be connected over a wide area network. Additionally, for the first time in the SEC's history, we invested in Enterprise Resource Planning to automate some administrative and financial-management processes, which helped in reducing overheads and improving our efficiency.

Concurrently, we were revamping our website, making it a lot more functional, user-friendly, and suited for our investor education and public awareness initiatives. The new website also simplified interaction with the SEC, making submitting investor complaints and feedback a lot easier. The website also highlighted our social media presence, especially on Facebook and what was then called Twitter, where all stakeholders could interact with us.

Training of human resources was severely lacking. In the aftermath of the most consequential financial crisis in almost a century, the regulatory environments internationally were getting more complex and constantly evolving, driven by changes in laws, market dynamics, and technological advancements. And our staff would have been incapable of keeping up with the trends without an intentional investment in world class relevant training. I saw continuous training as a crucial practice to ensure that my staff were up to date with the latest developments, enabling them to effectively interpret and enforce regulations. Knowledge is critical for maintaining the integrity and efficiency of markets, as well as for protecting investors and the public. Without ongoing education, staff may lack the necessary skills and understanding to address emerging challenges, potentially leading to regulatory failures.

When I arrived at the SEC, there was a sizable training budget, including for overseas courses and seminars. I was shocked to discover that this budget was being abused, with staff seeing it as an opportunity to get estacode and other travel allowances. In one particularly disturbing instance described by one of the staff, a training program billed as an "international corporate finance seminar" had as its venue a motor repair shop in an obscure corner of south London. The SEC was getting nothing for these considerable annual training expenditures. I was determined to revamp the entire training structure. We looked for institutions and providers of the highest quality, both at home and abroad, and put in place a system whereby the SEC verifies the quality of the program and pays directly on behalf of nominated staff. We negotiated strategic partnerships for training our staff with IOSCO, U.S. SEC, the IMF, Oxford University, many world class business schools, and other high-profile organizations. I am pleased that the SEC still adheres to this policy, which has helped boost capacity over the last decade.

The SEC also owned and ran the Nigerian Capital Market Institute (NCMI), which was created to not only provide ongoing relevant training to staff of the organization but to also be the go-to training provider for the entire market. Around 2010, the institute was practically redundant. We set out to revitalize the institute by selecting a new leadership team, redesigning their business model and service offerings, and refocusing the institute on the core capacity needs of the SEC.

Another area of worrisome deficit for me was in our research capability. Research, capable of supporting evidence-based policymaking, was grossly inadequate. And I was coming from the AfDB, which boasted of vast resources for high-quality research. Research is crucial for a securities market regulator in order to formulate effective evidence-based policies that ensure market integrity, protect investors, and promote economic development. Through rigorous research, regulators can analyze market trends, assess the impact of existing regulations, and identify emerging risks and opportunities. This empirical foundation enables the development of informed, data-driven policies that are responsive to actual market conditions and challenges, rather than relying on assumptions or outdated information. Furthermore, ongoing research allows regulators to stay ahead of technological advancements and evolving market dynamics, ensuring that regulatory frameworks remain robust and relevant. For me, building a strong in-house research team was important as it would empower the SEC to create policies that are both proactive and adaptive, fostering a more resilient and efficient capital market.

My front office

How to begin? I needed help. First, I had to build a competent team in my own office. One of my leadership secrets is to prioritize building a highly effective team of competent people who would be closest to me. Since my first management job in the 1990s, I have always believed that I am only as good as my team. The principle is that my success is intrinsically linked to the capabilities and performance of those around me. I actively seek out individuals with diverse skills, expertise, and perspectives, recognizing that a well-rounded team can tackle complex challenges more effectively. Then I work to foster a collaborative and inclusive environment that empowers each member of the team to bring their best self to work and excel. I value the input of everyone on the team, and I ensure my team knows that. I encourage innovation, out-of-the-box thinking, and accountability.

As a leader, it is imperative to take an active role in recognizing and harnessing the unique value each team member brings to the organization. Effective leadership involves more than merely overseeing tasks; it requires a deep understanding of individual strengths and contributions to fully leverage their potential. Research underscores the importance of this approach. For instance, a study published in the *Harvard Business Review* highlights that leaders who actively engage in identifying and nurturing employees' unique skills can significantly enhance team performance and job satisfaction.[121] By recognizing and capitalizing on these individual strengths, leaders not only boost productivity but also foster a more inclusive and motivated work environment. Furthermore, Gallup research indicates that employees who feel their talents are used and appreciated are twelve times more likely to be engaged at work, which directly correlates with increased organizational success.[122]

On my arrival at the SEC, I only had two messengers left in the office; the professional staff in the previous DG's office had been reassigned to other departments. I asked the three executive commissioners to each send one or two of their best staff to work temporarily with me until I settled in and had my own team in place. I was able to quickly identify those that I could work with and sent back a few that were not fit for purpose. This arrangement was a workable stopgap while I was in the process of bringing in new people to complement the resources we already had internally. By a combination of lucky coincidences and my active search within my known network, my inner circle was already taking shape.

A brilliant Nigerian lawyer who worked for me as an adviser at the AfDB suggested he would support me in the new role when he heard I was returning home to lead the SEC. He has a PhD in law and had worked as a senior counsel with the Independent Inquiry Committee, investigating allegations of fraud and corruption in the United Nations Oil for Food Programme. I knew, in addition to his obvious knowledge of the law, that his background in forensic investigation would be invaluable at the SEC. He would go on to play important roles in the actions we took against the management of the stock exchange. Another former colleague, an auditor at the AfDB, returned home to serve alongside me.

While waiting for my luggage on a flight home in 2009, I was introduced to a Nigerian woman who was managing a public relations firm in London. After several subsequent meetings, she joined my team and played a pivotal role in managing key events and public relations campaigns. Recognizing the need for even more exceptional legal expertise in the team, I asked another friend for help, and they recommended an outstanding Nigerian lawyer from a prestigious private practice in New York. She made the significant decision to return to Nigeria, where she proved to be not only an exceptional lawyer, but also a dependable and effective professional, providing top-notch legal opinions. She collaborated closely with a brilliant young lawyer I met in Washington, DC, following my testimony before the U.S. Congress. He approached me with insightful questions and revealed himself as a Nigerian Harvard Law graduate. He too left a sought-after clerkship in the United States to contribute to Nigeria's public service, offering invaluable legal analysis on some of our most crucial early initiatives.

With my amazing front office in place, I could finally shift my focus to replicating similar recruitments to improve capacity across the organization. I encountered several highly skilled and dependable professionals among the existing staff. One particularly memorable instance involved a senior staff member, who, having fallen out of favor with the previous management and been relegated to a remote regional office, wrote me a heartfelt letter detailing his situation and requesting an opportunity to demonstrate his capabilities. I reinstated him, and it soon became clear that he was both competent and reliable.

Next, we needed a proper assessment of the exact gaps we had to fill across the organization. I headhunted a human resources expert to join as an adviser to conduct this needs assessment and lead the recruitment and reorganization exercises to follow. The staff reorganization we implemented helped us to align the organization's structure with the fresh strategic vision and goals we were attempting to deliver. As best as we could with the capacity we had, we attempted to address existing inefficiencies, realign roles to better fit the evolving needs of the organization, and invigorate the different departments with new perspectives. I hoped the reorganization would make the commission a little more agile.

I was not going to allow the 'business-as-usual' way in which past recruitments into the SEC had been handled. This would typically involve people internally with connections to powerful politicians bringing in their nieces, nephews, relatives, or the like, whether they had relevant training or qualifications related to the core mandates of the SEC. This long-standing practice had deprived the organization of both competence and fresh perspectives, fostering a notable lack of enthusiasm for self-development. The resulting environment was one of stagnation and resistance to progress, particularly evident in the employees' vehement opposition to implementing exams before promotions – measures designed to ensure advancement based on merit and ability. Unlike the regular civil service employees in government ministries, who were required to pass exams for promotion, staff at the apex capital market regulator resisted these fundamental steps aimed at fortifying the institution. The situation was further exacerbated by the most troubled individuals, who even threatened to incite a riot if the promotion-exam policy was not abandoned. We did not back down, and to this day, every employee must sit for exams and interviews to be promoted to some higher positions.

SEC Young Professionals Program

Following thorough research and needs assessment, we had the exact number of resource gaps to fill. We needed about fifty additional resources with academic backgrounds in economics, law, accounting, finance, statistics, information technology, and risk management.

I wanted to implement something akin to the young professionals programs (YPPs) of the World Bank and the AfDB. The World Bank's and AfDB's YPP attract some of the brightest talent from around the world looking to kickstart their careers in international development.[123],[124] These programs are highly competitive, selecting candidates with outstanding academic credentials, leadership potential, and a passion for addressing global challenges. Participants receive comprehensive training and hands-on experience in various sectors, including economics, public policy, and sustainable development. This exposure allows them to develop a deep understanding of the intricacies of development work, build a global network of professionals, and gain insights into the operational frameworks of various sectors. The program includes structured rotations through different departments that provide a holistic view of the organization's functions.

The advantages of the YPP extend beyond individual career growth; they also contribute to the broader mission of these institutions by infusing fresh perspectives and innovative ideas into their operations. Young professionals (YPs) bring enthusiasm and contemporary knowledge, driving forward-thinking approaches to problem-solving. These programs serve as pipelines for future leaders who are well-equipped to design and implement impactful projects that promote economic growth, reduce poverty, and improve living standards in developing countries. During my tenure at the AfDB, I spearheaded the redesign of the Young Professionals

Program (YPP), revamping the mentorship framework, and increasing engagement from senior leadership. I organized sessions for the new YPs with the bank's president and other top executives. Eager to replicate these successful initiatives at the SEC, I took a hands-on approach, closely overseeing the process to ensure its effective implementation.

We engaged a leading Nigerian HR firm to oversee the recruitment process. In December 2010, we publicized the program in major national newspapers, on the SEC website, and various online platforms. We stipulated that only candidates with a minimum of a second-class upper degree in economics, law, accounting, finance, statistics, information technology, or risk management would be eligible for consideration.

The response was extraordinary, with 34,292 applications submitted before the deadline. From these, 2,283 candidates were invited to take aptitude tests, and subsequently, 219 top performers were selected for interviews and assessment center exercises. These exercises involved structured tasks – such as group discussions, roleplaying, case studies, and presentations – designed to replicate real workplace challenges. This rigorous process allowed assessors to evaluate each candidate's problem-solving skills, interpersonal abilities, leadership potential, and decision-making capabilities. Ultimately, fifty-two exceptional candidates were chosen, whom I proudly referred to as the "crème de la crème." Their arrival generated considerable anticipation within the organization, although some of the more senior staff viewed the excitement surrounding these "super YPs" with skepticism. To me, they were simply "my YPs."

Recruitments into the public service, especially one of this size, can be long, drawn-out exercises. A typical one can last as many as three years between the announcement and resumption of successful applicants. Ours took eleven months, which I considered too slow, but was told to celebrate as it was "unusually quick." Post-recruitment, we designed, as part of the onboarding process for the new fifty-two YPs, an intensive induction program that included a three-week training by a reputable UK-based training provider to major banks in London, a bootcamp in Lagos, and several months of internship with select groups of organizations and capital market operators.

By March 2012, my YPs were finally back in Abuja, ready to infuse the organization with new blood and fresh ideas. Among the fifty-two, I selected two to join my front office, giving them an opportunity to accelerate their learning through supporting me as the chief executive. They both worked diligently, and the exceptional quality of their work, which I could supervise directly, gave me confidence in the quality the other fifty YPs were bringing into the other departments and functions. Some of the YPs have now left the SEC, moving on to take up career-advancement opportunities around the world. A large crop of them are, however, still there, currently managers, as the SEC continues to depend on their extraordinary ability to deliver on complex projects and positions.

With the team and resources established, I also formed a "Transformation Office," led by a director-level executive who reported directly to me. Amid the collapse of oil prices, investors losing their savings, and profuse portfolio outflows, the SEC's board and leadership recognized the critical need to urgently salvage both the Nigerian capital markets and the nation itself, which was grappling with the fallout from the global financial crisis. By allocating the necessary resources to address capacity gaps and repositioning the SEC to confront this monumental challenge, the board and staff demonstrated remarkable foresight and commitment. Consequently, the SEC was now better positioned to set an example for the market community and effectively execute our ambitious reform initiatives.

Further strengthening the stock exchange

After our intervention removing the management of the exchange, the interim team was busy managing the transition while a substantive new team was being recruited. We engaged a global consulting firm to lead the rigorous and highly competitive selection process for a CEO and an executive director. The vacancies were announced worldwide to attract the best and most experienced leaders. After the rigorous process, in January 2011, we approved the appointment of a new CEO of the exchange who would bring deep experience working in the securities markets in the United States, including at the NYSE and the American Stock

Exchange. We also approved the appointment of a new executive director for IT and market operations. He had decades of experience in IT programs and business transformation for financial services institutions in the United Kingdom, including at Barclays Bank.

The new leadership team quickly announced an ambitious and bold five-year plan to build a credible market with five product ranges – equities, fixed-income, ETFs, options, and futures. They forecast that these products would enhance liquidity and market depth and lead to a robust market that would have a market capitalization of US$1 trillion by 2016.[125] The new leadership had some early quick wins rolling out a new trading engine, the X-GEN, which was the most robust trading platform on the continent at the time, with capability for trading in bonds, equities, ETFs, commodities, and derivatives.[126] The same sort of IT transformation was going on in our Central Securities Clearing System (CSCS), which deployed the Society for Worldwide Interbank Financial Telecommunication (SWIFT) messaging system to enhance transactions in the market and reduce the settlement period (the time between the trade date of a financial transaction and the date when the transaction is finalized, with the buyer receiving the asset and the seller receiving the payment). Our goal was to have all institutions participating in making our market strong and independent. We entrusted the exchanges with the tough task of rebuilding confidence in the exchange, implementing robust corporate governance structures, and implementing the demutualization of the stock exchange.

In September 2011, we inaugurated an industry-wide committee to develop a roadmap for demutualizing the exchange.

The demutualization of the Nigerian Stock Exchange was designed to mark a pivotal point in its transformation, transitioning from a member-owned mutual organization to a shareholder-owned public company. This process aimed to enhance governance, transparency, and efficiency within the exchange, aligning it with global best practices. By converting members' interests into shares, demutualization would open up the exchange to broader ownership, facilitating increased capital inflow and investment opportunities, and ultimately boosting the exchange's competitiveness on an international scale to serve as the gateway into Africa.

Another primary motivation for demutualization was to improve the exchange's ability to attract investment and facilitate capital accumulation in Nigeria. It could itself become a publicly listed entity, able to access additional capital through equity markets, essential for funding expensive modernization initiatives, technological upgrades, and expanding its service offerings. The new structure would also mean that the exchange was subject to more stringent regulatory oversight and corporate governance standards, which would help build greater investor confidence and trust in the market.

The demutualization process also aimed to address conflicts of interest inherent in the previous mutual structure, where members who were also market participants had dual roles as owners and users. By separating ownership from trading rights, the exchange could operate more independently and focus on its core mission of providing a fair, transparent, and efficient marketplace. This change was expected to foster innovation, improve service delivery, and enhance the overall market experience for investors and issuers alike, positioning the exchange as a more robust and dynamic player in the global financial markets.

The conclusion of the demutualization of the exchange in 2021 culminated in its transformation into the NGX Group, marking a new era for the organization.[127] Three distinct subsidiaries were created: NGX Exchange, NGX Regulation, and NGX Real Estate. In practice, demutualization involves the conversion from a company limited by guarantee to a company limited by shares. There was no existing legislation in Nigeria to govern such a legal restructuring. Our work involved thinking through all the possible scenarios for this legal conundrum. One option was to consider amending the Companies and Allied Matters Act (CAMA), the legislation that governs the establishment and management of companies in Nigeria. Another option was to seek standalone legislation that empowers the NGX to demutualize. Eventually, this was the option implemented with the passage of the Demutualization Act, authorizing the NGX to convert to a public company with the prior authorization of the SEC.

This restructuring allowed for a clear separation of trading operations, regulatory functions, and real estate activities, enhancing operational efficiency and governance. The transformation aimed to streamline processes, foster innovation, and provide a more robust framework for growth and development within the Nigerian capital markets. It now operates with greater flexibility and strategic focus. It is better equipped to meet the demands of modern financial markets. It has attracted more investments, both domestic and international, by demonstrating a commitment to transparency, accountability, and high governance standards. Additionally, the NGX Group is leveraging new technologies to expand its product offerings and enhance its competitiveness.

Resistance to change

During our "fit and proper" inspection of capital market operators, I became ever-more convinced that the status quo was unsuitable for the kind of robust capital market we were attempting to build. So many small, weak, and quasi-moribund operators proliferated in the market. At the end of 2010, the SEC had exactly 1,364 active licenses to different categories of market operators, including 104 issuing houses, 306 broker-dealers, 139 corporate/individual investment advisers, 126 fund/portfolio managers, and thirteen underwriters, among others. The top five brokers dominated, executing about 80% of daily transaction volumes. A logical direction to take would have been to significantly consolidate the industry, much like the case with banks in 2005.[128] I, however, knew to expect stiff opposition to any recapitalization plans. A predecessor had warned me not to take on the recapitalization issue based on the pressure he got from some broker-dealers.

We stubbornly decided to forge ahead and wanted to achieve this by requiring all categories of market participants to increase their capital base, which would necessitate mergers and acquisitions to meet the new capital requirements. This was going to naturally reduce the number of smaller, undercapitalized firms, and result in fewer, but larger and financially stronger, broker-dealers. These consolidated entities can benefit from economies of scale, enhanced operational efficiencies, and greater resources to invest in upgrading their technology and human capital. My goal was to convince the market that undergoing a recapitalization exercise would produce more robust and capable market intermediaries, providing higher-quality services, better risk management, and increased market stability, resilience, and confidence.

Unfortunately, we were unsuccessful. There was an entrenched inertia that mobilized all resources within its orbit to resist any attempt to require recapitalization. Considering the many battles ahead, I had no bandwidth to devote to this initiative. Nonetheless, I remained determined to bring it up again at some future date. To stiff opposition, we finally announced the recapitalization exercise in December 2013 following months of seeking, obtaining, and analyzing inputs from the market community. We increased the minimum capital requirement for a broker-dealer license more than four-fold; for a single broker license, five-fold; for underwriters, two-fold; for portfolio and fund managers, sixteen-fold; and varying magnitudes of increase for the other market functions.

I had hoped to pursue a more ambitious course of action, but the final decision represented a compromise. We granted the operators a full year to meet the new requirements. Throughout this period, however, we were inundated with excuses and pressure to extend the deadline. Brokers consistently cited the "bearish nature of the market" and "current economic conditions" as reasons for their resistance. Ultimately, we relented and extended the deadline by nine months to September 2015. Unfortunately, I would not remain in a position to resolve this matter. Successive leaders of the SEC have continued to grapple with the issue, which reflects a troubling lack of ambition among our capital market operators. Despite witnessing the banking sector's remarkable growth and transformation in the mid-2000s, their reluctance to emulate such success is perplexing and disappointing.

9
Financial Literacy

"The secret of change is to focus all your energy not
on fighting the old, but on building the new."
— Socrates

The SEC's dual mandate, enshrined in its enabling
law, is to regulate and develop Nigeria's capital markets. I saw no contradiction or even conflict between
these two overriding objectives. Indeed, I thought they
complemented each other. In designing rules and regulations aimed at improving regulation, we put on our
market development hat to ensure that we were not
going to be stifling innovation with the new rules. As a
regulator, I wielded a big stick and took decisive action
that aimed to sanitize the market. But undoubtedly,
the most fulfilling aspect of my work at the SEC was
spearheading various market development initiatives,

particularly because financial literacy is a subject close to my heart, as someone who fell in love with finance from the age of eight.

Regardless of where one lives, whether in a wealthy, advanced society or in a village in a third-world country, the pursuit of financial literacy is always a valuable endeavor. Financial literacy is crucial, especially in developing countries, as it equips individuals with the essential skills to manage whatever financial resources they own effectively, however small, helping to provide some degree of economic stability and personal empowerment. Improving one's financial literacy also comes with the added benefit of gaining life skills beyond mere money management. It cultivates discipline, as individuals learn to prioritize and limit their spending, set and adhere to financial goals, and be more strategic with money. These competencies contribute to greater resilience and are beneficial across various aspects of life. In developing countries, where economic challenges are often more pronounced, financial literacy challenges individuals to find ways to build a more secure future.

Even the most advanced countries are increasingly recognizing the critical importance of financial literacy for their citizens, particularly from a young age. As economies become more complex and financial products more sophisticated, these nations understand that equipping young people with robust financial knowledge is essential for fostering responsible money management and economic resilience. Initiatives in these countries often include integrating financial education into school curricula, promoting early financial planning, and providing resources to develop lifelong financial skills.

Personal finance education is increasingly becoming a staple in American schools, driven by new state mandates, according to a report in *The Economist*.[129] As of June 2024, twenty-five states, home to a majority of students in the United States, require high-school students to complete a personal finance course to graduate, a significant rise from previous years. This trend, supported by research, reflects a growing recognition of the need for financial literacy among young people. Courses cover essential skills such as investing, budgeting, managing credit, and saving, and are designed to equip students with practical financial knowledge.

Recent studies suggest that these courses are effective in improving students' financial behaviors and knowledge. Unlike earlier research that questioned their impact, newer randomized controlled trials indicate that students who take personal finance classes tend to save more, manage credit better, and make more informed borrowing decisions.[130] These educational programs not only help students manage their money but also prepare them to avoid high-interest loans and credit card debt in the future. As more states consider implementing such requirements, there is hope that these courses will foster a generation of financially savvy adults in the United States.

In developing countries, where formal financial systems may not be as deeply entrenched or widely accessible, financial literacy can also play a crucial role in promoting financial inclusion. By understanding how to use banking services, access credit, and take advantage of financial products such as savings accounts, insurance, and pensions, more people can participate in the formal economy. This inclusion can help reduce poverty levels by enabling individuals to build credit histories, secure loans for small businesses, and save for emergencies and future investments.

Financially literate populations are more likely to responsibly use financial services, which can, in turn, spur economic growth and development. It empowers individuals to protect themselves against exploitation and fraud, which are more prevalent in developing countries where regulatory frameworks might be weaker. A well-informed population can better navigate the financial landscape, avoiding scams and making choices that enhance their financial security. Understanding consumer rights, the terms of financial products, and the implications of high-interest loans are critical components of financial literacy that safeguard individuals from predatory practices and financial losses.

Overall, financial literacy contributes to the overall economic development of a country. When individuals make sound financial decisions, it leads to higher levels of savings and investments, fostering economic growth. A financially literate populace is also more likely to support and demand effective economic policies and reforms, leading to improved governance and economic stability. In essence, financial literacy is not only a tool for individual empowerment but also a cornerstone for sustainable economic development in developing countries, creating a more resilient and prosperous society.

Around 2010, the level of financial literacy in Nigeria was abysmally low. The low levels of financial literacy were particularly pronounced in rural areas and among women and youth, highlighting a critical need for targeted financial education programs. A study by the Enhancing Financial Innovation & Access (EFInA) in 2010 revealed that only about 26% of Nigerian adults were financially literate, defined as the ability to understand and use basic financial concepts effectively.[131] The survey highlighted that a majority of the population struggled with basic financial concepts such as budgeting, saving, and investing. For example, it was found that only 21% of adults could calculate simple interest rates on savings or loans, indicating a widespread lack of basic numerical and financial skills. This lack of understanding was a barrier to effective financial inclusion and economic empowerment.

As earlier noted, the level of financial literacy varied significantly between urban and rural areas, according to the same EFInA study. Urban residents, who generally had better access to educational resources and financial institutions, demonstrated higher levels of financial literacy compared to their rural counterparts. Additionally, the survey data indicated a gender gap, with men being more financially literate than women. Around 33% of men had basic financial knowledge compared to just 19% of women. This disparity was attributed to socio-cultural factors, lower educational attainment among women, and limited access to financial services in rural areas where traditional gender roles were more pronounced. In terms of financial inclusion, the EFInA survey showed that 39.2 million Nigerians, representing 46.3% of the adult population, were financially excluded.[132] Only 25.4 million Nigerians were banked, representing 30% of the adult population.

Recognizing the critical need to improve financial literacy and inclusion, the CBN set up a team of multiple stakeholders, including the banks, SEC, capital market operators, other government agencies, international development partners, and non-governmental organizations to develop the National Financial Inclusion Strategy (NFIS). This aimed to increase financial literacy through workshops, seminars, and partnerships with educational institutions. The goal was to reach underserved populations and empower them with the knowledge and skills necessary to participate fully in the financial system. The overarching goal of the NFIS was to reduce the percentage of adults excluded from financial services from 46.3% in 2010 to 20% by 2020.[133]

The NFIS outlined a comprehensive plan to enhance financial inclusion across Nigeria through several key pillars. These include the expansion of financial access points, the development of a robust digital financial services ecosystem, and the promotion of financial literacy and consumer protection. The strategy emphasized the importance of leveraging technology, such as mobile banking and agent networks, to reach underserved populations in remote and rural areas. Additionally, the NFIS focused on creating enabling regulatory environments, fostering public-private partnerships, and ensuring the availability of a diverse range of financial products tailored to the needs of different segments of the population. It also set specific targets for increasing the adoption of formal financial services, such as savings accounts, credit, insurance, and pension schemes, aiming to empower more Nigerians to participate in the financial system and improve their economic well-being.

Under my leadership, the SEC was focused on implementing various financial literacy initiatives aimed at achieving the targets set within the NFIS. Traditionally, the SEC relied on radio jingles, publications, and newspaper advertisements for its investor education campaigns. While these traditional media channels had broad reach, they became increasingly unsustainable for engaging young people, particularly in rural areas, due to the digital inflection at that time. Additionally, such media often offer limited interaction and feedback mechanisms, reducing the potential for public engagement and understanding. We needed a more integrated communication strategy that includes digital and social media, community outreach, and other innovative methods to ensure comprehensive and effective public enlightenment.

Project 50

October 1962 was the starting point of organized securities market regulation in Nigeria when the Capital Issues Committee was carved out of the central bank and inaugurated with the mandate to examine applications from companies seeking to raise funds from the capital market. October 2012 would mark the fiftieth year of continuous securities market regulation in Nigeria. I wanted the SEC to celebrate this milestone. From October 2011, we embarked on a year-long series of commemorative activities under a series of programs titled "Project 50." It commenced with a flagship event; an investment forum held on October 31, 2011. It was an opportunity for us to showcase the centrality of the capital market to the orderly development of the Nigerian economy.

The forum featured five panels, namely the Economists' Panel, the Regulators' Panel, the Market Panel, the Opportunities Panel and the Visioning Panel. The panel of distinguished economists examined the Nigerian economy and offered their perspective on how Nigeria could actualize its vision of becoming one of the world's leading economies. The panel of regulators outlined the key elements of effective regulation and its role in enabling the building of a leading economy. The Market Panel discussed the essential aspects of market development, notably how Nigeria could enhance market depth, breadth, liquidity, and efficiency. The opportunities panel offered an exposé into the opportunities in various sectors of the Nigerian economy, while the visioning panel outlined the trajectory the country needed to follow to actualize our vision for the capital market.

Knowing that a movie focused on saving and investing was an opportunity to broaden the general public's interest and understanding of the value of capital markets, we sought partnership with "Nollywood," Nigeria's vibrant film industry, which plays a crucial role in its cultural and economic landscape. Its dynamic storytelling and rich cultural narratives have captivated a vast international audience, fostering a unique cultural exchange and elevating African cinema on the world stage. Through its extensive reach via digital platforms and global distribution, Nollywood has become a powerful cultural ambassador, influencing perceptions, sparking dialogues, and inspiring filmmakers and audiences worldwide with its innovative and diverse cinematic expressions.

Tracing its history back to the early 1990s with the release of the groundbreaking film *Living in Bondage*, Nollywood emerged as a grassroots-driven industry characterized by rapid production and direct-to-video distribution.[134] Despite limited resources and modest budgets, Nollywood filmmakers leveraged their creativity and resilience to produce content that resonated deeply with local audiences. This approach led to the industry's exponential growth, making it the second-largest film industry in the world by volume, surpassing Hollywood and only trailing behind India's Bollywood.[135]

Iconic films such as *Osuofia in London*, *The Wedding Party*, and *Lionheart* have not only achieved commercial success but also garnered international acclaim, with *Lionheart* being Nigeria's first Netflix Original and the country's first submission for the Academy Awards.[136] The industry's achievements have created jobs, from actors and directors to technical crews and marketers, thus driving economic growth and supporting ancillary industries. Furthermore, Nollywood has been instrumental in promoting Nigerian culture and narratives on a global stage, fostering a sense of national pride and identity. Its continued evolution and success underscore its importance as a pillar of both cultural expression and economic development in Nigeria, as it further fueled the international popularity of the widely acclaimed Afrobeats music genre.

The investment forum we organized closed with the premiere of *Breeze*, a Nollywood movie we sponsored as part of Project 50 aiming to highlight the merits of a culture of saving and investing. We chose to collaborate with a promising young Nigerian filmmaker, Kunle Afolayan, who directed the movie. The movie starred A-list Nollywood stars, including Ayo Adesanya, Yemi Solade, Chioma Chukwuka and Afeez Oyetoro (popularly called *Saka*).

The year-long activities we packed into Project 50 were a resounding success, highlighting the evolution and impact of the capital markets on Nigeria's economic landscape while recognizing the contributions of key stakeholders, including regulators, market operators, and investors. It put the promotion of financial literacy back at the core of the SEC's investor education strategy, demystifying market operations and encouraging greater retail investor involvement as public understanding of investment opportunities and risks improved. Additionally, Project 50 emphasized the importance of regulatory reforms and innovations to adapt to the changing dynamics of global financial markets. By reflecting on past achievements and addressing current challenges, the initiative aimed to chart a course for a more resilient, inclusive, and robust Nigerian capital market, ultimately contributing to the nation's economic development and prosperity.

Other collaborations with Nollywood

Following the success of the *Breeze* collaboration, we saw Nollywood as a new means to further broaden our investor education reach. After the Project 50 commemorations, we continued the collaboration, sponsoring a whole season of Wale Adenuga's *Superstory*, a soap-opera-like series that has been a remarkable success on Nigerian television, captivating audiences since its debut in 2001 with its compelling storytelling and relatable themes.[137] The series, known for its tagline *"We are nothing but pencils in the hands of the creator,"* was known to consistently deliver high-quality, engaging content that reflects societal issues and everyday experiences of Nigerians. Its success is marked by its longevity, widespread popularity, and ability to address topical issues through drama, humor, and suspense. *Superstory* has garnered numerous awards and also set high standards for Nigerian television, contributing significantly to the growth and evolution of the country's entertainment industry. Through several episodes, we integrated educational messages about the capital market, investment opportunities, and the importance of financial literacy into the storyline of *Superstory*. We were able to reach a broad audience, using the power of entertainment to demystify complex financial concepts and promote a culture of informed investment decisions.

Health and Wealth Day

Another financial literacy initiative we introduced in 2013 was "Health and Wealth Day," which aimed at promoting both financial literacy and physical well-being among SEC staff and the general public. Held annually, this event combines health-related activities with financial education sessions, underscoring the SEC's holistic approach to wellness and productivity. The program typically includes health screenings, fitness activities, and seminars on maintaining a healthy lifestyle, alongside workshops and presentations on various financial topics such as investment strategies, retirement planning, and risk management. By addressing both health and wealth, the SEC emphasizes the interconnectedness of physical health and financial stability in achieving overall well-being.

We marked the first edition with early fitness activities before converging on the busy Kuje markets near the international airport in Abuja, inviting market men and women to join us. It was a unique opportunity for us to share inspirational life stories of successful Nigerians in the creative arts with people at the local market. We had respected Nollywood veterans Zack Orji and Paul Obazele, as well as the entertaining pair of Bosede Ogunboye ("Lapacious Bose") and Sani Danja, to share their stories with the market men and women. Our collective goal at the occasion was to share knowledge about saving and investing and maintaining a healthy lifestyle. In line with the common saying "Health is Wealth," participants had one-on-one interactions with financial experts as well as health professionals from the Pro-Health International medical team and the Center for Disease Control in Atlanta, USA.

The impact of "Health and Wealth Day" has been significant in fostering a more informed and health-conscious community within and beyond the SEC. Employees benefit from the convenience of on-site health services and gain valuable insights into managing their health, which can lead to increased productivity and reduced absenteeism. Concurrently, the financial education components of the event empower participants with the knowledge and tools to make sound financial decisions, thereby enhancing their economic security and quality of life. This dual focus on health and financial literacy helps create a more resilient workforce capable of navigating both personal and professional challenges.

Moreover, "Health and Wealth Day" serves as a model for other organizations and underscores the SEC's commitment to corporate social responsibility. By prioritizing the well-being of its employees and the public, the SEC not only improves individual health and financial outcomes but also contributes to broader societal benefits. The initiative promotes a culture of wellness and proactive financial management, encouraging other institutions to adopt similar practices. This holistic approach ultimately supports the SEC's investor outreach strategy, and I am delighted that it is still being observed to this day.

Catch them young

My own story, learning about saving and investing from the age of eight, shows how early exposure to financial literacy can lead to lifelong responsible money management, including sensible debt management, building wealth, and contributing to society. As in my case, it can also spark interest in a career in finance. This informed my decision to introduce a series of initiatives targeting children under a "catch-them-young" program.

The SEC introduced capital market clubs in junior and senior secondary schools across the country. In May 2010, we symbolically chose to launch that year's edition of the clubs in Sokoto State, the furthest northwestern state in Nigeria, where financial literacy rates were among the lowest in the country. The governor of the state at the time graciously accepted to champion the initiative as its patron. The capital market clubs in schools were to promote financial literacy and understanding of concepts in basic economics among schoolchildren. The clubs would provide a hands-on, interactive platform for students to learn about the fundamentals of the stock market, investing, and personal finance.

By simulating real-world financial scenarios and

investment strategies, students can gain practical knowledge and skills that are not typically covered in standard curricula. This early exposure could demystify complex financial concepts, making them more accessible and engaging for young minds, especially as they grow older. They could also promote critical thinking, analytical skills, and a deeper understanding of economic principles. Students involved in capital market clubs can learn valuable skills in any career path and could be inspired to future careers in finance, economics, and business. Furthermore, these clubs were to encourage a culture of saving and investing from a young age, setting students on a path toward financial independence and stability. We wanted to start building a more financially savvy and economically empowered generation.

To complement and deepen the capital market club, we introduced an annual national secondary school quiz competition also aimed at promoting financial literacy and awareness among young students across Nigeria. These competitions involve students from various secondary schools competing in a series of quizzes that test their knowledge on a wide range of topics related to the capital market, financial management, and economic principles. The competition is structured to encourage learning and understanding of the financial sector in a fun and engaging way, making complex concepts more accessible to young minds. By involving schools from different regions, we ensured broad participation and fostered a spirit of healthy competition and national unity.

Participants not only gain a deeper understanding of financial concepts but also develop important skills such as critical thinking, teamwork, and public speaking. Additionally, these competitions help to raise awareness about the importance of financial literacy in the wider community, encouraging parents, educators, and policymakers to prioritize financial education.

In the second half of 2010, we rolled out the year's edition of the competition throughout the geopolitical regions of Nigeria, with the finale taking place in Abuja at a well-attended ceremony. Federal Government College, Enugu, emerged the champions, beating finalists the School for the Gifted, Gwagwalada and Birabi Memorial Grammar School, Bori, who came first and second runners-up, respectively. The competition is still held annually.

As an anecdote to buttress the success of this initiative to inspire a career in finance, one of the winners of the early editions recently reached out to me on LinkedIn after several attempts to reach me since 2021 to tell me how being part of the competition inspired her to pursue a career in finance. She shared with me a group picture I had taken with the winning team, with her the lead of the winning team, a young girl standing graciously in her neat school uniform. Nine years later, she was accepted into the Harvard MBA program and was taking the Chartered Financial Analyst (CFA) designation courses. It was so heartwarming to read her story, which reminded me of the SEC's very valuable and impactful catch-them-young program.

Higher education

At the tertiary level, we wanted to sponsor capital market studies in some universities, including Ahmadu Bello University, Zaria, my alma mater, the University of Nigeria, Nsukka, and the University of Lagos, with plans to include many others. The goal was to support the development of a knowledgeable and skilled workforce equipped to handle the complexities of the financial markets. This can also enable quality academic research and innovation into understanding of market dynamics, investment strategies, regulatory frameworks, and financial technologies. I believe that Nigerian universities can become hubs for cutting-edge ideas and solutions to current and future challenges in the securities markets. Further, we went into partnership with the NYSC management to include topics related to the capital market, saving, and investing at the orientation camps organized for fresh graduates starting their mandatory year of national youth service.

Under my leadership, the SEC also instituted an annual SEC Journalists' Academy, in keeping with my early promise to make the media our partners in the quest to build world class capital markets. The academy was designed as a skills-improvement workshop to promote transparency and accountability in the markets through improved professional journalism. This was in addition to a journalists-only essay competition, inviting write-ups of the highest quality about the capital market from practicing journalists in Nigeria. We hoped this would stimulate interest in reading and writing about the markets, especially among young journalists. The prize winnings at this competition were designed to be in the form of the SEC sponsoring the training at elite local and international learning centers for the winners. We did a similar thing with an "SEC Shareholders' Academy," to educate individual shareholders about their rights as key stakeholders and investors in the capital market. This initiative was intended to address long-standing issues, such as the accumulation of unclaimed dividends, where shareholders are unaware of how to retrieve the dividends declared by the companies in which they hold investments.

In a similar vein, we began sponsoring "Eye on Nigeria's Capital Market," which aired monthly on CNBC Africa, with each edition focusing on a topical issue within the Nigerian market.[138] In addition to its financial literacy objective, the program also provided international investors with reliable reporting about opportunities and relevant news on Nigeria.

The capital markets committee

An important domestic collaboration that I nurtured was the Capital Market Committee (CMC). It was set up long before I joined the SEC, and I quickly saw immense value in it. I am unaware of any other jurisdiction in the world that brings together all relevant stakeholders in the capital market every quarter for "state of the market" meetings. The CMC plays a crucial role in shaping the policies and regulatory frameworks that govern Nigeria's capital markets.

As an advisory body composed of key stakeholders, including regulators, market operators, trade groups, and representatives from various financial institutions, the CMC facilitates a collaborative approach to market oversight and development. It provides a platform for discussing and addressing critical issues impacting the capital markets, such as regulatory changes, market innovations, and emerging risks. This inclusive dialogue ensures that the perspectives and needs of different market participants are considered in the decision-making process, leading to more balanced and effective policies.

Furthermore, the CMC is instrumental in driving initiatives aimed at enhancing market efficiency, transparency, and investor protection. By promoting best practices and cooperation among stakeholders, the committee helps to build a more resilient and competitive capital market environment. Quarterly CMC meetings and consultations allow us, as the apex regulator, to stay abreast of global trends and adapt local regulations to align with international standards. It also gave me an opportunity to set the agenda for the market and rally support for implementing our priorities.

In 2012, I introduced the CMC retreat as an opportunity to occasionally convene for a whole weekend to address urgent market issues or big-ticket items. My plan was for these retreats to showcase the pivotal role of capital markets in Nigeria, particularly in driving infrastructure development, wealth creation, and financial literacy. By inviting prominent figures such as the state governors of Akwa Ibom and Delta, as well as the Minister of the Federal Capital Territory (FCT), these retreats provided a valuable platform for raising awareness and understanding of the capital markets' potential. The presence of these high-profile leaders not only lent credibility to the discussions but also raised the awareness of state government officials of the benefits of leveraging capital markets for the development of their states. The retreats facilitated meaningful dialogue on how capital markets can be harnessed to finance critical infrastructure projects, create investment opportunities, and promote financial education among the populace.

The SEC Integrity Awards

Despite its poor image with respect to integrity, Nigeria is home to some of the most upright people anywhere in the world. In most Nigerian cultures, integrity is a core ethic expected from everybody. In 2012, I became aware of the story of an ordinary Nigerian, Mr. Imeh Usuah. His friends call him Jaja. After many years working as a workshop foreman at the construction giant Julius Berger, Jaja retired. With no savings and mouths to feed, he became a taxi driver. His favorite route was the Nnamdi Azikiwe International Airport to the central business district axis. One fateful day, Jaja picked up two British nationals who had arrived early in the morning on a British Airways flight. He drove them safely through a 45-kilometer trip to their hotel in the Maitama area of Abuja.

Much later in the day, at the carwash, Jaja discovered a brown briefcase tucked underneath the driver's seat. Opening the briefcase, he quickly realized it belonged to the two Oyinbo passengers from his first trip for the day after discovering it contained wads of foreign currency. Jaja quickly drove to the hotel, where he met the two men frantically pacing back and forth with a sad demeanor. They laid eyes on him but did not recognize him until they looked closely and saw their lost bag in his right hand. The agonized look on their faces suddenly disappeared. They collected their bag and thanked Jaja profusely as he made his way out of the hotel lobby. Jaja would discover that the money he returned contained the GBP equivalent of about 300 times the average annual salary at the time. A few months later, that same year, Jaja returned a passenger's expensive camera forgotten in his cab.

When I heard Jaja's story, it spoke to me of the integrity of the kind of Nigerian I meet daily. People outside of Nigeria never hear of such uprightness from our country because we do not celebrate or publicize it. I would never have even heard of Jaja's story if we had not introduced the SEC Integrity Award that year to recognize Nigerians who exemplify the values strongly encouraged in our society. We did not establish this award only to celebrate extraordinary acts of integrity but rather to showcase the integrity of the average Nigerian. The process of choosing a winner involves broad calls for nominations from individuals, the police, the EFCC, and other law enforcement agencies. When nominations are received, a selection comprising SEC staff and some market participants applies a set of criteria to determine the winner. After this rigorous process, Mr. Imeh, a.k.a. Jaja, emerged as the maiden winner of the award in 2012.

Monopoly

Who does not love Monopoly? Not that kind of monopoly! I am referring here to the beloved classic board game that simulates real estate investment and management. The game was initially developed by Elizabeth Magie in 1903 under the name "The Landlord's Game."[139] Magie created the game to illustrate the economic principles of land monopoly and the negative effects of wealth concentration. Her design aimed to teach players about the disparities between private monopolies and the benefits of shared resources. However, the game evolved significantly over time. Charles Darrow, a Philadelphia salesman, popularized a modified version of Magie's game in the 1930s, which was later purchased and distributed by Parker Brothers, leading to the modern version of Monopoly that we recognize today. The game is renowned for its educational value, as it introduces players to fundamental financial concepts such as investment, asset management, and strategic planning. I first encountered Monopoly as a little girl and instantly fell in love with it. Later, when I had my own real money, not Monopoly money, I became an avid collector of the various editions.

Research supports the educational benefits of Monopoly in enhancing financial literacy. A study published in the *American Journal of Business Education* found that playing Monopoly can improve understanding of basic financial concepts and decision-making skills. The game's mechanics require players to manage resources, negotiate deals, and plan investments, which can translate into practical financial skills.[140] Additionally, a study in the *Journal of Economic Education* demonstrated that playing Monopoly helps individuals better grasp the consequences of financial decisions and the importance of strategic thinking.[141]

The nation we call Nigeria today became a geographic reality in 1914 following the amalgamation of the Northern and Southern Protectorates, along with the Lagos Colony, by the British colonial administration. This consolidation was orchestrated by Sir Frederick Lugard, the then Governor-General of Nigeria, with the goal of creating a more manageable and economically cohesive territory. The amalgamation aimed to streamline administrative processes and optimize resource management, laying the groundwork for the modern Nigerian state. This unification was a pivotal moment in Nigerian history, setting the stage for the country's eventual independence in 1960.

To commemorate Nigeria's 100 years of nationhood, the Nigerian government launched a series of activities under the "Nigeria Centenary Celebration" initiative in 2014.[142] Key events included a major national conference, cultural festivals, and historical exhibitions that showcased the country's rich heritage and progress over its century. The government also organized various public lectures and seminars to discuss Nigeria's achievements and future prospects. A significant highlight was the release of the centenary edition of Monopoly, featuring landmarks and institutions integral to Nigeria's history, symbolizing the nation's journey and aspirations. We ensured that the SEC was among these landmark institutions.

The edition was a collaborative effort involving the Nigerian government, and Bestman Games, a Nigerian company founded by Ambassador Nimi Akinkugbe that had the exclusive license for creating games using the iconic global Monopoly brand. The game's design features prominent locations such as the Nigerian SEC, alongside other notable sites such as the Aso Rock, seat of the Nigerian presidency, and Nigeria's parliament, the National Assembly. They were all integrated into the game's property spaces to provide players with a deeper understanding of Nigeria's national symbols and institutions while enjoying the educationally stimulating game.

By including the SEC in the Monopoly game, we hoped to educate players about the role and significance of the Securities and Exchange Commission, increasing awareness of its functions and importance. Our hope was that as the game reaches more homes and classrooms, it will spark greater interest in the capital market among a broader audience.

Our work cut out for us

Knowledge about the SEC in Nigeria is abysmally low. I first discovered this within my first week on the job when letters addressed to me would read "To the DG, Security and Exchange Commission." One day in 2013, I got a vivid reminder of this when an association of Nigerian university students was expected to come to our head offices to confer an award on me. They had written a letter weeks earlier extolling my public service and asking for a date to visit us at the commission to present the plaque to me. Seeing this, as with most occasions, my team thought it was a great idea to accept the invitation, as it was an opportunity to further raise awareness about our work amongst Nigerian university students. The day had arrived, and we gathered in the auditorium that was filled to capacity on the ground floor of the SEC building in Abuja.

The leader of the awarding delegation rose up to speak. The audience was expecting him to give an eloquent speech about our reform initiatives in the capital market that prompted the association to consider me for the award. He was loquacious, praising me for my amazing impact on improving the "security" situation in the country. None of us laughed because we saw that he was not delivering a punchline in a joke routine, but rather was unaware of the role of SEC Nigeria, even though they were in our offices to give me an award for our successes. This young man, a leader of students in a tertiary institution, apparently thought our job at the Securities and Exchange Commission is to ensure the physical security of Nigerian citizens.

After the event, I asked my staff if they caught that moment, and I was relieved to know that I was not just hearing voices. At that point, I knew that we had to redouble our financial literacy efforts if a university student thought our work was similar to the work of the Nigerian military. As of 2013, Boko Haram, an extremist group opposed to what they termed "Western education," based in northeastern Nigeria, was involved in a violent insurgency characterized by a series of attacks against government targets, military personnel, and civilians. The group was known for its brutal tactics, including bombing incidents, assassinations, and kidnappings.[143] Notably, Boko Haram gained international attention in April 2014 with the abduction of over 250 schoolgirls in Chibok, which highlighted its growing threat and the severe impact of its activities on Nigerian society and security.[144]

As Boko Haram's atrocities raged, Nigerians would still find ways to maintain their happiness by finding anything amusing to share with family and friends. Around that same time in 2013, the "My Oga at the Top" story was becoming a viral sensation following a television interview with a state commandant of the Nigeria Security and Civil Defense Corps (NSCDC). This time, "security" really meant physical security. During the interview, the NSCDC official struggled to answer basic questions about his organization's website and gave the URL as "ww.nscdc" containing only two "Ws" instead of three, inadvertently referring to his superior as "my oga at the top." In Nigerian parlance, "oga" is a term derived from Yoruba that means "boss" or "supervisor." Across Nigeria, it is commonly used in informal settings to address someone in a position of authority or someone who holds a higher rank in a workplace or social setting. The clip of this NSCDC official, highlighting his lack of familiarity with the organization's online presence and his fumbling responses, quickly became a source of national amusement, leading to widespread memes and jokes across Nigerian media and social platforms.

Collective investment schemes

Among our major goals with all these financial literacy and investor education programs was to encourage investors who had fled the market following the painful losses from the 2008 collapse. And we thought a clear way to know if we were succeeding or not was to look at the developments in the collective investment schemes (CIS) approved by the SEC. These CIS included mutual funds of various kinds, exchange-traded funds, which became available after we issued enabling rules, unit trusts, real estate investment trusts (REITs), and so on. According to SEC data, the number of registered CIS in Nigeria more than tripled between 2010 and 2024, reflecting an increasing interest among Nigerian retail investors.[145] This shift marks a move away from the traditionally entrenched culture of direct self-investing toward seeking diversification and professional management through the available, more sophisticated, investment vehicles.

The assets under management (AUM) in Nigerian collective investment schemes have experienced substantial growth. As of February 2024, the total AUM reached approximately 2.8 trillion naira, over 110 times the amount at the inception of our financial literacy program in 2010.[146] This significant increase highlights the growing confidence investors have in these schemes. To sustain this growth, it is essential that robust and evolving investor education programs remain relevant to the young, dynamic demographic of investors.

10
Product Innovation And New Platforms

"Innovation distinguishes between a leader and a follower."
— Steve Jobs

The SEC's dual mandate, enshrined in its enabling law, is to regulate and develop Nigeria's capital markets. I saw no contradiction or even conflict between these two overriding objectives. Indeed, I thought they complemented each other. In designing rules and regulations aimed at improving regulation, we put on our market development hat to ensure that we were not going to be stifling innovation with the new rules. As a regulator, I wielded a big stick and took decisive action that aimed to establish market integrity.

But regulation should enable, and not stifle, innovation within well-functioning capital markets. Product innovation in the capital market is crucial for several reasons. First, it enhances market efficiency by introducing new financial instruments and services that cater to the evolving needs of investors and issuers, thereby broadening the range of investment opportunities. Innovative products can improve liquidity and risk management, making it easier for market participants to hedge against potential losses, diversify their portfolio, and optimize their investment strategies. Additionally, product innovation can attract a diverse pool of investors, including those with varying risk appetites and investment horizons, which contributes to the overall growth and dynamism of the market. Ultimately, continuous innovation ensures that the capital market remains competitive, resilient, and capable of supporting economic development. Even the most developed markets need to maintain environments that support continued product innovation.

The shallowness of Nigeria's capital market hampered market liquidity. This deficiency meant that investors had fewer options for diversifying their portfolios, leading to over-reliance on traditional equity (stocks) and debt instruments (bonds). The absence of more sophisticated financial products limited the ability of market participants to effectively manage risk and capitalize on various market opportunities. It stifled the market's growth potential and reduced its attractiveness to both domestic and international investors seeking more comprehensive and advanced investment options. Moreover, the limited product offering failed to cater to the evolving financial needs of the economy, thereby restricting the capital market's role in mobilizing savings, allocating capital efficiently, and facilitating economic development.

The SEC uses rulemaking to set standards, shape behavior, and create a level playing field for market participants. The rulemaking process begins with the identification of a need for new regulations or amendments to existing ones, which may arise from market developments, stakeholder feedback, or regulatory reviews. Following this, the SEC conducts extensive research and analysis to understand the implications of the proposed rule changes. This phase involves benchmarking against international best practices, assessing the potential impact on market participants, and consulting with internal experts and advisory committees.

Once a draft regulation is prepared, the SEC engages in a public consultation process to gather input from a wide range of stakeholders, including market operators, investors, legal experts, and the general public. This consultation is crucial for ensuring that the proposed rules are well-informed, practical, and reflective of the market's needs. Feedback received during this period is carefully reviewed and incorporated into the final draft, where appropriate. The final step involves the approval of the regulations by the SEC's board, after which the rules are officially published and communicated to the market participants. This transparent and participatory rulemaking process helps to foster a regulatory environment that is fair, effective, and responsive to the evolving dynamics of the market. To usher in an era of product innovation in the market, we needed to reinvigorate and streamline the SEC's rulemaking process. We redesigned it to be a structured and iterative process through which necessary regulations could be developed, looking at what works, and making adjustments as needed.

Among the first set of rules I made sure were introduced after streamlining the rulemaking process, were the rules on margin lending, a framework for borrowing funds to purchase securities, ensuring that both lenders and borrowers adhere to strict requirements. By setting clear guidelines on collateral valuation, margin requirements, and the handling of margin calls, these rules would enable the mitigation of the risk of excessive leverage and prevent situations where market volatility could lead to widespread defaults and financial instability. Many in the market, including the banks, had their fingers burnt with margin calls without adequate rules to guide the process.

The establishment of AMCON was motivated by the need to reduce the Nigerian banking system's exposure to toxic assets.[147] These included problematic loan categories, primarily to the oil and gas sector, which faced significant challenges due to a sharp drop in oil prices, margin loans used for speculative trading on the NGX, and insider lending, where inadequate risk management allowed banks to exceed prescribed lending limits to insiders. The margin lending rules we issued were intended to set allowable boundaries and exclude bank stocks due to the inherent conflict of interest that could arise. Banks, as both lenders and borrowers in the financial system, are uniquely positioned to influence market conditions and access privileged information. Allowing margin lending on bank stocks could exacerbate systemic risk, as it might lead to excessive leverage and speculative trading. Which is exactly what happened in the absence of rules on margin lending. We therefore had to restrict margin lending on bank stocks to maintain market integrity, ensure fair practices, and safeguard against destabilizing effects that could threaten the broader financial system.

By allowing investors to leverage their existing portfolios, these rules helped increase trading volumes and enhanced market depth in a responsible way, subject to regulatory oversight. This increased liquidity can lead to more efficient price discovery and smoother market operations. Moreover, well-regulated margin lending practices can attract a broader range of investors, including those seeking to optimize their returns through leverage, thus contributing to the growth and dynamism of the securities market, a trend gradually underway in Nigeria, which should continue to be monitored.

Index funds

Stock exchange indexes are vital indicators of market performance, reflecting the overall health and trends of financial markets by tracking a selected group of stocks. These indexes serve as benchmarks for investors and provide insights into the economic climate. For instance, the Dow Jones Industrial Average (DJIA) in the United States comprises thirty major blue-chip companies and has long been considered a barometer of American economic vitality. In Europe, the FTSE 100 represents the 100 largest companies listed on the London Stock Exchange, highlighting the United Kingdom's market strength. Similarly, the Nikkei 225 tracks 225 prominent companies on the Tokyo Stock Exchange, offering a gauge of Japan's economic pulse. The Shanghai Composite Index likewise encompasses all stocks traded on the Shanghai Stock Exchange, reflecting China's dynamic market. Each index, through its curated selection of representative companies, encapsulates the broader economic landscape of its respective region, providing investors with essential data for making informed decisions.

Like the other stock exchanges around the world, the NGX also features several key indexes that serve as barometers for market performance and investor sentiment. The NGX All-Share Index, introduced in 1985, tracks the performance of all listed equities on the exchange, offering a comprehensive snapshot of the overall market movement and health. The NGX 30 Index, launched in 2008, focuses on the top thirty companies based on market capitalization and liquidity, providing insights into the most influential players in the Nigerian market. Additionally, the NGX Premium Index, introduced in 2015, highlights the performance of the exchange's most liquid and high-quality stocks, comprising eight stocks as of August 2024 who are expected to reflect the highest standards in terms of corporate governance and financial performance.[148]

We issued rules for the creation, operation, and management of ETFs within Nigeria with a focus on transparency, efficiency, and investor protection. The new rules clarified the approval process for launching ETFs, listing requirements, ongoing disclosure obligations, and the roles and responsibilities of ETF sponsors and fund managers. The aim was to facilitate the growth of ETFs as a viable investment option, offering investors diversified exposure to different asset classes, while maintaining robust oversight to uphold market integrity and investor confidence.

Less than a year after we issued the ETF rules, in December 2011, the first ETF, the "NewGold ETF," was launched by ABSA Capital, a South African investment bank. This ETF was designed to track the price of gold and provided Nigerian investors with an opportunity to invest in the commodity without the need to hold physical gold. The introduction of the NewGold ETF marked a significant milestone in the development of Nigeria's capital markets, offering a new, innovative investment product that enhanced market depth and provided investors with greater diversification options. Since then, the NGX has continued to support the growth of the ETF market, encouraging the introduction of more ETFs to cater to the evolving needs of investors.

The next ETF to follow was the Vetiva Griffin 30 ETF, which mirrors the performance of the NGX 30 Index, offering investors exposure to the top thirty companies listed on the NGX. One of the biggest fund managers in Nigeria, Stanbic IBTC, also introduced the Stanbic

IBTC ETF 30, which equally tracks the NGX 30 Index. Lotus Capital, a leading ethical investment management firm based in Lagos, also launched the Lotus Halal Equity ETF, catering to specific investment strategies, including sharia-compliant investments. These diverse offerings enable investors to diversify their portfolios, manage risk more effectively, and tap into various market segments with ease and cost-efficiency. Empirical research underscores the cost-efficiency of ETFs, driven by their lower expense ratios and added tax benefits. A study by Morningstar Canada found that, on average, ETFs have expense ratios 0.43% lower than actively managed mutual funds, directly translating into cost savings for investors.[149]

Globally, ETFs continue to grow in popularity. According to a new study by professional services firm PwC, global ETF assets under management (AUM) have experienced an impressive compound annual growth rate of 18.9% between 2018 and 2023.[150] The PwC report states that by the end of 2023, ETF AUM surged by over 25% from December 2022, reaching a new peak of nearly US$11.5 trillion. Additionally, PwC revealed that the number of asset managers offering ETFs has more than doubled since 2013, rising to 582 from 233, with 60% of the top 100 asset managers now providing ETFs. This substantial growth underscores the significant opportunities in the ETF market, which, according to a PwC survey, show no signs of diminishing.

Research demonstrates that passive investment strategies, including ETFs, often outperform actively managed funds in terms of performance. A study conducted by Morningstar found that, over a ten-year period, more than 60% of actively managed equity funds underperformed their benchmark indexes, whereas ETFs, which typically track these indexes, delivered superior returns with lower costs.[151] Another study published in the *Journal of Financial Economics* analyzed performance data of actively managed mutual funds and ETFs across various market conditions. The study revealed that ETFs not only had lower expense ratios, but also exhibited better performance consistency compared to their actively managed counterparts. This is largely due to the passive nature of ETFs, which minimizes the risk of manager underperformance and reduces transaction costs. The findings affirm that, over the long-term, ETFs tend to outperform actively managed funds, providing investors with both cost-efficiency and robust returns.[152]

Real Estate Investment Trusts (REITs)

Real Estate Investment Trusts (REITs) were first introduced in the United States in 1960 through the Real Estate Investment Trust Act, which was signed into law by President Dwight D. Eisenhower. This groundbreaking legislation allowed individual investors to invest in large-scale, income-producing real estate, similar to how they would invest in stocks and bonds. By providing a structure for real estate companies to pool capital from numerous investors and distribute income in the form of dividends, REITs democratized real estate investment, making it accessible to a broader audience. Over the decades, the concept of REITs expanded globally, with many countries adopting similar frameworks, and REITs have since become a significant and popular asset class, offering liquidity, diversification, and regular income to investors.

According to the National Association of Real Estate Investment Trusts (NAREIT), as of 2023, forty-one countries and regions, representing 83% of global GDP and home to over 5 billion people, have enacted specific legislation for REITs. Since 2015, five countries – China, Oman, Portugal, Sri Lanka, and Saudi Arabia – have introduced REIT legislation. Over this period, the number of listed REITs has surged by 33%, adding 222 REITs, with the majority of this growth occurring in Asia, where the count rose from 141 to 223, according to data from NAREIT.[153]

The first REIT in Nigeria, the Union Homes Hybrid REIT, was launched in 2008, offering a mix of residential and commercial real estate investments. In 2012 we strengthened the rules which saw renewed interest in the issuance of new REITs. Following this, the Skye Shelter Fund REIT was introduced in 2010, focusing primarily on residential properties. In 2013, the UPDC REIT entered the market, providing a diversified portfolio of commercial, residential, and industrial properties. These REITs were enabling investors to benefit from the income and capital appreciation of real estate while enjoying the liquidity and regulatory protections of the capital markets.

Empirical research shows that REITs often outperform other asset classes in terms of investment returns. A study by NAREIT and the University of California, Berkeley, revealed that over a twenty-year period, REITs delivered an average annual return of 11.6%, surpassing the performance of both the S&P 500 and bonds.[154] This superior performance is largely attributed to REITs' unique structure, which combines the income stability of real estate with the liquidity of stocks. By focusing on income-producing properties and adhering to the distribution requirements mandated for REITs, these entities often generate higher yields compared to traditional equities and fixed-income investments. Moreover, their diversification across various property sectors mitigates risks and enhances overall return potential.

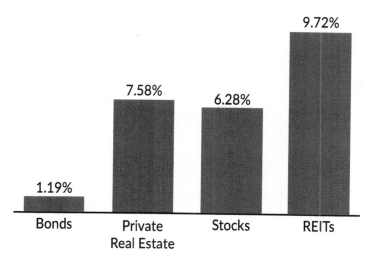

REITs Outperform International Stocks and Bonds, 2009–2022 (Source: NAREIT)

In addition to their investment return performance, REITs have a notable positive impact on the housing and commercial real estate sectors. Another study by NAREIT highlights that REITs contribute significantly to the development and modernization of real estate infrastructure.[155] For instance, REIT investments in residential properties have been linked to increased housing supply and improved property standards, benefiting renters and homeowners alike. Commercial REITs, on the other hand, play a crucial role in revitalizing urban areas, attracting businesses, and fostering economic growth. Their investments in office spaces, shopping centers, and industrial properties not only enhance local real estate markets, but also generate employment opportunities and stimulate economic activity.

Further empirical evidence underscores the broader societal benefits of REITs. A study published in the *Journal of Real Estate Research* found that regions with a high concentration of REIT investments experienced higher property values and improved local infrastructure.[156] This is due to the capital inflows from REITs that drive redevelopment projects and upgrades to existing properties. Additionally, REITs' focus on maintaining high occupancy rates and quality standards ensures that properties remain attractive to tenants and buyers, contributing to stable and prosperous real estate markets. Overall, REITs offer a compelling blend of return potential and positive real estate impact, making them a valuable asset class for both investors and the communities they serve.

Market making and securities lending

In 2012, we amended the rules on market making, which enabled the Nigerian Stock Exchange to first introduce market making in September 2012, with ten stockbroking firms qualifying as market makers. United Bank of Africa (UBA) Plc and Stanbic IBTC Plc were appointed securities lending agents for equities and bond transactions at the exchange. Concurrently, we approved the Nigerian Stock Exchange's implementation framework for appointing fixed-income market makers.

Market making and securities lending significantly enhance liquidity by ensuring that there are always buyers and sellers available for securities, thus facilitating smoother and more efficient trading. Market makers provide continuous bid and ask quotes, narrowing spreads and enabling investors to buy or sell securities without substantial price changes. This constant presence of market makers helps in maintaining orderly markets and improving price discovery. Securities lending complements this by allowing investors to borrow and sell securities they do not own, thereby increasing the volume of securities available for trading. This not only boosts market liquidity but also enables short selling, which can contribute to more efficient pricing and reduced volatility.

Before we introduced market making, daily trading volumes were relatively modest due to liquidity constraints and wider bid-ask spreads. The average daily trading volume in the first half of 2012 was approximately 183 million shares.[157] The impact of market making quickly became evident, with a year-over-year 46.5% increase in the average daily trading volume as average daily volumes topped 268 million shares by the end of 2013. The upward trend continued in 2014, supported by the ongoing activities of market makers and the introduction of securities lending. These mechanisms contributed to a further increase in market liquidity. The average daily trading volume reached the 300 million shares mark in 2014. Despite economic challenges and market volatility, the stock exchange maintained relatively high trading volumes in 2015, the average daily trading holding up at approximately 290 million shares. The resilience in trading volumes, amid an unfavorable macroeconomic environment during this period, highlighted the effectiveness of market making and securities lending in sustaining market activity even in less-favorable economic conditions (the backdrop was uncertainty related to the general elections that year and the significant collapse of oil prices).

Securitization

Complementary to securities lending, we began working on the SEC rules on securitization, providing a legal framework for the issuance and regulation of asset-backed securities (ABS) and mortgage-backed securities (MBS). Our rules specified the registration and disclosure requirements for issuing ABS and MBS, including submitting a detailed prospectus or offering a memorandum that provides comprehensive information about the securitized assets, their underlying collateral, cash flows, and risk factors, in addition to all other relevant information. The CBN complemented this with rules and regulations for banks engaged in securitization, covering risk management, capital adequacy, and accounting requirements.

Asset-backed securities (ABS), created through securitization, are financial instruments secured by contracts on future cash flows, typically backed by assets such as auto loans or residential mortgages, and occasionally by other types of receivables including credit card debts and even book or music royalties. Unlike traditional corporate loans or bonds, which are secured by a company's promise to repay, ABS are collateralized by specific assets, allowing for more tailored financing solutions that align with distinct risks and return goals. Asset-backed securities are designed with investor-friendly features that enhance protection against losses and boost liquidity. These include bankruptcy remoteness, payment prioritization, overcollateralization, excess spread, amortization, professional servicing, and a diverse range of payers within the underlying asset pool. Overcollateralization simply means pledging more assets than required to back the issued securities, offering investors an additional cushion in the event of default.

Securitization commences with the establishment of a special purpose vehicle (SPV), which acquires a portfolio of assets and concurrently secures debt financing by issuing ABS to fund the acquisition of these assets.

Typically, securitizations aggregate similar types of contractual assets, such as auto loans, aircraft leases, credit card receivables, or corporate loans, into a unified pool. For a securitization to be viable, the underlying assets must consist of contractual obligations to make payments. Each asset involves a payer – such as a borrower, lessee, or insurer – and a corresponding contract, such as a mortgage, lease, loan, or receivable.

The size and complexity of the securitization market have grown significantly over the past few decades, driven by innovations in financial engineering and increasing demand for diversified investment products. Major financial centers, such as the United States, Europe, and Asia, play pivotal roles in this market, with the United States holding the largest share due to its well-established securitization infrastructure and extensive range of securitized products. As of December 2023, the global securitization market, encompassing structured credit and government-backed structured finance, was valued at over US$13.8 trillion, dominated by the United States, which accounts for 90% of this total, according to data from SIFMA.[158]

Historically, banks were the primary source of asset financing, but their role has diminished since the 2008 global financial crisis due to regulatory changes and strategic shifts. This gap has been filled by non-bank financiers, such as investment funds, insurance companies, and high-net-worth individuals, who now provide capital in the evolving ABS market. The market features various terms, including asset-backed finance and structured credit, with specific types such as collateralized loan obligations (CLOs), collateral-ized debt obligations (CDOs), and residential mort-gage-backed securities (RMBS).

Indeed, through RMBS, securitization is particu-larly transformative for the housing sector. By convert-ing mortgage loans into tradable securities, financial institutions can offload these assets from their balance sheets, freeing up capital to issue more mortgages for residential buildings. This process increases liquid-ity in the housing market, allowing lenders to offer more competitive mortgage rates and terms. Mortgage-backed securities played a central role in the United States housing market during the early 2000s, driving increased lending to a diverse range of homebuyers. By pooling mortgages into securities and selling them to investors, financial institutions could offload the risk associated with individual loans, allowing them to extend credit to more borrowers, fueling the 2003 to 2006 credit boom. Although this expansion of credit contributed to a surge in homeownership rates, many point to it as the origin of the 2008 global financial crisis.

As the housing market peaked and began to decline, the vulnerabilities of this credit expansion became starkly apparent. The collapse in housing prices led to a wave of mortgage defaults, particularly among sub-prime borrowers, which severely impacted the value of MBS and CDOs. Subprime borrowers are individ-uals with a less-than-stellar credit history, often char-acterized by past delinquencies, high debt-to-income ratios, or a limited credit record. These borrowers are considered higher risk compared to those with prime credit scores, which typically qualify them for more favorable lending terms. Because of their elevated risk profile, subprime borrowers usually face higher interest rates on loans, designed to compensate lenders for the increased likelihood of default.

During the credit boom, subprime mortgages were specifically designed and massively marketed to these borrowers, often with terms that reflect their riskier credit status. Financial institutions and investors holding these assets faced massive losses, especially from private label RMBS and MBS-backed CDOs that had subprime mortgages as part of their underlying assets. This revealed the risks of relying on ratings, monoline insurance guarantees, and historical performance during the 2003–2006 credit boom. The interconnectedness of these securities and the widespread reliance on optimistic credit ratings amplified the crisis, culminating in a systemic collapse that affected global markets.

A key lesson from the global financial crisis is that, while product innovation should be encouraged, regulators must maintain a vigilant oversight of the entire financial ecosystem. This diligence is crucial for promptly identifying emerging risks and deploying regulatory tools effectively to protect the stability of the broader financial system. Following regulatory intervention in the post-global financial crisis era, the structured credit market underwent significant reform, requiring market participants to adopt more sustainable credit underwriting practices.

This transition was marked by the entry of well-capitalized, cautious investors, enhancing market liquidity and stability. However, despite these improvements, structured credit remains vulnerable to volatility and potential losses. During the early stages of the COVID-19 pandemic, structured credit experienced downward rating adjustments, but it still performed better than other asset classes. For instance, CLOs saw no defaults in 2020 and only five in 2021, according to Standard & Poor's, contrasting favorably with the high-yield bond market, which had a default rate of up to 9% in August 2020, and the leveraged loan market, with a 4.2% default rate in September 2020.[159]

Non-interest products

In December 2012, we introduced rules on sukuk issuance in Nigeria. In Islamic finance, sukuk are financial certificates that comply with shariah law, which prohibits the charging or paying of interest. Instead of representing a debt obligation, sukuk certificates represent a share in an asset or a business venture, with the investors earning returns through profit-sharing, lease payments, or other income generated by the underlying asset. This structure ensures that investments are backed by tangible assets and that returns are derived from legitimate commercial activities, aligning with Islamic principles. Sukuk have gained popularity as a means of raising capital for infrastructure projects and other investments while catering to the ethical preferences of Muslim investors, contributing to the growth and diversification of global financial markets.

A sukuk is similar to a zero-coupon bond in that it typically does not provide periodic interest payments and is issued at a discount of its face value. Instead of earning periodic interest, sukuk holders receive a lump-sum payment upon maturity, reflecting the appreciation of their initial investment. Like zero-coupon bonds, sukuk generates returns through the difference between the discounted purchase price and the face value paid at maturity, aligning with sharia principles that prohibit interest payments but allow for returns derived from profit-sharing and asset-backed structures.

Many prominent sukuk issuances are managed by leading conventional investment banks. For instance, global giants such as JPMorgan Chase, HSBC, and Standard Chartered have played pivotal roles in structuring and underwriting major sukuk deals. In recent years, these banks have facilitated significant sukuk transactions for high-profile issuers, including sovereign entities and large corporations, demonstrating their expertise in blending conventional financial practices with Islamic finance principles. Their involvement underscores the integration of conventional banking expertise in the thriving global sukuk market.

In 2014, the United Kingdom became the first non-Muslim country to issue sukuk, demonstrating its commitment to becoming a global center for Islamic finance. The UK government issued £200 million in sovereign sukuk, attracting orders of over £2.3 billion, which highlighted strong investor interest.[160] This landmark issuance was part of broader efforts to diversify funding sources and showcase London's capability to support shariah-compliant financial products.

The global sukuk market has experienced substantial growth in the recent past, reflecting increased demand for shariah-compliant financial instruments around the world. According to the Islamic Financial Services Industry (IFSI) Stability Report 2020, the total sukuk issuance reached US$162 billion in 2019, up from US$125 billion in 2018. By 2021, global sukuk issuance had further surged, with the total value surpassing US$200 billion, driven by strong activity in key markets such as Malaysia, Saudi Arabia, and the United Arab Emirates.[161] This rapid expansion highlights the growing appeal of sukuk among both issuers and investors seeking ethical and diversified investment opportunities.

According to S&P, global sukuk issuances totaled US$168.4 billion in 2023.[162] Investors drawn to ethical and sustainable investing often find a natural alignment with Islamic finance products, as both approaches emphasize principles of social responsibility and ethical stewardship. Islamic finance operates on the foundation of sharia law, which mandates that investments be free from activities deemed harmful or unethical, such as gambling or usury. This commitment to ethical practices resonates with investors who seek to align their portfolios with values that promote environmental sustainability, social justice, and economic fairness. The core tenets of Islamic finance – such as risk-sharing, asset-backed financing, and the prohibition of speculative activities – mirror the principles of responsible investing.

Furthermore, the principles of transparency, fairness, and stakeholder welfare embedded in Islamic finance attract investors who are keen on supporting sustainable development and ethical business practices. The emphasis of Islamic finance on equitable profit and loss sharing, along with its focus on real economic activity and tangible assets, aligns with the broader objectives of sustainable investing. This synergy not only appeals to those who are motivated by moral and ethical considerations but also to those who seek to contribute to a more balanced and responsible financial system.

Nigeria is particularly suitable for the growth of the sukuk market due to its substantial Muslim population, which provides a strong foundation for demand. Nigeria is home to at least 90 million Muslims, the fifth largest population of Muslims in the world.[163] This significant demographic factor creates a natural market for shariah-compliant financial products such as sukuk. Additionally, Nigeria's urgent need for infrastructure development and economic diversification makes sukuk an attractive financing mechanism.

Less than a year after we issued the sukuk rules, the state government of Osun became the first issuer of sukuk in Nigeria, raising 11.4 billion naira (US$62 million at the time) in Ijarah sukuk to build schools.[164] Later, Lotus Capital Limited raised 1 billion naira of private sukuk of Al-Istisna to finance the construction of apartments in Lagos.[165] More recently, the Nigerian federal government has been issuing sukuks to finance infrastructure construction. The maiden sovereign sukuk issuance in September 2017 raised 100 billion naira (approximately US$326 million) with a seven-year tenor, and was heavily oversubscribed, confirming strong market interest and confidence in shariah-compliant instruments.[166] The funds were allocated to critical road projects across the six geopolitical zones of Nigeria. A year later, the government issued another sukuk of equivalent size and tenor to expand the infrastructure works.

When compared to other major Islamic finance hubs, such as Malaysia, Saudi Arabia, and the United Arab Emirates, Nigeria significantly lags behind. For instance, Malaysia, with a Muslim population of approximately 20 million, accounted for 40.3% market share of global sukuk outstanding and 43.3% of global sukuk issued in 2022.[167] Nigeria accounts for less than 0.1% on both counts.

The development of Islamic index funds in Nigeria naturally followed the introduction of products such as the sukuk and other shariah-compliant investment options within the country's financial market. These funds track indices that include only companies that are not explicitly involved in practices considered "haram" in Islamic philosophy, therefore excluding businesses involved in activities such as gambling, alcohol, and conventional interest-based banking. The previously mentioned Lotus Halal Equity ETF, launched in 2015, is a notable example, providing investors with a diversified portfolio of shariah-compliant stocks listed on the exchange.[168] This initiative has broadened the range of ethical investment opportunities available to Nigerian investors, attracting both domestic and international investors interested in aligning their financial goals with their religious or ethical beliefs.

New trading platforms

Unregulated over-the-counter (OTC) markets present significant challenges to the global financial system due to insufficient transparency and oversight. Unlike regulated exchanges, OTC markets operate without stringent regulatory frameworks, which can lead to a higher risk of fraud, manipulation, and financial instability. The opacity of these markets makes it difficult for investors to obtain accurate and timely information about securities, resulting in increased vulnerability to deceptive practices. For example, the 2008 financial crisis highlighted severe issues in the OTC derivatives market, where complex financial instruments such as mortgage-backed securities and credit default swaps were traded with minimal oversight, contributing to the systemic collapse. This lack of regulation allowed the proliferation of high-risk assets and ultimately led to significant economic fallout. Another illustrative case that happened even before the 2008 global financial crisis is the scandal involving Enron's use of OTC markets to conceal its financial health through complex derivative transactions. The subsequent collapse of Enron and the revelations about its accounting practices underscored the dangers of insufficiently regulated markets and led to calls for increased transparency and oversight on OTC markets that went largely unheeded.

Following the global financial crisis, my colleagues at IOSCO, particularly from advanced markets severely impacted by OTC market issues, were exploring ways to regulate OTC transactions. During the 2011 annual meeting, I recounted the story of Nigeria's Financial Markets Dealers Association (FMDA), previously known as the Money Market Association of Nigeria (MMAN), which had approached the SEC to register their platform as an officially recognized exchange. This was an unusual situation; typically, industries operate unregulated until problems prompt regulatory intervention. However, the FMDA sought proactive oversight, recognizing that official registration and supervision would enhance their platform's credibility.

After a thorough review of the FMDA's proposal – including its structural design, governance rules, and member-conduct monitoring – the SEC approved the platform in 2013, initially named the FMDQ OTC Securities Exchange. This development was a significant advancement in Nigeria's financial infrastructure, aimed at improving the OTC market's efficiency and transparency. In 2019, the platform was rebranded as FMDQ Securities Exchange, reflecting its expanded role and adherence to global standards. The exchange has greatly enhanced Nigeria's financial markets by providing a robust platform for trading fixed-income securities and foreign exchange, fostering transparency, efficiency, and liquidity. Its innovative trading solutions and strong regulatory framework have attracted a diverse array of participants, including both domestic and international investors, thus boosting market liquidity and investor confidence.

Since its inception, FMDQ Securities Exchange has achieved impressive growth, establishing itself as a cornerstone of Nigeria's financial market. By April 2024, the total value of securities listed on FMDQ had exceeded 177 trillion naira (approximately US$404 billion), with an average annual turnover reaching the same amount, indicative of substantial increases in trading volumes and market engagement.[169] The platform supports a diverse range of products, including bonds, commercial papers, treasury bills, open market operation (OMO) bills, mutual funds, repos, unsecured placements, foreign exchange (FX), OTC FX futures, FX forwards, swaps, money market derivatives, FGN bond futures, ETFs, depository receipts, and warrants. The effective management of the FMDQ platform registration impressed my colleagues at IOSCO, who were eager to learn from our experience as they undertook their own reform efforts.

The flaws uncovered by the 2008 global financial crisis include unmanageable counterparty risks, a lack of transparency regarding market activities and credit exposures, and operational inefficiencies that underscored the need for greater standardization and automation. In response, the G20 Leaders in 2009 endorsed a series of reforms to address these issues. These reforms aimed to introduce central clearing and, where feasible, exchange or electronic trading for standardized OTC derivatives, mandate transaction reporting to trade repositories, and impose stricter capital and margin requirements for transactions not centrally cleared. In response, IOSCO issued the IOSCO Principles for the Regulation and Supervision of Commodity Derivatives Markets in 2011, building upon the so-called Tokyo Communiqué of 1997, which endorsed best practices for commodity contract design and market surveillance.

The United States has implemented these reforms through the Dodd-Frank Wall Street Reform and Consumer Protection Act and associated regulations enforced by agencies such as the Commodity Futures Trading Commission, the U.S. SEC, and the Federal Reserve. In Europe, European Market Infrastructure Regulation (EMIR) has established requirements for clearing certain derivatives through central counterparties (CCPs), standardizing contracts, and reporting trades to trade repositories. These measures aim to enhance market transparency, reduce counterparty risk, and improve the overall stability of the financial system by ensuring that all trades are documented and accessible to regulators, thereby reducing the potential for hidden systemic risks. The push toward central clearing aims to mitigate counterparty risk by having a central clearing house assume the role of guarantor in transactions, thus reducing the risk of default by any single party. The Basel Committee on Banking Supervision has also introduced stricter capital and liquidity requirements for financial institutions engaging in OTC trading, ensuring that they maintain sufficient reserves to absorb potential losses. Collectively, these reforms have sought to enhance the resilience of the global financial system by improving oversight, increasing transparency, and ensuring that risk-management practices are robust enough to withstand market shocks.

According to a 2022 progress report from the Financial Stability Board (FSB), the implementation of the G20's OTC derivatives reforms was in broadly advanced stages across the twenty-four FSB member jurisdictions, though progress on remaining gaps has been rather incremental.[170] Notably, eighteen jurisdictions now have higher capital requirements for non-centrally cleared derivatives (up from fifteen), and interim measures are in place universally. Margin requirements remain in effect in sixteen jurisdictions, with some adopting final standards and others planning implementation. Trade reporting requirements are active in twenty-three jurisdictions, with ongoing enhancements to trade repositories. Central clearing requirements are enforced in seventeen jurisdictions, with some moving toward mandatory clearing. Platform-trading requirements remain unchanged at thirteen jurisdictions. Most jurisdictions have reverted or made permanent changes to the temporary measures introduced during COVID-19 to address operational burdens and procyclicality.[171]

Just like the FMDA, the Nigerian National Association of Securities Dealers (NASD) approached us with their intention to register a platform for dealing in securities. Their intention was to begin with a focus on facilitating the trading of the shares and securities of unlisted companies. We also reviewed and approved the platform in 2013. The NASD facilitates the trading of unlisted public securities, thereby bridging a crucial gap in the Nigerian capital market. Before the establishment of NASD, there was no formal market for trading shares of unlisted companies, leading to illiquidity and a lack of transparency. NASD has addressed these challenges by offering a regulated environment where investors can buy and sell shares of companies that are not listed on the Nigerian Stock Exchange. This has improved price discovery, liquidity, and investor protection for these securities, contributing to the overall depth and breadth of the Nigerian capital market.

In terms of commodities trading, the Nigeria Commodity Exchange (NCX), originally established as the Abuja Securities and Commodities Exchange in 1998, had been attempting to provide a structured marketplace where buyers and sellers of agricultural products can transact with greater efficiency and transparency. Being a state-owned and controlled entity, the NCX has not lived up to expectations.

In 2014, we received an application to register another commodity exchange called Africa Exchange (AFEX) to address the very challenging task of improving price discovery and providing liquidity to producers and traders of mostly agricultural products. I am delighted that one of my final decisions as DG SEC was to approve AFEX as a commodity trading platform. The platform has since introduced products and services, such as warehouse receipts and commodity futures contracts, to facilitate efficient trading and investment in commodities such as maize, soybeans, and rice, all aligned with Nigeria's broader goals of modernizing agricultural finance and boosting the agricultural sector's overall productivity.

AFEX is attempting to become pan-African, currently operating 200 warehouses in Nigeria, Kenya, and Uganda, and serving over 450,000 farmers in multiple African countries.[172] In November 2023, they received US$26.5 million in committed support from British International Investment (BII), the United Kingdom's development finance institution, to build twenty additional modern warehouses in strategic locations in Nigeria, Kenya, and Uganda.[173] The new warehouses will add 230,000 metric tons of storage capacity, allowing up to 200,000 additional farmers to benefit from affordable storage solutions and optimize their crop sales. This could potentially boost farmer incomes by over 200%.

I was elated to read the news of their progress and the support from British International Investment (BII), so I congratulated them on LinkedIn, to which the group CEO, who was among the people that came to us in 2014, responded so heartwarmingly:

"Thank you so much, Ma Arunma (AEEM) Oteh. Most people would not have taken a bet on a very young (all under 30) team and gave them a license when you did. You have also consistently been in our corner. History will continue to remember you for all the good you did for Nigeria, and indeed across the globe."[174]

His message reminded me of the richly rewarding fulfillment in the work we did at the SEC.

The establishment and support for these new trading platforms – FMDQ, NASD, and AFEX – have collectively transformed the landscape of Nigeria's financial system. They have introduced greater diversity and sophistication into the market, offering tailored solutions for different types of securities and commodities. These platforms have also encouraged the adoption of best practices in trading, transparency, and regulatory compliance, thereby fostering investor confidence and participation. The continued development and integration of such platforms are crucial for the sustained growth and resilience of Nigeria's capital markets, ensuring that they can continue to support the country's broader economic development objectives.

11
Beyond Finance

"The best way to ensure a better future is through good governance."
— Peter Drucker

Capital markets hold profound significance beyond providing access to affordable long-term money, a lot of which is usually underappreciated, including playing a crucial role in enhancing governance and transparency in society. Companies listed on stock exchanges must adhere to stringent regulatory frameworks that require frequent disclosures, including audited quarterly and annual financial statements, management discussions, and analyses. In the United States, the U.S. SEC mandates detailed disclosure requirements for publicly traded companies, including filing 10-K and 10-Q reports, which provide extensive information on a company's financial condition and business operations. At the Nigerian SEC, we also require such regular filings to boost transparency and allow investors to make informed decisions.

These requirements create a strong incentive for firms to implement robust internal control measures and transparent reporting practices. A report by the World Bank highlights how the increased scrutiny from analysts, investors, and the media, which comes with being publicly traded, leads to more disciplined management and better alignment of executive compensation with shareholder interests.[175] This heightened accountability not only mitigates the risk of corporate mismanagement but also fosters a culture of ethical conduct and long-term value creation.

Listing on the stock exchange and corporate governance

For me, it was crucial to increase the number of listed companies on the stock exchange for several reasons. The first reason was for the obvious benefit of expanding the adoption of best corporate governance practices in Nigeria. Secondly, we wanted the stock market to better reflect the economy in terms of the composition of listed companies, thereby reducing concentration risk. Following the market correction of 2008, by the time I assumed office at the SEC, the stock exchange had 216 listed equities on the exchange, with banks dominating, accounting for about 45% of capitalization. The next-most capitalized sectors were breweries, food, beverages and tobacco and building materials. Strangely, for a country known for its regional leading status in oil and gas, petroleum was a minuscule sector on the exchange. Even the listed companies in that sector were mostly in oil marketing, the downstream subsector. We were determined to change this by pushing for the listing of companies from all important sectors of the economy, including agriculture (which has been the largest sector in the Nigerian economy), oil and gas, and telecommunications.

Our advocacy bore fruit with the attraction of significant listings. In April 2014, Seplat Petroleum Development Company, an indigenous oil and gas firm that had commenced operations in June 2009, achieved a milestone by listing its shares on both the Nigerian Stock Exchange and the London Stock Exchange. This landmark dual listing, the first of its kind for a Nigerian company, followed extensive preparation and a thorough review of listing regulations. The company successfully raised US$500 million in an oversubscribed IPO in both Lagos and London, enhancing its global visibility and broadening its access to a diverse range of investors. While celebrating its tenth listing anniversary, the company disclosed it had paid out US$575 million in dividends to shareholders, its shares appreciating by almost 500% since getting listed.[176] We also held targeted engagements with other companies in the industry, prodding them to get listed, including the government behemoth, the Nigerian National Petroleum Company (NNPC), and the partly state-owned Nigeria Liquefied Natural Gas (NLNG) company. These engagements continue as many in Nigeria recognize the clear advantages of listing such significant national assets, democratizing ownership, fostering social cohesion, and enhancing the depth of the capital market.

Based on our enhancement of the listing rules and the advocacy we championed, I was delighted that MTN, Africa's leading telecommunications group, eventually listed its shares on the Nigerian Stock Exchange in 2019 after eighteen years of operating in the country as a subsidiary of the South African group.[177] Both MTN and Seplat are listed on the premium board of the exchange, representing a commitment to hold themselves to the highest standards of corporate governance.

The NGX premium board is similar to the Brazilian Novo Mercado, which was launched in 2000 by Brasil, Bolsa, Balcão.[178] Its introduction represented a landmark in corporate governance and market transparency in Brazil. As an innovative listing segment, Novo Mercado is dedicated to companies that adhere to the highest standards of corporate governance, including stringent requirements for board independence, enhanced disclosure, and equitable treatment of shareholders. It dramatically elevated Brazil's capital markets by fostering an environment of trust and transparency, which in turn has attracted both domestic and international investors.

The success of Novo Mercado is evident in its ability to attract prominent Brazilian firms seeking to bolster their credibility and investor confidence, thereby enhancing their market capitalization and liquidity. These include Petrobras, the state-controlled oil giant and a significant player in the Brazilian and global energy markets, as well as Itaú Unibanco, one of the largest financial institutions in Latin America. The total market capitalization of companies listed on Novo Mercado fluctuates with market conditions. As of recent reports, the total capitalization of the Novo Mercado segment is approximately 1 trillion Brazilian real (about US$200 billion).[179] The platform has not only contributed to the maturation of Brazil's financial markets but has also served as a model for other emerging markets aiming to enhance their own market integrity and governance standards.

Corporate governance is crucial for ensuring the integrity and efficiency of financial markets and the overall health of organizations. Research consistently underscores that strong corporate governance practices lead to better financial performance and stability. According to a study by the IFC, companies with robust governance frameworks experience lower costs of capital, higher firm value, and improved stock performance.[180] This is attributed to enhanced transparency, accountability, and the alignment of management's interests with those of shareholders.

Moreover, corporate governance plays a pivotal role in strengthening institutions and promoting sustainable business practices. The OECD's Corporate Governance Principles highlight that effective governance mechanisms encourage ethical behavior and long-term strategic planning.[181] Companies with strong governance practices are better equipped to navigate economic downturns and regulatory changes. By ensuring that companies adhere to high standards of conduct, governance frameworks not only protect shareholders but also contribute to broader social and economic stability, reinforcing the trust and integrity essential for a well-functioning market system.

In 2000, the SEC and the Corporate Affairs Commission (CAC) were keen to elevate the importance of good governance practices in Nigeria. They jointly appointed Atedo Peterside, then a highly respected bank CEO, to chair a committee charged with identifying weaknesses in the nation's corporate governance practices and recommending necessary improvements. This committee's diligent work culminated in the release of Nigeria's first Code of Best Practices for Public Companies in October 2003, setting a benchmark for corporate conduct in the country. Peterside continues to be instrumental in pushing for governance improvements across public and private sector institutions and is renowned for his unwavering integrity and his consistent efforts to hold the government accountable. His Anap Foundation is dedicated to advocating for enhanced governance standards across Nigeria.[182]

To reinforce corporate governance in Nigeria, we issued a new Code of Corporate Governance for Public Companies in 2011. The new code aligned with global best practice, mandating quoted companies to disclose their level of compliance with the code in their reporting. The code set out principles and guidelines for board structure, risk management, internal controls, shareholder rights, and disclosure practices, aiming to foster a culture of good governance and protect investor interests. Compliance with the code by listed companies has been progressively improving, driven by regulatory enforcement and increasing awareness of the benefits of good governance. While many companies have embraced the code and integrated its principles into their operations, some challenges remain in achieving full compliance across all sectors, with ongoing efforts by the SEC to ensure more consistent adherence to these governance standards.

One of the most high-profile examples of corporate governance breaches we encountered involved the pan-African financial services group Ecobank Transnational Incorporated (ETI), which is listed on the Nigerian Stock Exchange. A media outlet reported that in June 2013, the group CEO of ETI "sacked the executive director for finance (EDF), who had been in the role since 2010,... citing a lack of trust and confidence in her competence."[183]

Subsequent reports indicated that the ETI board met and resolved to commute the EDF's dismissal to a suspension pending its own internal review. The EDF, however, wrote a detailed petition to the SEC alleging that the ETI board had made many misrepresentations in the group's 2012 annual reports and financial statements.

The petition further alleged that the chairman of the board and the group CEO were attempting to sell assets of the bank at below market value, and that both the chairman and the CEO manipulated the 2012 results to make the performance appear rosier. It also raised questions regarding a massive increase in the CEO's bonus approved in 2012, and alluded to being pressured to write off debts owed by a real estate company belonging to the chairman. Months earlier, ETI had been in the news over debts owed by businesses associated with its chairman, who eventually resigned in October 2013 after enormous public pressure.

As part of the SEC investigation into these allegations, all the directors of ETI were invited to make statements. SEC also commissioned KPMG to conduct an independent corporate governance audit. Meanwhile, the *Financial Times* reported that the CEO "would forego a controversial US$1.14 million bonus for 2012 and launch an internal inquiry into allegations of mismanagement, in a bid to draw a line under a crisis of confidence in the pan-African lender's leadership."[184]

After completing the investigation in December 2013, the SEC met again with the ETI board to share its findings. The findings confirmed serious corporate governance breaches, including a culture of lack of transparency and several instances of conflicts of interest. In January 2014, the ETI board terminated the appointment of the EDF. The SEC, however, considered this termination by the board as an act of retaliation against the EDF for whistleblowing. Consequently, the SEC ordered the reinstatement of the EDF. The CEO, in defiance, refused to comply with this directive.

The Investment Securities Act, Nigeria's enabling securities law, empowers the SEC to remove the CEO of a listed company found to have contravened provisions of the act or the regulations issued pursuant to the act. This was clearly the case with the ETI CEO, but as always, we chose the least dramatic option. Behind the scenes, the chairman and CEO were both reaching out to the most powerful levers of power in Nigeria to get SEC to back off. Leading a pan-African bank that has important operations in more than thirty-five countries can confer considerable leverage. Nigeria was by far the bank's largest market, although its head office is in Lomé, the capital of Togo. Again, to the great credit of President Goodluck Jonathan, despite this pressure campaign against our actions, he allowed us full independence to deal with the situation as we deemed appropriate.

A few months later, after weeks of negative media coverage globally, and amid mounting pressure from shareholders, including South Africa's Public Investment Corporation, Ghana's state pension fund, and the IFC, along with past board members and other stakeholders, ETI's board finally relieved the CEO of his position on March 11, 2014.[185]

According to the *Financial Times* article, "the ousted CEO initiated legal proceedings and was awarded damages by a court in Côte d'Ivoire... The bank and the former CEO finally reached an out of court settlement in February 2016."[186] This case underscores the complexities inherent in regulation. Throughout this period, our primary focus remained on restoring investor confidence. We emphasized the importance of ETI and the broader market community, learning from this prolonged corporate dispute. To facilitate necessary corporate governance reforms, we mandated ETI to appoint a new, substantive chairman with proven qualities of integrity and independence. The board also complied with our directive to reinstate the EDF.

This ETI case was considered by many as a significant test for the SEC as an apex regulator because it cast a spotlight on the integrity of financial institutions in the African region. It threatened to jeopardize the remarkable progress made by leaders over a twenty-five-year period to build a reputable pan-African bank. It also threatened to undermine the integrity of our capital markets, which we had painstakingly restored. The manner with which we handled it helped strengthen confidence in our market as investors were reassured that the regulator will not allow wrongdoing, regardless of the perceived powers wielded by the perpetrators.

The ETI case underscores the importance of strong corporate governance for companies. One of the major principles in corporate governance is accountability. Boards need to develop strong internal controls that are properly monitored and reporting systems that are accurate and transparent with adequate checks and balances. Strong corporate governance will naturally emphasize high levels of ethics, honesty, and integrity. In this regard, policies on code of business conduct, conflict of interest, and whistleblowing are best practice requirements. The bank would have been spared the scandal and perhaps the huge costs incurred had the board instituted strong corporate governance in its affairs.

Capital markets and SMEs

Listing on the main board of a major stock exchange can be a long, onerous process that excludes most small and medium-sized enterprises (SMEs). Some stock exchanges have therefore introduced alternative boards to attract SMEs and facilitate their access to capital markets.

For example, the London Stock Exchange's AIM (Alternative Investment Market) platform offers exceptional value to smaller companies seeking to access capital markets with greater flexibility and fewer constraints compared to the main board. AIM is designed to support the growth ambitions of emerging businesses by providing a more accessible entry point into public markets. Unlike the main board, AIM has less stringent regulatory requirements, which allows for a streamlined listing process tailored to the needs of smaller, high-growth companies. The platform's flexible rules are geared toward fostering innovation and attracting diverse sectors, offering relaxed admission standards and ongoing reporting obligations. This enables such smaller companies to raise capital more efficiently and at a lower cost, while still benefiting from the prestige and visibility of being listed on a major exchange. AIM's supportive environment, coupled with its investor-friendly framework, provides smaller companies with the opportunity to grow and thrive, while improving their corporate governance practices. This makes a crucial difference to the United Kingdom's financial ecosystem. Since its inception in

1995, AIM has facilitated the raising of over £130 billion for 4,000 companies.[187]

We encouraged the Nigerian Stock Exchange to introduce an alternative platform similar to AIM, and in April 2013 they relaunched the Alternative Securities Market (ASEM), a new platform designed to enable small businesses and SMEs in Nigeria to trade their equities.[188] Listing on the ASEM offers numerous advantages for SMEs in Nigeria. One of the key benefits is access to more affordable long-term capital, which provides these companies with the financial resources they need to sustain and grow their operations over time. ASEM also facilitates the long-term sustainability of listed companies by opening ownership to a more diversified set of investors. This can be particularly beneficial in a country such as Nigeria, with numerous successful family-run businesses that sometimes struggle when the founder or patriarch of the family passes on. It also leads to natural improvements in corporate governance practices. Additionally, listing on ASEM can help reduce financial burdens and spreads risk among a broader base of shareholders, enhancing the company's financial stability. The ASEM, being part of the stock exchange, attracts investors who are particularly interested in high-growth potential SMEs, thus providing access to a targeted investor base internationally. Furthermore, ASEM ensures liquidity for shareholders and features a transparent price-discovery mechanism, which collectively contribute to a more efficient and dynamic market.

Evidence of the impact of alternative platforms for

listing such as AIM and ASEM is seen when companies that join these alternative platforms grow, mature and are eventually promoted to the main boards of exchanges. According to the Quoted Companies Alliance, in a ten-year period between 2008 and 2018, sixty-five companies moved from AIM to the main board.[189] In 2010, the NGX created a new board for companies that had outgrown the ASEM, migrating four companies to the Growth Board on November 30, 2020.[190]

Capital markets improve public sector governance

In the public sector, capital markets act as a catalyst for good governance by promoting transparency and accountability. Research conducted by the World Bank emphasizes that the availability of public capital markets provides a platform for governments to raise funds in a manner that is subject to rigorous scrutiny by investors and regulatory bodies. This scrutiny forces governments to adhere to higher standards of financial reporting and disclosure, thus enhancing transparency. The World Bank's report highlights that the process of issuing bonds or other securities requires governments to disclose detailed financial information and maintain stringent compliance with regulatory requirements, which in turn promotes better governance practices and reduces the potential for corruption and mismanagement.[191]

Furthermore, a study published in the *Journal of*

Financial Economics underscores the impact of capital markets on governance by demonstrating that countries with well-developed capital markets exhibit stronger institutions and more effective public sector management. The research finds that the pressure to maintain favorable credit ratings and attract investors encourages governments to implement sound fiscal policies and reforms. This market discipline acts as a catalyst for good governance by aligning public sector practices with international standards and expectations, thus fostering a more stable and accountable governance framework.[192]

Between 2010 and 2015, the issuance of state government bonds in Nigeria experienced significant growth, reflecting the states' increasing reliance on the capital markets to fund infrastructure projects and other subnational priorities. This period marked a strategic shift as many state governments turned to bond issuances to bridge funding gaps due to declining federal allocations as a result of fluctuating oil revenues. SEC data showed that the total value of state government bonds issued more than quadrupled between 2010 and 2015.[193]

One of the pivotal years during this period was 2012, which saw a notable surge in state bond issuances. For example, the Lagos State Government issued an 80-billion-naira tranche, as part of a 500-billion-naira shelf program, which was oversubscribed. Similarly, the Rivers State Government registered its own 250-billion-naira shelf program, launched to critical infrastructure projects in the state.

These issuances demonstrated a robust appetite

for subnational bonds among investors, driven by attractive yields and the enabling regulatory regime we established. This regime included enforcing strict disclosure requirements, introducing the Irrevocable Standing Payment Order (ISPO), which mandates that a portion of the state's federal allocation is automatically deducted to service the bond obligations, and encouraging the use of credit ratings to assess the creditworthiness of issuing states. These measures provided greater transparency and security for investors. The growth trajectory continued through 2015, with more states entering the bond market. By 2015, states such as Osun, Ekiti, and Edo had successfully issued bonds, contributing to the cumulative increase in state bond issuances.

We viewed the interest of Nigerian state governments in the capital market as an embracing of transparency, rigorous scrutiny, and high governance standards essential for market participation. This has largely proven to be true, as the states that have engaged with the market most frequently are among the best managed in Nigeria, underscoring the capital market's ability to catalyze governance improvements. A recent conversation with a colleague highlighted the significant impact that capital markets have had on Lagos. He pointed out that these improvements in governance ensure that, regardless of the governor elected, the state is likely to operate effectively and uphold high standards of public stewardship.

Research underscores the potential of capital markets to enhance social cohesion through their role in fostering economic growth and inclusiveness. A study published in the *Journal of Financial Economics* highlights how well-functioning capital markets contribute to economic stability and prosperity, which in turn supports social cohesion.[194] By providing a platform for diverse financial instruments and facilitating investments, capital markets create opportunities for individuals and businesses across various socioeconomic backgrounds. This inclusivity helps to bridge economic disparities, reduce social tensions, and promote a sense of shared economic interest and stability within communities. Furthermore, the increased transparency and accountability mandated by capital markets' regulatory frameworks help ensure that economic benefits are more evenly distributed, thereby reinforcing social trust and cooperation. This was the reasoning we presented when advocating the listing of shares of major government-owned entities, especially those operating in communities that felt abandoned by the government and were often resorting to vandalism of critical infrastructure.

Additional research by the World Bank further supports this view, emphasizing that capital markets play a crucial role in strengthening social cohesion by enabling governments to finance public infrastructure and services effectively.[195] By raising funds through bond issuance and other securities, governments can invest in projects that improve social welfare, such as education, healthcare, and transportation. These investments not only boost economic development but also enhance the quality of life for citizens, contributing to a more cohesive and equitable society. The involvement of capital markets in financing public goods fosters a sense of collective progress and shared benefits, reinforcing social bonds and contributing to a more inclusive and stable social fabric.

12
Partnerships For Success

"Success is not final, failure is not fatal: It is the
courage to continue that counts."
— Winston Churchill

To succeed, you need help, especially if you are a
developing country daring to overcome humon-
gous challenges and lay enduring foundations for long-
term sustainable development. What we were striving
to achieve at the SEC was monumental, both in the
scope of work required and in the resources needed.
Seeking help is a hallmark of successful leadership,
reflecting a leader's recognition of their limitations
and their commitment to continuous improvement. By
seeking help, leaders demonstrate humility and a proactive attitude toward addressing challenges, which
can contribute to their overall effectiveness and the

achievement of organizational goals. This approach not only allows leaders to gain diverse perspectives and expertise, but also fosters a culture of openness and learning within the organizations they lead. Throughout my time at the SEC, we sought help wherever we could find it, but especially from the most reputed institutions in the world who have had experience supporting other regulators around the world.

Deepening the local bond market

The International Finance Corporation (IFC), a member of the World Bank Group, focuses on investing in private sector growth and supporting high-impact projects that can stimulate the private sector in developing countries. I recognized the IFC as a crucial partner for advancing our market development goals, especially in building a robust secondary bond market. I learned that the IFC was undertaking a US$4.8 million project aimed at strengthening the capacity of financial institutions in emerging markets, particularly in securities markets and transactions. This project specifically included the development of well-functioning securities markets in African nations, making it an ideal platform to engage the IFC. At that time, the Nigerian capital market was predominantly focused on equities, with the bond market, though smaller, largely composed of sovereign bonds. In 2010, the total new issues by companies and state governments amounted to 356 billion naira, compared to 1.2 trillion naira of federal government of Nigeria (FGN) bonds raised by the Debt Management Office (DMO).[196]

We sought assistance from the IFC to sponsor a resident adviser to help us develop the bond market. Our objective was to expand the corporate and sub-national bond segments to be on par with the FGN bond segment. The IFC generously provided us with a bond market expert, whose contribution was invaluable. He conducted numerous seminars for pension funds, portfolio managers, policymakers, and other stakeholders, addressing the current state of Nigeria's non-government bond markets, the opportunities available, the challenges hindering progress, and the necessary steps to overcome these challenges. Additionally, he trained our SEC staff and assisted in amending rules to foster the growth of domestic nongovernment bond issuances. This enabled us to streamline the bond issuance process, introduce shelf registration and book-building, and reduce bond issuance costs. Furthermore, we organized a well-attended bond market conference in collaboration with the IFC, which drew international attention to the ongoing reforms in our bond market.

These reforms yielded fruit. The IFC registered a shelf program committing to issue naira-denominated bonds in Nigeria, which they called "Naija Bonds," to support the development of the local bond market and to raise funding domestically for their other private sector projects in Nigeria. The first tranche was issued in 2013, in which they raised 12 billion naira (approximately US$75 million at the time), marking a significant milestone as the IFC's first local currency bond in Nigeria.[197] These bonds served to attract local and international investors by offering an opportunity to invest in Nigeria's growth while mitigating exchange rate risk. The proceeds from the Naija Bonds are used to finance critical projects in public infrastructure, healthcare, and agriculture.

Africa's paradox of abundant natural resources and a youthful, growing population amid widespread poverty highlights a profound economic developmental challenge. The continent is home to vast reserves of minerals, oil, and gas, and its demographic profile boasts a significant proportion of young people, whose potential for productivity is hindered. Yet, despite these advantages, many African nations grapple with extreme poverty, high unemployment rates, and underdeveloped infrastructure.

This conundrum arises from a complex interplay of factors, including political instability, corruption, insufficient investment in human capital, and the historical exploitation of resources by external actors. The challenge lies not in the scarcity of resources but in the ineffective management and distribution of wealth, which undermines the potential for sustainable economic growth and equitable development. Addressing these issues requires a multifaceted approach, focusing on improving governance, enhancing institutional capacities, and ensuring that resource wealth translates into tangible benefits for the broader population. Often, implementing this approach requires foreign aid or concessionary loans.

There are growing calls from many quarters for these international aid and loans to be denominated in local currencies rather than in foreign currencies to mitigate the debt burden often faced by developing countries resulting from local currency devaluations. Research from the International Monetary Fund (IMF) highlights that foreign currency-denominated debt can significantly exacerbate financial vulnerability in developing nations, especially during periods of exchange rate volatility.[198] When developing countries hold debt in foreign currencies, any depreciation of their local currency can lead to a sharp increase in the cost of debt servicing, often resulting in economic strain and potential debt crises. Other studies, documented in an IMF working paper, have shown that local currency debt can provide more stability and reduce the risk of debt distress, allowing for better management of economic shocks and more predictable fiscal planning.[199]

Supporting this point of view, the World Bank has advocated for a shift toward local currency financing as part of its broader strategy to enhance financial stability and promote sustainable development. In its 2020 report, the World Bank underscored that local currency borrowing can align better with the economic realities of developing countries, as it eliminates the exchange rate risk that can otherwise lead to unsustainable debt burdens.[200] By supporting local currency financing, international aid and loan programs can help countries manage their debt more effectively, stabilize their economies, and foster long-term development. This approach is seen as a critical step toward achieving more equitable and resilient economic growth, as it empowers developing countries to navigate global financial markets without the added pressure of foreign exchange volatility.

I believe that developing deep, liquid, and sophisticated local capital markets in Africa offers the most sustainable solution to overcoming the continent's economic challenges while minimizing reliance on foreign debt. This view is supported by many empirical studies. One such study, conducted by the IFC, underscores the importance of local financial markets in enabling countries to mobilize domestic resources for development. Documenting this research in a 2021 report, the IFC highlighted that well-developed local capital markets not only facilitate long-term investments but also provide governments with more stable and predictable sources of funding, thus reducing their dependency on volatile foreign capital flows.[201] By fostering robust local markets, African nations can enhance their financial resilience, attract private investment, and support infrastructure and social projects that drive inclusive growth.

Similar studies by the World Bank emphasize that local currency bonds and other financial instruments mitigate the risks associated with exchange rate fluctuations and global economic uncertainties.[202] This aligns better with the economic realities of developing countries, as it minimizes the risks of currency mismatch and helps maintain fiscal stability. By strengthening local financial systems, African countries can better manage economic shocks, foster investor confidence, and support sustainable development initiatives. As such, investing in local capital market infrastructure is not only a strategic necessity but also a pathway to achieving long-term economic stability and prosperity.

A year after the maiden multilateral naira-denominated bond was issued by the IFC, the AfDB followed suit, also registering its shelf program to issue "Naira Bonds" in 2014, aiming to support Nigeria's economic development and strengthen its local capital markets. They raised 12.95 billion naira (approximately US$80 million at the time) in the first tranche.[203] The bond likewise attracted both local and international investors, especially impact investors, by offering an investment in Nigeria's economic development. The proceeds from the Naira Bonds were used to finance key infrastructure projects and other development initiatives in the country.

These two landmark issuances by the triple-A-rated IFC and the AfDB positively impacted the corporate bond market, just as we anticipated. Between 2010 and 2015, Nigeria witnessed significant growth in corporate bond issuances as companies sought alternative financing sources amid a difficult credit environment. Data from the SEC showed that the total value of corporate bonds issued during this period surged four-fold from 2010 to 2015. This growth was driven by several factors, including the need for long-term capital, the development of regulatory frameworks, and growing investor confidence in the corporate debt market.

One of the most notable corporate bond issuances during this period was by the telecommunications giant MTN, which registered 200 billion naira in bonds in 2013 (about US$1.25 billion at the time).[204] The first tranche of this program was massively oversubscribed, demonstrating strong investor demand and confidence. Other significant issuers included Lafarge Africa, which registered a prospectus of 100 billion naira (about US$625 million at the time) through multiple tranches between 2011 and 2014, and Fidelity Bank, which issued 30 billion naira (approximately US$260 million at the time) in 2015 to support its lending activities and increase its capital base.[205],[206]

The period also saw increased participation from various sectors, including banking, manufacturing, and infrastructure, contributing to the diversification of the corporate bond market. The regulatory environment played a crucial role in this growth, with the SEC implementing policies to enhance market transparency, improve the issuance process, and protect investors. The partnership with the IFC contributed in no small measure to these successes in our bond market.

Adopting international reporting standards

I also believed that best practice in reporting and disclosure standards was critical to building world class capital markets. I therefore ensured that SEC led the process of helping listed companies transition from the Nigerian Global Accounting Standards to International

Financial Reporting Standards (IFRS). This entailed in-depth training for relevant teams within listed companies in addition to high-level, more strategic training programs for C-suite executives. The SEC corporate governance team also led the redesign of relevant reporting templates. This culminated in a successful transition of the companies to IFRS by 2012. In implementing the IFRS, we received great support internationally, including from the Institute of Chartered Accountants of England and Wales (ICAEW) to provide professional consultancy services for the completion of our transition to IFRS. ICAEW is a prestigious professional organization established in 1880 that represents and supports accountants. It plays a crucial role in setting high standards for accounting practice, providing training and development for its members, and promoting the accounting profession. It is known for its rigorous ACA qualification process and its work in advocating for transparent financial reporting and governance standards. The institute also engages in policy development, contributes to public debate on financial issues, and supports businesses through guidance on financial management and regulatory compliance. Its influence extends globally, impacting both national and international accounting practices and standards.

We received their support with our implementation of the IFRS in Nigeria through an initiative that was supported by the World Bank. They assisted us in building the necessary skills within the SEC and ensuring the alignment of our relevant regulations, processes, and procedures with the IFRS. Adopting IFRS has been shown to significantly benefit a country's capital markets and overall economy. A 2014 study by the World Bank highlights that IFRS adoption enhances financial transparency and comparability, which are crucial for attracting foreign investment and improving market efficiency.[207] The report indicates that countries transitioning to IFRS experience greater foreign direct investment (FDI) and improved market liquidity due to the higher quality and consistency of financial statements, which reduce information asymmetry between investors and companies. Furthermore, a study by Barth, Landsman, and Lang in a 2008 issue of the *Journal of Accounting Research* found that, at the corporate level, the adoption of IFRS leads to improved earnings quality and more timely recognition of losses, which supports more accurate pricing of financial assets and better risk assessment in capital markets.[208]

Further economic benefits of IFRS adoption are well documented. A study in 2011 published by the Accounting Review found that countries implementing IFRS experienced a decrease in the cost of capital and an increase in the overall market valuation of firms. This is because IFRS standards facilitate more reliable and comparable financial information, which helps investors make more informed decisions and reduces the risk premium associated with investing in less transparent environments.[209] Additionally, research by the European Commission highlights that IFRS adoption has contributed to the integration of European capital markets by providing a common financial reporting language, which has enhanced cross-border investments and economic integration within the EU.[210]

For our investment management industry, we were also looking at adopting the Global Investment Performance Standards (GIPS) for our fund management industry to meet international performance measurement standards. We reached out to the CFA Institute for support. The GIPS provide a standardized framework for calculating and presenting investment performance, ensuring consistency, comparability, and integrity. Their adoption would align Nigeria's investment industry with international best practices, attracting more global investors by boosting their confidence in the accuracy and reliability of reported performance data. As more Nigerian asset managers and financial institutions embrace GIPS, the overall quality of performance reporting is expected to improve, fostering greater trust and competitiveness in Nigeria's capital markets.

Beyond its pivotal role in setting and maintaining the GIPS, the CFA Institute plays a crucial part in advancing the investment management profession through its comprehensive suite of programs and services. It fosters the highest ethical standards in financial analysis and portfolio management, providing rigorous certification and continuing education opportunities to finance professionals globally. The institute also conducts influential research that informs best practices and shapes investment strategies, while advocating for strong ethical practices and transparent market conduct. Additionally, it offers a robust platform for professional networking and knowledge sharing, contributing to the overall enhancement of global financial markets and investor confidence.

I first encountered the depth of the CFA program during my time as a portfolio manager handling the AfDB's fixed-income portfolios in dollars. Although I had enrolled in and prepared for the CFA exams, I ultimately was unable to take them. I often encourage colleagues to take up the challenge and pursue the CFA certification, as it exposes you to phenomenal training for professions in business, economics, and finance. Nigerians are known for their quest for knowledge and global credibility in diverse professions. Many Nigerians in the finance profession were having to travel worldwide to take the CFA exams, a testament to their commitment to achieving international recognition in finance.

I was disheartened by the lack of a CFA exam center in Nigeria, a country with a population of over 220 million. During a meeting with the CFA Institute, I highlighted this gap, emphasizing the need for a local examination center to support the growing demand for CFA certification in our capital markets. Our goal was to integrate CFA certification as a standard in the industry, thereby enhancing local expertise and aligning with global best practices. I am happy that, today, Nigerians can take the CFA exams within the country, a significant advancement that allows students to begin their CFA journey while still in undergraduate programs. This development not only reflects the increasing investment in building financial capacity locally but also enhances our capital markets' global credibility and competitive edge.

As the World Bank Treasurer, I took great pride in the success of the Risk and Asset Management Program (RAMP), which uniquely combined fund management with capacity building for central banks. RAMP is a distinguished initiative within the World Bank Treasury that offers a comprehensive suite of services, including expert advisory, executive training, and asset management, all within an extensive network of global public asset managers. Founded in 2001, RAMP supports more than seventy members, predominantly central banks, as well as international financial institutions, pension funds, and sovereign wealth funds, who collectively oversee over US$2 trillion in sovereign assets.[211] During my tenure, we managed a substantial US$170 billion on behalf of these institutions, but the program's true value lay in its dual approach. Not only did we provide sophisticated fund management services, but we also focused on enhancing the capabilities of central banks through targeted training and development. This capacity-building component was instrumental in equipping central bank staff with the skills and knowledge necessary to manage their financial assets more effectively and adapt to the evolving global financial landscape. By fostering both financial acumen and practical skills, RAMP helped central banks achieve greater stability and efficiency in their operations, ultimately strengthening the broader financial system and contributing to global economic stability.

13
My Leadership Philosophy

"When the best leader's work is done the people say,
'We did it ourselves.'"
— Laozi (Ancient Chinese philosopher)

nscribed on the forecourt of the Temple of Apollo at
Delphi is one of my favorite sayings from ancient wisdom: "Know thyself." It was one of the Delphic Maxims,
a set of aphorisms inscribed on the temple's forecourt
that were meant to guide individuals in their pursuit of
wisdom and ethical conduct. The maxim was famously
associated with the Greek philosopher Socrates, who
emphasized the importance of self-awareness in his
philosophical inquiries. Socrates believed that understanding one's own nature, limitations, and place in
the world was crucial for leading a virtuous and examined life.

"Know thyself" has come to signify the foundational principle of self-awareness and introspection, central to both personal development and philosophical thought, particularly important in shaping one's leadership philosophy. A leader's understanding of their own values, strengths, and weaknesses profoundly influences their leadership style and approach. For example, a leader who values collaboration and inclusivity may foster a participatory work environment, encouraging team input and shared decision-making. A leader who prioritizes decisiveness and efficiency might adopt a more authoritative style, emphasizing clear directives and swift action. According to a study published in the *Journal of Leadership & Organizational Studies*, leaders who align their actions with their personal values and self-perceptions are more likely to build trust and inspire loyalty among their teams.[212] This alignment not only enhances their effectiveness but also fosters a work culture that reflects their leadership philosophy.

Early influences, such as personal experiences and formative interactions, play a crucial role in shaping a leader's philosophy and, consequently, their effectiveness. Leaders who are mindful of these early influences can better understand their own biases and preferences, leading to more deliberate and authentic leadership practices. For instance, a leader who had positive early experiences with open communication and feedback may naturally emphasize these values in their leadership style, fostering an environment of openness and continuous improvement. By reflecting on and learning from these formative experiences, leaders can refine their approaches and cultivate a leadership style that is both effective and true to their core principles. This self-awareness and intentionality in leadership development are crucial for achieving long-term success and fostering a positive organizational culture.

I believe that a leadership philosophy rooted in values is deeply influenced by one's early experiences and upbringing. My own philosophy is inspired by my parents, who not only imparted their values on me but also exemplified them through their actions. These core values – character and integrity, trust, respect, accountability, and empathy – have evolved over time into what I refer to as my four Cs: character, compassion, competence, and courage. They have been crucial to my success as a leader.

Primary education

My primary school, St. Louis Primary School Kano, was a significant early influence on my development. This esteemed institution, run by nuns, was situated in the predominantly Muslim city of Kano and was renowned for its exceptional educational standards. The school's reputation attracted a diverse student body, including local Kano indigenes and children from various expatriate communities such as Americans, Britons, Indians, and Malaysians. This blend of cultural backgrounds provided a rich, multicultural environment that fostered tolerance, respect, and understanding among students from different ethnic and religious backgrounds.

The exposure to such a diverse group not only broadened my perspective but also ingrained in me the value of inclusivity and respect for different cultures from a young age.

Furthermore, the values and discipline instilled by the nuns who managed St. Louis were instrumental in shaping my character. Their dedication to education went beyond academic excellence, emphasizing moral and ethical development. The school's ethos – rooted in compassion, integrity, and service – mirrored the values I later adopted as foundational principles in my personal and professional life. The nurturing environment at St. Louis helped to cultivate a strong sense of responsibility and a commitment to personal growth, which I have carried forward into my leadership philosophy. The lessons learned and the diverse experiences shared with peers from various backgrounds have significantly influenced my approach to leadership and my understanding of the importance of fostering inclusive environments in all aspects of life.

At a young age, this gave me cultural awareness and appreciation. It helped me gain an understanding of diverse customs, traditions, and viewpoints. I had Christian, Muslim, Hindu, and Buddhist friends. This early multicultural interaction enhanced my social skills, empathy, and adaptability, preparing me to thrive in the more interconnected and cosmopolitan societies in which I would later live. I also attribute a lot of my curiosity and open-mindedness to those cherished times at St. Louis in Kano.

Nigerians are predominantly practicing Christians

or Muslims. As a Christian family, you pray every morning together and go to church every Sunday. I believed from a very young age that I could have a relationship with God, a fact I still strongly believe is anchoring my faith. I recall as a young girl, the then-patriarch of our family, my father's oldest brother, would lead family prayers from 04:00 to 05:00 every day. This is a sort of discipline; to wake up so early daily, people in other parts of the world only learn if or when they join the military. I was not even ten years old when I had to be doing that. My Muslim friends of the same age would pray five times a day and fast for about thirty days annually during the Ramadan.

Learning discipline as a child is a cornerstone for developing a well-rounded and successful life. My parents strongly believed this, much like practically every Nigerian parent of their time. My father was the disciplinarian. From his stern look when I was not on my best behavior, to his commanding baritone voice, he always kept me alert and focused on doing the right thing. Discipline instills a sense of structure and responsibility that becomes the foundation for all future endeavors. It teaches kids the importance of setting goals and the perseverance required to achieve them, fostering a mindset that values hard work and dedication. This early understanding of discipline helps children navigate the complexities of life with a clear sense of purpose and direction, enabling them to manage their time effectively by prioritizing tasks.

Discipline also cultivates emotional resilience and self-control. Because of the discipline of my father, I learned to handle setbacks and frustrations with grace, and I developed the ability to delay gratification in pursuit of long-term rewards. It also gave me emotional maturity early on, crucial in building relationships in school and making sound decisions about my future. The discipline instilled in me is also the bedrock of my lifelong respect for rules and order.

Secondary education

For my secondary school education, I attended the Federal Government Girls College (FGGC) Owerri, in southeastern Nigeria, close to the village where both of my parents were born. It is one of the 104 unity schools, which are federal government-managed schools that bring together students from different backgrounds. The unity schools are a melting pot. At FGGC Owerri, a boarding school, I met Nigerians from all over our vast country and some from other African countries. There I deepened my discipline, valued resilience, and gained a much deeper appreciation for Nigeria's unity in diversity.

Nigeria is an incredibly diverse country; a collection of peoples of breathtaking heterogeneity, a mosaic of cultures, languages, and traditions. With over 250 ethnic groups, each contributing its own unique customs, dialects, and art forms, Nigeria exemplifies the richness of pluralism. The landscape itself mirrors this diversity, ranging from the arid Sahel in the north, to the lush rainforests of the Niger and Benue river deltas in the south. As a preteen on the 990-kilometer Kano to Umuahia train rides to resume school, I remember being struck by the graduating contrast from the scant vegetation of the savanna across the Kano plains to the rubber plantations dotting the forests in southeastern Nigeria. The train terminus was in Umuahia, and I would have to secure a connecting vehicle that took me to Owerri, where my school was located.

Owerri sits along the great African rainforest, Africa's *Amazon*, an awe-inspiring expanse of verdant life. It begins along the western coast of the continent in Sierra Leone and Liberia, stretching eastward across the heart of Africa. This lush tapestry weaves through the dense canopies of the Ivory Coast and Ghana, unfurling into the emerald depths of Nigeria and Cameroon. It reaches its zenith in the sprawling Congo Basin, the green lungs of the continent, before tapering off into the eastern fringes of Uganda. In those days, largely untouched by the deforestation that came after, that region was a majestic kaleidoscope of biodiversity, from towering ancient trees to the vibrant chorus of wildlife.

I was chosen to serve as the school's Timekeeping Prefect, a position that taught me invaluable life lessons. As Timekeeping Prefect, my responsibility was to ensure that I rang the "wake-up" bell at 5:30 AM every day. This kickstarts the whole series of activities that make up a school day. One morning, however, I overslept, and many of my mates ran late for the day's morning activities because I rang the bell too late. Of course, this also meant that many were late to class and other early morning activities. The weight of that mistake was profound – I learned the true burden of responsibility in that moment. But more importantly, I learned about grace and second chances. Instead of harsh reprimands, my principal and the matrons extended grace, giving me the opportunity to redeem myself. It was a moment that shaped my outlook on leadership and accountability, instilling in me the importance of compassion, responsibility, and the growth that comes from learning from our mistakes. It never happened again.

When you spend most of your year in boarding school with other teenage and preteen girls, one other leadership value you internalize is forgiveness. In the bustling corridors and shared hostels, years are spent living in close quarters with several other teenage girls. Amid the inevitable clashes and misunderstandings, a girl discovers the grace in letting go of grudges and the strength in mending fractured friendships. Through the daily rhythm of communal life – where secrets are shared, arguments flare, and loyalties are tested – she becomes adept at navigating the emotional landscapes of others, realizing that forgiveness is not a sign of weakness but a testament to her resilience and empathy. Each apology accepted and each slight overlooked becomes a stepping stone, building a foundation of compassion and understanding. By embracing forgiveness, she learns to find peace within herself, creating lasting bonds that transcend the fleeting conflicts of adolescence. That was my story.

In secondary school, I was in the same dormitory as one of the South African girls at FGGC Owerri. I consequently learned more about apartheid. My heart was always heavy hearing stories of the horrible realities of living under the apartheid regime in South Africa. I also closely followed apartheid news on radio broadcasts and the stark newspaper headlines. Each report painted a vivid picture of a world far removed yet intimately felt – a land where racial injustice and brutality carve deep scars into the lives of black South Africans. But I also learned about the unyielding spirit of those who fight against injustice. Many years later, when I was a young professional, I would learn, again, one of the most powerful lessons in human forgiveness from my childhood hero, Nelson Madiba Mandela. He exemplified tolerance by his capacity to forgive those who perpetrated apartheid and imprisoned him for twenty-seven years.

Madiba expressed his forgiveness to those who wronged him in his inaugural speech as President of South Africa on May 10, 1994. In this historic address, delivered at the Union Buildings in Pretoria, Mandela spoke of reconciliation and the need to move past the injustices of apartheid to build a united and democratic South Africa. He emphasized forgiveness and the importance of working together to heal the nation, embodying his commitment to peace and reconciliation. This made an indelible mark on me. As a leader, I have found that it is far easier to forgive than to hold a grudge. And whenever it is difficult to forgive due to the gravity of the offense or betrayal, I prefer to look at the bigger picture. I never allow a past wrong to inhibit my organization's progress or damage relationships with the perpetrator of that wrong.

An important element of my success has been my commitment to ensuring that mistakes or missteps do not overshadow the positive qualities that individuals or ideas may possess. I believe strongly in giving people and concepts the opportunity for redemption and growth, understanding that everyone and everything can have redeeming attributes despite occasional failures. This perspective has enabled me to approach situations with a sense of optimism and openness, allowing for second chances and fostering an environment where constructive development is prioritized over past errors. This approach not only helps in building a more forgiving and innovative atmosphere within an organization but also in unlocking the potential for meaningful progress and improvement.

Attending boarding school further reinforced my independence and appreciation for multicultural environments, qualities that have become defining aspects of my career and personal life. The experience of living away from home in a diverse, ethnic setting at FGGC laid a foundation for my adaptability and global outlook. These traits have been pivotal throughout my career, allowing me to live, work, and thrive in various cultural contexts across Africa, Europe, and the USA. My tenure at the World Bank, where I led a team of professionals from sixty different countries, exemplified this adaptability. Leading such a diverse team required not only an understanding of different cultural perspectives but also the ability to integrate diverse viewpoints into a cohesive, effective strategy, crucial for a team, during my time, responsible for the careful management of a US$200 billion debt portfolio, a US$200 billion asset portfolio for institutions within the World Bank Group, and about sixty-five clients, in addition to US$600 billion in transactions related to hedging and risk management. This global experience has further enriched my leadership style, enabling me to continue navigating complex international environments and fostering collaboration among individuals from varied backgrounds.

Post-secondary education influences

After secondary school, choosing a field of study for university was a pivotal decision that needed to balance my childhood aspirations with the available opportunities. From a young age, I dreamed of becoming a scientist, driven by the vision of inventing something revolutionary that would leave a mark on the world. This ambition fueled my academic pursuits and fostered a deep curiosity about the natural world. As I approached the end of my secondary education, the choice of a university major became a crossroads where my passion for innovation met the evolving landscape of technology. The allure of computer science, with its promise of shaping the future of technology, seemed like a natural extension of my desire to be at the forefront of scientific advancement.

Admitted to study computer science at one of Nigeria's most prestigious universities, I immersed myself in a field that was both nascent and challenging.

During this era, computers were not as ubiquitous as they are today. I vividly recall the painstaking process of submitting my code to the punch card operators. In those days, instead of typing directly into a computer, we would write our programs on paper, and the operators would convert them into punch cards, which were then fed into the computers linked to those imposing mainframes. On one occasion, I encountered a persistent bug in my program that baffled me. I kept revisiting my code, analyzing it line by line, certain that the error lay in my logic. Yet, no matter how many times I resubmitted the program, the bug remained. Frustrated and determined, I finally decided to review the punch cards themselves, and there it was – an error introduced not by me, but by the operator. The same mistake had been repeated every time. That experience taught me the importance of diligence and thoroughness, but more importantly, it was a valuable lesson in the realities of working with imperfect systems and relying on human collaboration in technology.

Relying on such arduous manual writing of our codes required us to engage deeply with the fundamentals of programming and mathematics. We often relied on manual calculations and theoretical problem-solving, which honed my numeracy and analytical skills to a remarkable degree. As I transitioned into a career in finance, my sister would humorously point out that, while my childhood dream of inventing something grand might not have materialized, I was indeed "inventing" valuable insights through my work. The rigorous training and problem-solving skills I developed during my computer science studies became indispensable in my financial career, where analytical precision and quantitative expertise are crucial. This blend of early ambition and practical skill development not only shaped my professional trajectory but also reinforced the value of adaptability and lifelong learning in navigating career paths.

In Nigeria, every corner offers a different story, a different song, and a different dance, all woven together by the unifying thread of national pride and resilience. This incredible diversity not only shapes the country's identity but also fuels its dynamism and creativity, making Nigeria a beacon of cultural wealth and human potential. Today it is home to over 220 million people, who are competitive, proud, and resilient.[213] I saw a lot more of these qualities during my mandatory one year of national youth service (NYSC) in Benin, the heart of the ancient Benin Kingdom, from September 1984 to September 1985. Many of my lifelong friends are from my time in boarding school and my NYSC.

The NYSC experience in Nigeria is a pivotal rite of passage for many young graduates, characterized by its rigorous and transformative nature. Upon arrival at the orientation camp, such as the one I attended in Auchi, Benin State, participants undergo an intensive one-month program that includes early morning military drills, army-style endurance training, and various activities designed to foster discipline and teamwork. In the evenings, you undergo another round of physical exercises, and extra drills aimed at building resilience and unity among corps members. After completing the one-month camp, participants are assigned to serve in regions of the country where they have not previously resided, often distant from their former homes or academic settings, immersing them in new environments and cultures. This geographical and cultural diversity not only broadens their perspectives but also encourages adaptability and a deeper understanding of Nigeria's multifaceted society. Through these experiences, NYSC helps to cultivate a sense of national service and solidarity, contributing to personal growth and a more cohesive national identity.

After the NYSC orientation camp, I was posted to the University of Benin, one of the federal government-owned universities in Nigeria. As a graduate of computer science, I was assigned to serve at the university's Institute of Computer Science that, at the time, provided consulting services. My job for the few weeks I served in that role included supporting different functions in the university with the information management systems. As providence would have it, a lecturer of the computer science 101 course had to leave for an extended period to the United States, creating a resource gap that the university had to fill. It was decided that, as a fresh graduate with a first-class honors degree in computer science, I would be a worthy substitute. I relished the opportunity to teach, so I was delighted to take up the challenge.

At barely twenty years old, stepping into the lecture hall for my first day teaching computer science 101 was an experience both exhilarating and daunting. But I was confident because I was well prepared.

As I entered, a sea of expectant faces greeted me, their expressions a mix of curiosity and indifference. Clad in my most professional-looking dress, I felt a wave of apprehension as I approached the front of the class, but the room remained abuzz with chatter. It was not until I cleared my throat and addressed the class that the realization dawned on them: the young woman they had initially perceived as just another student was, in fact, their lecturer. The collective shock and murmurs that followed were palpable, as they struggled to reconcile their expectations with the reality before them.

The initial disbelief soon gave way to a test of authority. Some of the older students, presuming my youth as a weakness, began to push boundaries with disruptive behavior. Their attempts to undermine my credibility were met with swift and resolute action. I maintained composure, addressing their misbehavior directly and firmly. With a blend of assertiveness and professionalism, I asked the unruly students to leave, making it clear that respect and discipline were non-negotiable in my classroom. This decisive stance not only restored order but also established my role as an authoritative yet fair educator, setting the tone for the rest of the semester.

Character

Character is the set of moral and ethical qualities that define an individual's nature and guide their behavior. It encompasses traits such as honesty, integrity, and responsibility, reflecting how a person interacts with others and navigates life's challenges. Character is demonstrated through consistent actions and decisions that align with one's values, revealing the true essence of who they are, especially in difficult or testing circumstances, or when no one is looking.

My parents taught me character through the power of their example and intentional guidance. They both embodied integrity. My parents always told us that we must stand up for the right thing. They taught us by their own examples that if you are standing up for what is right, it is OK to stand alone, if need be. Character and integrity are deeply intertwined. Integrity, the quality of being honest and having strong moral principles, is a fundamental component of a person with character. It is the steadfast adherence to ethical values, even when it is difficult or inconvenient. Character is the consistent alignment with one's values and beliefs. Through consistent behavior that aligned with their values, in the privacy of our home and in public alike, they exemplified character. From simple acts such as keeping promises, treating others with respect, and admitting mistakes, they exuded authenticity and accountability.

Character is a cornerstone of effective leadership, fundamentally shaping a leader's interactions, decisions, and overall influence within an organization. A leader with strong character consistently exhibits integrity, honesty, and ethical behavior, fostering a culture of trust and respect. These qualities ensure that their actions align with their words, creating a reliable and transparent environment. When leaders demonstrate unwavering principles, they set a powerful example for their team, encouraging colleagues to uphold similar standards in their own work. This alignment between values and behavior is critical in building credibility and maintaining the moral compass of the organization, guiding it through challenges, and ensuring long-term sustainability.

Moreover, character in leadership is pivotal in building and nurturing meaningful relationships within and outside the organization. Character was the leadership value I relied on the most as my team and I worked to restore investor confidence in Nigeria. At the peak of the market in 2008, domestic investors accounted for 85% of total trades. Most pulled out following the crash later that year. Many, having had their fingers burned, had been reluctant to come back. We were more successful in convincing foreign investors to return. Foreign participation, which was 15% at the height of the bull market, quickly grew to 67%, driven by various factors, including the inclusion of Nigeria in major international financial indices.

In October 2012, Nigeria's government bonds were included in the JP Morgan Government Bond Index – Emerging Markets (GBI-EM), enhancing the visibility of our domestic bond market in global financial markets.[214] Not long after that, in 2013, Nigeria was added to the MSCI Frontier Markets Index, recognizing its emerging status and growing potential in our capital market. This move was a testament to the country's increasing appeal to international investors and its improving market infrastructure. These inclusions were pivotal in attracting foreign investment, boosting liquidity, and providing Nigerian assets with greater credibility on the international stage. The addition of Nigeria to these indices signaled that the Nigerian capital market was regaining the confidence of foreign investors because of our reforms.

Our local investors were still unconvinced, particularly the retail investors. At that time, domestic investors accounted for only 33% of trade volumes, with this contribution predominantly coming from institutional sources rather than traditional direct retail participation. The Nigerian pension sector, once mired in unfunded liabilities of US$12 billion, had undergone a profound transformation, quickly rising to over US$30 billion of contributions in a robust, fully funded system.[215],[216] This overhaul led to pension assets rapidly accumulating to trillions of naira. The introduction of the contributory pension scheme played a crucial role in this growth, channeling substantial capital into the equities market. However, the Nigeria Pension Commission (Pencom) adopted a highly cautious approach, imposing strict limits on asset allocation to equities and other perceived riskier investments. Consequently, pension funds, adhering to these conservative regulatory guidelines, invested conservatively, often falling well short of the allowable regulatory limits in their investment strategies.

The integrity demonstrated through our early initiatives, such as the rigorous implementation of the fit and proper test, the decisive removal of the stock exchange's leadership, and our strict zero-tolerance policy, played a pivotal role in restoring investor confidence in our markets. This led to a steady and sustained return of retail investors. Within several months in 2014, data from the exchange indicated that retail investors had even surpassed institutional investors in terms of contribution to trading volume.

Both domestic and foreign participation in trading volumes continued to grow, approaching a near 50:50 split. By December 2014, my final full month in charge, foreign portfolio managers represented 58% of trading volumes, compared to 42% from domestic sources.[217] The Central Bank of Nigeria recognized the significance of this renewed confidence in Nigeria's capital markets. As confidence in the markets increased, foreign portfolio investments – an essential component of the central bank's reserves – rose to over US$6 billion in 2013, up from less than US$1 billion in 2009.[218] This growth, however, was followed by fluctuations due to global economic conditions and domestic challenges leading up to Nigeria's 2015 general elections.

As we approached the end of 2013, our reforms were working; the market had been cleaned up and had tripled in size; reduced concentration as the share of the banking sector was reduced from about 60% to about 25% of total capitalization; liquidity was improving; investor confidence was restored; market integrity was solidified; institutions were strengthened; and enabling rules required for product innovation were in place. It was now time to look ahead. We needed a long-term plan that envisioned what world class capital

markets would look like in Nigeria and which specified the steps to take to get us there. Nigeria had not
previously had a long-term plan to guide capital market development.

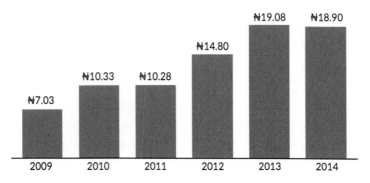

Total Market Capitalization (Trillion Naira) (Source: SEC)

During my visit to Malaysia in 2012, I was impressed
to see what they had achieved through their master
plan strategy. They developed a ten-year master plan
for their capital market in 2001. By the end, they had
implemented 95% of the recommendations in the plan,
which led to a doubling of the market size from US$317
billion to US$606 billion.[219] The plan further established
Malaysia as one of the world's most important Islamic
finance centers while moving it from a narrow market
dominated by equities and bonds to other products
including REITs, ETFs, derivatives, and non-interest
products. Malaysia's first master plan was so successful
that, in 2011, they developed a second one for their market, implementing it up to 2020. Closer home, Kenya
had also launched a ten-year master plan in 2013 to
guide the development of their capital market. At the

time, even developed markets such as the European Union (EU) were mulling plans to produce a long-term plan for their market. In 2014, the EU's financial services commissioner announced plans to unveil a long-term master plan in mid-2015 that would lead the growth and integration of European capital markets while reducing their companies' reliance on banks.

Through the Capital Market Committee (CMC), our market's consultative framework, we established industry-wide committees to assess the current state of our market and to chart its future direction. We created three distinct committees, each tasked with developing strategic blueprints in key areas: the first was to formulate a comprehensive capital market master plan, the second focused on crafting a development roadmap for non-interest finance, particularly given our significant Muslim population, and the third aimed to design a master plan for enhancing financial literacy, a cause I am deeply passionate about. This collaborative effort, which engaged with market participants and stakeholders over the course of a year, culminated in a detailed ten-year master plan for the Nigerian capital markets. This plan is complemented by standalone volumes with specific strategies for capital market literacy and the expansion of non-interest financial products.

The strategic plan outlines several key initiatives aimed at enhancing market depth, improving investor confidence, and fostering economic growth. Central to the master plan is developing and maintaining robust regulatory frameworks and governance standards that ensure transparency, market integrity, and protection for investors. The plan also highlights the need for innovation in financial products, including the development of derivatives, commodities, and fixed-income markets, to provide diverse investment opportunities and manage risks more effectively.

Furthermore, the master plan prioritizes financial inclusion and literacy as critical components for broadening market participation, by promoting initiatives that encourage retail investment and support SMEs, basically seeking to democratize access to capital. Under the plan, the SEC would leverage technology to streamline operations, enhance market efficiency, and reduce transaction costs. Partnerships with international financial institutions and stakeholders were also highlighted within the plan to facilitate knowledge transfer, capacity building, and adherence to global best practices. Through the comprehensive strategies articulated in the plan, the Nigerian capital market aspires to not only boost the nation's economic resilience and growth but also to position Nigeria as a leading financial center in the world and the main gateway into Africa.

I invested a lot of the last twelve months of my time at the SEC working on this master plan. It was such an important project for me, as I believe strongly in preparation, especially long-term preparation, where possible. In November 2014, we launched the master plan at a well-attended ceremony during which major ministers from the government commended the SEC's foresight in developing the master plan and committing to collaborating with us in its implementation.

At this juncture, I knew that I would not be present to lead the implementation of this critical master plan. As my first five-year term approached its conclusion, I was worn out and preferred to close the curtain on my time leading the transformation of the Nigerian capital markets. I decided to take a break, get some rest, and to later look ahead for other opportunities.

A few weeks after launching the master plan, at the CMC retreat, I gave my last public remarks to the market community. We introduced the CMC retreats to hold at the end of the year and give the market community a platform to reflect on what worked well and what required more work for the next year. At this point, I knew that I would not be continuing as SEC DG, but the market – my audience – was unaware. Many were expecting that I would stay on to lead the implementation of the master plan and consolidate the remarkable gains we had made together. But I knew this was it. I spoke to the market community from the heart.

I reflected on the significant progress made in Nigeria's capital markets since the initiation of our comprehensive reforms in 2010, emphasizing the pivotal role of capital markets in driving socioeconomic development by providing long-term finance, fostering innovation, promoting good corporate governance, and enabling wealth creation and distribution. I went down memory lane, tracing the history of capital market development in Nigeria, noting its initial promise and subsequent challenges, including the severe market correction in 2008 that eroded investor confidence and exposed systemic weaknesses.

In what was like my valedictory speech, I outlined the strategic initiatives we had implemented during my tenure to restore confidence and enhance market infrastructure, such as strengthening regulatory oversight, implementing global best practices, and fostering market innovation. I highlighted key achievements, including the establishment of the National Investor Protection Fund, the introduction and expansion of new products such as ETFs, REITs, and sukuk, and significant improvements in market transparency and liquidity. I acknowledged the support from President Goodluck Jonathan and his administration, which facilitated critical reforms, including the elimination of value-added tax on market transactions and providing forbearance on the margin loans of stockbrokers.

I shared a little more of my vision of a transformative future for Nigeria's capital market, guided by the newly developed ten-year master plan aimed at achieving a deep, liquid, and diversified market that would significantly contribute to Nigeria's development. I ended by calling for dedication to the faithful implementation of the master plan, aspiring for a capital market that not only supports infrastructure and housing finance but also fosters entrepreneurship and inclusive economic growth. As I ended my remarks, I knew I was handing over the master plan, my legacy, to a committed community willing and able to implement it. Looking back, I am very pleased that successive administrations at the SEC have made the master plan their guidebook, faithfully implementing the recommendations it contains. In 2021, the SEC launched a revised edition of the master plan to include new and emerging issues.[220]

Several recommendations from the master plan have already been successfully achieved and implemented, driving significant improvements in the market. These include the strengthening of the NIPF to safeguard investor interests, the permanent elimination of VAT on capital market transactions, the introduction of new products, including derivatives, and the expansion of ETFs, REITs, sukuk, and green bonds. Additionally, substantial progress had been made in enhancing market transparency and governance through the completion of IFRS adoption and strengthening of the code of corporate governance. Activities such as market making and securities lending were improving market liquidity and depth. Meanwhile, just as recommended in the master plan, the trading platforms NASD, FMDQ, NGX, and AFEX were all making great strides toward improving market transparency, efficiency, and liquidity.

Courage

Courage is the mental and emotional strength to face fear, danger, or adversity, whether physical or moral. It enables a leader to take bold actions despite potential risks or challenges, driven by conviction, determination, and resilience. As Franklin Roosevelt famously said, courage is not the absence of fear but the ability to act in the presence of it. It is standing up for what is right, defending the vulnerable, and striving to achieve one's goals with unwavering resolve. Growing up, I admired my father as a paragon of courage and leadership. Observing him daily, I was deeply struck by his unwavering resolve and composure in the face of challenges. To my young eyes, he seemed almost impervious to fear, embodying a sense of strength and determination that was both inspiring and reassuring. His fearless approach to overcoming obstacles and his ability to lead with conviction left an indelible impression on me, shaping my understanding of true leadership and resilience.

Courage, at its core, involves more than just the absence of fear; it is the resolve to act in the face of imminent threats and severe repercussions. Despite the clear and present dangers of unwarranted reputational damage and potential physical harm from powerful entities who were threatened by changes to the status quo, true courage is exemplified by the willingness to move forward with necessary reforms. Even when one is acutely aware of the significant costs and risks associated with challenging entrenched systems, the essence of bravery lies in the commitment to forge ahead, driven by a conviction to achieve meaningful change despite the personal and professional peril. This profound courage manifests not merely in the absence of fear but in the determined pursuit of justice and progress amid adversity.

Taking up a public sector role in a developing country often entails significant personal risks, including threats to one's physical safety and that of loved ones, particularly when one challenges entrenched interests. As we initiated reforms at the SEC and reinforced our zero-tolerance stance against misconduct, I received an unsettling call one evening from the national security adviser (NSA) inviting me for a meeting at his office. I went to see him later the same day. He spoke softly but with an authoritative tone, his voice carrying the weight of someone accustomed to command and deference. His demeanor exuded the seriousness of the disconcerting news he was about to deliver. Their intelligence had uncovered active threats to my life. He relayed that our market reforms were stepping on many toes, and he said something to the effect of "some powerful people are not happy with you, and they are plotting to kill you."

Receiving this news was frightening, but I remained composed and calm. I made it clear that the work we were doing at the SEC – reforming the capital markets in the wake of the global financial crisis and restoring investor confidence – was critical for our nation and for the average Nigerian. I emphasized that this work was so important that it was worth risking my life, if necessary, to eliminate market malpractices and disgorge bad actors of their illegally gained profits. The NSA responded by commending my efforts and assured me that Nigeria needed me alive to continue the good work. He informed me that he would assign a security detail – similar to the Secret Service in the United States – to ensure my safety. The following day, he dispatched two highly trained officers from the Department of State Security. Although it took a little while to adjust to their presence, they soon became an integral part of my daily life for the remainder of my tenure at the SEC. They provided near-constant protection, including daily escorts to and from the office, church on Sundays, and my travels within the country. Their commitment was unwavering; they were prepared to risk their lives for my safety.

Courage fosters resilience, enabling individuals to face and overcome challenges with determination, even amid fear and uncertainty. By embracing courage, one takes bold actions despite potential risks, thereby enhancing their capacity to endure adversity. In a country of over 220 million people, the intense competition for limited resources, opportunities, and positions is far more pronounced than in many other parts of the world. In such an environment, where individuals relentlessly strive to surpass each other and secure the necessary resources for success, one must continually excel in education, employment, and other endeavors. This relentless pursuit drives both innovation and resilience, as individuals are compelled to differentiate themselves and thrive despite fierce competition.

Unfortunately, the complexities of Nigerian politics have made achieving success in public office even more challenging. I experienced this firsthand after just two weeks on the job. One afternoon, after a meeting – ostensibly to defend the budget of the SEC for fiscal year 2010 – at the National Assembly complex with members of the House of Representatives' Capital Market Committee, the committee chairman dismissed other participants and asked me to stay behind. In the off-the-record discussion that followed, their intent was clear: to bully me into conniving with them to alter a budget that had already been approved by the relevant authorities. I remained unyielding and firmly rejected their demands, which earned me formidable adversaries from that day onwards. Although I was taken aback by the encounter, it was not entirely unexpected, as I had been forewarned. A predecessor had told me of the challenges I would face, ominously predicting that "untoward and fraudulent requests" would be made of me. The stark reality of these warnings became painfully evident on that day.

Navigating the intricate landscape of public service, particularly in a developing country with a nascent democratic framework, presented formidable challenges, especially when it came to dealing with legislators. Throughout my five-year tenure as the DG of the SEC, I had to deal with the often-grueling task of appearing at thirty different hearings of various legislative committees. Each appearance was fraught with its own set of difficulties and various forms of intimidation that could threaten to undermine even the most well-prepared individual. The experience highlighted the additional layer of complexity inherent in public service roles within less mature democracies, where the political environment can be particularly challenging. This realization underscored that managing such complexities requires not just individual resilience, but a collective effort – an entire 'village' – to navigate the political landscape effectively. Finding a way to manage these challenges while maintaining one's integrity and focus is crucial in this realm of public service.

Later, I would discover that the parliamentarians escalated their threats, going so far as to pressure the President of Nigeria, Goodluck Jonathan, with the demand that I be dismissed, or they would block the approval of the entire federal government's budget. Despite the gravity of their threats, President Jonathan, to his great credit, refused to bow to their demands. His decision to stand firm not only upheld the integrity of his office but also appeared to reinforce his support for my reform efforts at the SEC. This was especially commendable given that I had been appointed by his predecessor, not by him.

Later that year, after we removed the leadership of the stock exchange, the same group of legislators launched a campaign to reverse our decision. Members of the Capital Market Committee sent me threatening letters requiring the SEC to reinstate the leadership of the Exchange. Some in the media reported it as "the house committee on capital market [is] directing the Securities Exchange Commission to reverse the sack of [the DG of the stock exchange]."[221] But the committee had no such powers. Their letter asked that, at a minimum, the SEC should allow the Exchange's DG to "quietly retire rather than being sacked." But we did not back down. Our decision stood, further entrenching the animosity toward me from those quarters.

This all came to a head in March 2012 when, under the guise of a parliamentary investigation into the reasons for the 2008 collapse of the Nigerian capital market, the lawmakers saw an opportunity to get back at me on live national television during a series of public hearings. This is the story of the most publicized episode of my entire time in Nigeria, a topic that dominated news headlines for weeks. In the twelve years since that experience, the video clip has gone viral multiple times each year. Every time it goes viral, I receive a fresh flurry of messages from Nigerians of all walks of life who continue to express their support and appreciation of me. I believe that this is because the average Nigerian desires their leaders to act with integrity and uphold what is right, and they perceived my actions during that period as a steadfast commitment to these values. Their widespread support reflects their recognition of my efforts to do the right thing and stand firm in the face of adversity.

It all began when I received a proposal from our corporate communications team, based on a letter from the National Assembly, regarding an upcoming public hearing to be overseen by the Capital Market Committee of the House of Representatives. They presented a plan, complete with a detailed budget, for a hearing on "the root causes of the collapse in the capital market in 2008." I was taken aback by the choice of topic, given that, by 2012, our market had made substantial progress and was far removed from the aftermath of the crisis. However, I was intrigued, as this committee had historically shown little interest in the market's progress. I wondered if this new group of committee members genuinely cared about the state of our market.

As a point of context, serving on the Capital Market Committee was once considered a highly lucrative position in the House of Representatives. The committee had long been associated with significant personal and financial benefits, contrasting sharply with other less profitable committees. However, by the time I took office as DG, the kickbacks ceased completely, disrupting the status quo. The perceived profitability of the committee had diminished significantly, leading to a high turnover of its members. No one seemed eager to serve on the committee anymore, as my being in charge of the capital markets had effectively turned it into a less attractive post.

In late 2011, a young Nigerian parliamentarian was appointed as the chair of the Capital Markets Committee, along with a crew of new members. The two predecessors in this role had transitioned to more "lucrative committees." The SEC, as part of its market development efforts, had a tradition of supporting the training of various stakeholders, including legislators, judges, and journalists. This initiative aimed to ensure that we had a well-informed team of legislators capable of effectively collaborating with us and facilitating any necessary amendments to support our reform efforts.

Therefore, in October 2011, the SEC sponsored the new chairman of the committee to attend the Emerging Market Committee meetings of IOSCO held in the Dominican Republic. These IOSCO meetings offer invaluable learning opportunities, including presentations on subjects pertinent to emerging markets and their legislators. Unfortunately, despite receiving the estacode intended for travel expenses, the chairman did not attend the conference. I was unaware of this at the time and only discovered it much later. Several months later, we received a letter from the House Committee detailing their plans for a public hearing with a budget of 39 million naira. The SEC's Corporate Communications team recommended supporting the committee, emphasizing that such a hearing was essential for market development. Consequently, the SEC board approved covering expenses for live television broadcasts and some secretarial services, totaling 30 million naira. They also stipulated that payments be made directly to established vendors, including the reputable national networks that would be covering the hearing. Unexpectedly, just days before the hearing commenced, a House Committee staff member approached us, requesting that 5 million naira be delivered in cash to the committee chairman – a highly irregular request that we promptly rejected.

We had only a few weeks to prepare a presentation for the parliamentary committee on the causes of the market collapse. I saw this as an opportunity to highlight not only the reasons behind the market's downturn but also the significant strides we had made toward its recovery. In the forty-five-page presentation, I planned to briefly outline the history of the Nigerian capital market before pinpointing the vulnerabilities that exposed it to the 2008 global financial crisis. Most of the presentation would then focus on the various reforms we had implemented, supported by evidence of the market's recovery and improvements since the crash.

On March 13, 2012, I went to the National Assembly buildings in Abuja for the scheduled hearing. As I began to deliver our comprehensive presentation, I observed the disinterest of the committee members seated at the high tables before us, in a setup reminiscent of the U.S. Congress's public hearings. It later became evident that the committee had made no arrangements for live broadcasting the proceedings for that day. We made our presentation as did various other stakeholders, including the stock exchange, trade groups, and shareholder associations. Thus, the first day concluded without incident.

The next day, it was time to receive feedback from the legislators. We anticipated and were prepared to address inquiries regarding the origins of the crisis, the reforms we were implementing, and any necessary legislative proposals. However, what transpired was an urgent attempt by the committee members to divert the focus of the hearing. On this particular day, the proceedings were broadcast live on national television, with major networks including the Nigerian Television Authority (NTA), Channels TV, and AIT covering the event.

In a coordinated effort, the committee members took turns leveling baseless accusations against me, misrepresenting facts, and deceitfully suggesting that they had obtained evidence from internal SEC documents. Various members falsely accused me of extravagant spending, questioned my competence, and criticized our hiring choices, especially those concerning my front office team. They brandished documents purportedly from the SEC, but which clearly were unauthorized.

This was profoundly infuriating, as in nearly three decades of my career, my integrity had never been questioned, either privately or publicly. I had anticipated an opportunity to respond that day, but the hearing was adjourned, leaving me even more outraged.

In the evening, I reached out to my beloved sister, my Nwannem, who is both my closest confidant and dearest friend. We prayed together, and she offered words of encouragement, urging me to remain steadfast. The following day, I attended the resumption of the hearing without a prepared speech, ready to address any further questions and defend every decision made since my appointment at the SEC. However, I was uncertain how to tackle the absurd and unfounded personal attacks on both myself and the SEC's reputation, particularly at a time when we had successfully restored fragile investor confidence.

As the committee members took their places and the hearing began, we were asked to introduce ourselves, and I knew this might be my only chance to get a word in. Still unsure of exactly how to address the situation, I spoke extemporaneously, expressing thoughts that would come to define me to many Nigerians:

> "When I accepted this position [DG SEC], I was told that when I fight corruption, corruption would fight me back. But I could not have imagined that...that would happen in the house committee on capital markets. Now I question, honorable chairman, your credibility in carrying out this hearing. The reason I question your credibility in carrying out this hearing

is that on October 20th [2011], the SEC gave you an estacode and business class ticket to travel to an emerging market conference in the Dominican Republic. Please tell the Nigerian people whether you actually went there. And this was supposed to happen in November [2011]. Please also tell the Nigerian people, if you did not go, whether you have returned the monies."

As I paused, my gaze remained fixed on the high table. I observed the committee members shifting uncomfortably in their seats, their expressions reflecting a dawning realization of the serious mistake they had made. The hearing was being broadcast live to millions of viewers, leaving them unable to halt the proceedings. I pressed on, raising my voice when necessary to emphasize my points:

"I would also like to say that yesterday, you had indicated that we should … you had implied that, as a regulator, that by having people on secondment, from the private sector in the SEC, that it could have undermined our capacity as the regulator to make our decisions. In asking the SEC to contribute 39 million naira to this hearing, do you think it undermined your capacity to conduct this hearing?"

At this point, the chairman was making frantic efforts to cut me off. I ignored him and persisted:

"I do not think you have given me a fair hearing. I do not think, honorable chairman …, that it is appropriate for you to have [purportedly] gotten information from the SEC, and without even asking us to verify that information, to respond to the issues, that you then made the judgments that you made yesterday. We're trying to build a democracy. But people told me that corruption will fight me hard. It's been two years and a few months...I am still standing...I have not been killed...all of the shenanigans so far have not affected me. But I think that because the integrity of the apex regulator of the Nigerian capital market is so important, it is very important that I state these facts very publicly. And I believe that if we want to carry out an investigation, and as you said, in the interest of Nigeria, and not in your own interest, I should not be subjected to what you subjected me to because the SEC did not give you 5 million naira in cash on Tuesday the 10th of March. It should not be. It should not be. Honorable... And I am sorry because we need to start running this country *differently*. We *need* to start running this country differently. We need to start running this *country* differently."

I continued relentlessly while members of the committee looked visibly restless, swiveling their chairs to consult with aides:

"I cannot have had the auditable career that I have had, and you want to rubbish my person, the reputation...of the apex regulator of the Nigerian capital markets, and the reputation of the Nigerian capital market. If you say that we are here trying to find out why the things that happened in the Nigerian capital market happened ... and we're trying to propose solutions, then please can you explain to me why even the presentation that I made on the 13th of March was not aired live."

Undeterred by further attempts to interrupt me, I proceeded to conclude my statement:

"Can you explain to me why, if our market..., if our equities market peaked at 12.6 trillion naira in March of 2008 and then declined to a bottom of US\$32.9 billion by February of 2009 ... that what you have decided is in the interest of Nigeria is to try and undermine the regulator, and undermine my person. You have questioned my competence, you have made frivolous accusations of me, of having done things that compromised myself and the integrity of the organization that I am the CEO of. Please is this the House that we all know? That gives people fair hearing?"

I concluded that this was akin to "a kangaroo court."

As the committee chairman tried talking over me, I concluded: "no...no...no...my issue is, I question your credibility in doing this. We need an independent arbiter." In his sorry attempt at responding to my remarks, the chairman appeared rattled. He claimed the hearing was not about personalities but about getting to the root of a crisis that happened four years prior, which, through the reforms we were leading, was in the rearview mirror. He began to spout falsehoods, conflating issues I did not allege. As I interrupted to correct some of his falsehoods, he would instruct me to put off my microphone, asking, "Why are you doing this?"

In a Freudian slip, he admitted collecting money for the aforementioned emerging market conference trip and that he did not travel for it. He glibly gave "permission" to the EFCC to investigate him "deeply." They did, just as he asked. Two months later, an Abuja high court granted the EFCC "leave to arraign him."[222],[223] Under probe by the ethics committee of the House of Representatives, the chairman would be forced to step down from the Capital Market Committee during a speech on the floor of the house in which he absurdly alleged that I offered him a 30-million-naira bribe.[224] He did not say what the bribe was for or when the bribe was offered to him.

My encounter with the house committee significantly elevated my profile among Nigerians, including those who were not previously acquainted with capital market issues. The weekend after the contentious live TV confrontation, as I disembarked the plane after a trip outside Abuja, I saw a large crowd waiting on the tarmac and initially feared it might be a protest. To my relief, I discovered that these were Nigerians eager to express their gratitude and commend me for the courage I displayed in standing up to the House of Representatives committee. So many more from across the country reached out to me, praising my "bold stand against the committee." Others lauded my "courage and integrity." In one public opinion piece, an anonymous writer said of my actions, "Her actions are rare and commendable, displaying accountability and transparency in the face of systemic corruption." Another said that my "willingness to challenge the powerful legislative body resonated with a populace increasingly frustrated by corruption and impunity in the country's governance." Someone relayed to me the reaction of my dear late uncle to the whole debacle. When a friend had expressed surprise at how I handled the situation, my uncle replied, "Nobody who knew Oteh Oteh [as my beloved father was called in the community] would be surprised by the courage of his daughter."

Among the most moving calls and letters I received from Nigerians after this episode was a call from Prof. Alele-Williams, a pioneering Nigerian professor of mathematics. At the time, she was around eighty years old and hospitalized. Mrs. Alele-Williams, who was the first Nigerian woman to earn a doctorate and the first female vice chancellor of a Nigerian university, called me to express her immense pride in the courage I had shown. She said she felt compelled to reach out immediately rather than wait until she was discharged from the hospital. I also received a call from Chief Olaniwun Ajayi, one of Nigeria's most esteemed legal scholars, who conveyed his support and pride. Chief Ajayi was an activist in his youth and was among the prominent disciples of the great Chief Obafemi Awolowo, who served as Premier of the Western Region of Nigeria. Throughout that month, I was inundated with hundreds of calls and letters of solidarity from Nigerians, particularly many young people, from all walks of life, most of whom I had never met.

A few commentators viewed the episode with skepticism, questioning the motives and timing of my accusations. The drama unfolded in a highly charged political environment, with various stakeholders having vested interests in the outcome. Despite these differing perspectives, most people agree that the episode brought issues of corruption into the public discourse. Amid the ongoing turmoil and public lynching I was facing from some members of the House of Representatives, President Goodluck Jonathan, during a meeting of the Economic Management Team (EMT), in his usual calm and unassuming voice, publicly commended my steadfast anti-corruption stance and the bold reforms I was spearheading at the SEC, to the hearing of the ministers and other members of the EMT in the room. "If there were two or three more people like Arunma Oteh," he said, "Nigeria would be in a much better place." His words were a strong support, an endorsement that bolstered my resolve amid the storm.

This public affirmation from the President was not merely a gesture of solidarity, but a profound leadership lesson: even small actions, seemingly inconsequential to those in power, can profoundly impact those they lead. By standing firm and voicing his support, President Jonathan not only validated my efforts but also set a powerful example of leadership, courage, and integrity. Such acts, while perhaps routine for a leader, can make a world of difference to those navigating the challenges and pressures of their roles.

Meanwhile, my opponents continued their efforts to undermine me by filing frivolous lawsuits designed to distract me from my primary goal of reforming the capital market. I needed a competent and trustworthy lawyer to handle these cases so that I could stay focused on my work. I was fortunate to receive a referral from Lagos State Governor Babatunde Fashola to his former colleague, Prof. Yemi Osinbajo, who was then running his private practice after serving as Attorney General of Lagos. Prof. Osinbajo, a distinguished Senior Advocate of Nigeria, was a legal luminary I thought I could never afford. To my surprise, he agreed to take on my case pro bono, and remained deeply committed, personally appearing in court throughout the proceedings. His dedication was particularly meaningful to me, especially when, in December 2014, while my case was still ongoing, Prof. Osinbajo was announced as the vice-presidential candidate for the All Progressives Congress. Despite this significant development, he continued to represent me in court, combining that with a hectic schedule of a presidential campaign. I will always be grateful to him for his unwavering support, which ultimately led to a successful outcome in our case. Prof. Osinbajo was later elected Vice President alongside President Muhammadu Buhari, a role he held for two full terms.

As the overwhelming public support continued in my favor, my detractors took it as a temporary setback only. They kept sharpening the knives; however, unfortunately, the controversy was far from over. In coordination with some on the SEC board, they began making a fresh set of frivolous allegations regarding the budget of the one-year program to commemorate fifty years of capital market regulation, "Project 50." Some members of the SEC seemed to have aligned with my detractors, I suspect, because they were uncomfortable with my zero tolerance to corruption and unwavering commitment to integrity. It became evident that they sought my removal.

This situation further escalated into an attempt to scapegoat one of my finest staff members, who had meticulously managed "Project 50." Despite maintaining the highest standards, instead of being commended, there was an effort to undermine his promising career. It became apparent that certain SEC board members were motivated by the personal financial benefits they had hoped to gain from the project, which we prevented by adhering strictly to procurement best practices. I was determined not to allow this injustice, knowing it would weigh on my conscience. As CEO, I insisted that any issues should fall on me, not my staff, who had carried out his duties impeccably.

True leaders stand by their teams, protect them from unjust treatment, and foster a culture of accountability, where excellence is rewarded, not punished. When your team sees that you will defend them when they act with integrity, they are motivated to go the extra mile, knowing they have a leader who will fight for them.

Eventually, the board, displeased with my stance, retaliated by deciding that I should go on compulsory leave, citing the need for an external investigation into Project 50. Their rationale was that, as CEO, my leave would ensure unrestricted access to information during the investigation. Fortunately, one of the Big 4 audit firms, with a global reputation to protect, was chosen to conduct the investigation. I proceeded on leave but was not particularly worried because I was confident in the integrity of the work we had done.

The following morning newspapers announced my "suspension," a term in Nigeria that often signifies a permanent dismissal.[225] My detractors viewed this as a decisive victory, assuming my departure was final. Unaware that suspensions typically meant permanent dismissal and confident in my integrity, I believed that any investigation would reveal Project 50 as a paragon of accountability. While on leave, I continued to fulfill my other responsibilities, such as participating in the Economic Management Team meetings, as the situation unfolded.

The report of the external auditor contracted by the board to look into Project 50 cleared me of any wrongdoing. After only three weeks of compulsory leave, I received the letter from the then-Secretary to the Government of the Federation reinstating me to my position. I applaud him for the role he played in that whole episode, ensuring that justice was done to me. Many told me how "lucky" I was to come back after a "suspension." One of them, a high-ranking government official, mentioned to me that he could not recall any other Nigerian government official returning to their position after being placed on compulsory leave. I was, perhaps naively, absolutely convinced that I would return to my role, and I was gearing up to resume the important work that had been unfortunately interrupted.

One consequence of this experience was the significant impact it had on my team. They were disheartened and angered by the injustices I was facing. I urged them to renew their commitment to our mission, emphasizing that we were making progress toward the governance reforms we sought. To my great admiration, my steadfast team persevered, continuing their diligent work despite the challenges. By the end of that arduous year, we received positive feedback from market participants, who were impressed by our swift and efficient handling of transactions, despite the numerous distractions we had encountered.

A proactive approach to difficulties fosters a mindset that views setbacks as opportunities for growth and learning rather than insurmountable obstacles. During tough times, I take time to fortify my emotional and mental fortitude, relying more on the support system around me, which enhances my capacity to recover from hardships and persist on the goal. In this regard, my sister has been an absolute rock, on whom I have been able to lean for literally my whole life. Over time, the repeated exercise of courage in overcoming challenges cultivates a robust inner strength, further deepening resilience.

A courageous leader must be willing to confront challenges head-on, even in the face of uncertainty or potential failure. This boldness enables the leader to make tough decisions that are essential for the long-term success and growth of their organization – particularly when taking calculated risks to pursue new opportunities. Courage empowers leaders to act decisively and with conviction.

Competence

Of my four Cs, competence is the most malleable and least innate. It can be learned and re-learned. Competence is the harmonious blend of knowledge, skills, and abilities that empowers an individual to perform tasks effectively and efficiently. It embodies the depth of understanding and proficiency in a particular field, allowing one to navigate complex challenges with confidence and precision. It is not merely about possessing theoretical insights, however, but also about applying this wisdom practically to achieve desired outcomes. It reflects a commitment to continuous learning and adaptation, ensuring that one remains adept in a dynamic and ever-evolving environment. Competence is the hallmark of reliability and excellence, inspiring trust and respect from peers and stakeholders alike.

Preparation builds competence and gives you confidence. It is fundamental to success in any endeavor, as it equips individuals with the knowledge and skills necessary to face challenges with confidence. Just as regular exercise strengthens muscles and improves physical endurance, thorough preparation fortifies one's ability to handle various situations effectively. Research underscores the importance of preparation in enhancing performance and confidence. For example, a study by K. Anders Ericsson and colleagues highlights that deliberate practice, a form of focused preparation, significantly improves expertise and performance in fields ranging from music to sports and beyond.[226] This process of systematic preparation builds a solid foundation, instilling confidence and reducing anxiety when confronted with complex or high-stakes scenarios.

Furthermore, preparation not only boosts individual confidence but also enhances organizational performance by reducing uncertainty and enabling proactive problem-solving. According to a study by Collins and colleagues, thorough preparation and planning can lead to better decision-making and higher performance levels, as individuals are more adept at anticipating challenges and devising effective strategies.[227] This principle applies across various domains, including business, education, and sports. By investing time and effort into preparation, individuals build the mental resilience and competence required to navigate obstacles successfully, just as exercise conditions the body to meet physical demands.

My parents encouraged me to be the best version of myself. Growing up, my parents constantly encouraged me to work hard, study hard, and seek to improve constantly. It worked, and I recall excitedly showing my dad my results, telling him I was now at the top of my class. I was dumbfounded when he simply said, "Next time, I hope you will do better and make 'first plus plus'." Later, I have heard similar stories from Nigerian friends and colleagues who were similarly pushed by their parents. A particular friend mentioned how he excitedly showed his dad that he scored 95% in an exam, and his dad asked him, "What happened to the remaining 5%?"

While this is not a formula I would recommend for bringing up every child, I suspect it is the reason I have always put in my best in everything I do. The pressure to do well also comes from the fact that a community brings up a child. Specifically, since most children will usually have to disclose their results to an extended community that includes uncles, aunts, and family friends, they are further inspired to do well as they do not want to be considered the "laggard" of the family.

I was very fortunate to begin my journey toward competence in finance at a very young age. I feel like I have been a finance professional for half a century at this point, because I started my finance career at the age of eight. My parents were teaching us about investing in stocks while simultaneously involving us in their small businesses (block molding business, poultry farm, piggery). After school and on holidays, my siblings and I helped with various aspects. I liked to write invoices, collect payments, and count the money at the end of each day.

Before finance stole my heart, my ambition as a child was to become an inventor. I was constantly inspired by great female inventors such as Ada Lovelace, often considered the first computer programmer, who laid the foundation for modern computing with her visionary work on Charles Babbage's early mechanical general-purpose computer. Marie Curie is another, a pioneer in radioactivity who became the first woman to win a Nobel Prize, and many others. These remarkable women have shown that, with determination and intellect, girls can achieve groundbreaking successes and transform the world. I decided to study computer science for my degree, thinking it could be a bridge for me between my love for science and technology and my passion for finance. Later, I would yearn for even more competence in finance, eventually, in 1988, becoming the first Nigerian woman to be accepted into the prestigious Harvard Business School (HBS) MBA program.

Competence enhances ambition by providing individuals with the confidence and capability to pursue their goals effectively. When individuals possess the necessary skills and knowledge, they are more likely to set higher aspirations, believing in their ability to overcome challenges and achieve success. This sense of mastery fuels their drive and determination, encouraging them to tackle ambitious projects and strive for continuous improvement. As competence grows, so does the willingness to take on new opportunities, further expanding the horizons of what can be accomplished. This is true for an organization as well.

Ambition fuels entrepreneurship by driving individuals and organizations to pursue innovative ideas and take calculated risks to bring those ideas to fruition. It is the engine that powers entrepreneurial success and innovation. I grew up admiring several entrepreneurs. Madam CJ Walker's journey to becoming the first female self-made millionaire is a tale of resilience, innovation, and unwavering determination. Born in

1867 to former slaves on a cotton plantation in Louisiana, her early life was marked by hardship and struggle. Yet it was her personal battle with hair loss that ignited her entrepreneurial spirit. In an era when opportunities for African American women were scarce, she created a line of hair care products specifically for black women, revolutionizing the beauty industry.[228] With sheer grit and an astute business acumen, she built a thriving business empire, employing thousands of women and empowering them with economic independence. Walker's legacy transcends her wealth; she became a beacon of hope, philanthropy, and activism, advocating for social change and uplifting her community. Her story is a testament to the transformative power of ambition and the boundless possibilities it can unlock.

I was similarly inspired by technology startups from the days of Microsoft and Apple. More recently, I have been very pleased to see similar entrepreneurial verve with a rave of African fintech unicorns such as Flutterwave and Paystack. They represent the continent's burgeoning innovation and entrepreneurial spirit. These companies are changing the financial landscape on the continent, bridging gaps in payment systems and enabling transactions across borders. Flutterwave, with its cutting-edge technology, facilitates online payments for businesses globally, while Paystack simplifies payment processes for African merchants, driving e-commerce growth. Their meteoric success, with their multimillion-dollar valuations and strategic acquisitions, not only highlights the immense potential within Africa's tech ecosystem but also showcases the talent and resilience of famous risk-taking African entrepreneurs. These fintech pioneers are not just creating wealth; they are empowering businesses, fostering financial inclusion, and shaping the future of digital finance on the continent. I am confident that African entrepreneurs will continue to be part of a dedicated group around the world with a relentless desire to revolutionize industries and solve humanity's most complex problems.

Compassion

I was raised by parents who taught me, both by their actions and their words, the importance of compassion. Compassion is the ability to understand and empathize with the suffering of others. It sometimes manifests in a strong desire to alleviate that suffering. I have found that being compassionate has been very helpful in managing tough situations, both for the "victim" of the circumstance and for myself. Compassion involves recognizing the emotional and physical challenges that people face and responding with kindness, support, and a willingness to help. Compassion goes beyond mere sympathy; it is an active commitment to improving the well-being of others through thoughtful actions and understanding. It is a fundamental human trait that fosters deep connections and promotes a sense of community and shared humanity.

As a leader, compassion is an invaluable quality that enhances your ability to connect with and inspire your team. A compassionate leader is attuned to the needs and concerns of their employees, creating a supportive and inclusive work environment where individuals feel valued and understood. This does not only boost morale but also fosters loyalty and trust, as team members are more likely to engage and contribute their best efforts when they know their leader genuinely cares about their well-being. Compassionate leadership also encourages open communication, where employees feel safe to voice their ideas, concerns, and feedback, leading to better decision-making and innovation.

My mother's most obvious quality was her compassion. As a nurse at the main government hospital in our community in Kano, she helped many mothers deliver their babies. Many of these families revered her and considered her one of them. She was welcoming to all who came in need, and although we were not wealthy, she would always dig into our supplies at home to help someone in need.

During vacations, our whole family made the trip down south to my parents' village, where my mom was considered the "women leader." She would rally other women who put their resources together to fund beneficial projects for the community, and directly provided primary healthcare services to the less fortunate. Her compassionate leadership and philanthropy were intrinsically connected, both rooted in a deep-seated desire to uplift others and make a meaningful difference in the world. Her philanthropy has continued to inspire and influence my own approach to philanthropy. She taught me to always help those less privileged. Knowing the society I was coming from, I considered myself being in Harvard a great privilege. During my program there, I often volunteered locally in Boston at soup kitchens and other initiatives caring for the homeless.

Like my mom, I love giving because it gives me the greatest joy to give, whether to individuals in need or to causes that are important to me. Over the years, I have found that helping another person has one of the highest returns on investment. Helping one person can create a profound ripple effect on society, akin to a single stone causing waves across a calm lake. When we extend our support to an individual, we often enable them to improve their circumstances, empowering them to positively impact others in their community. In my giving to individuals, I support educational opportunities, help cover healthcare bills, or support a young business venture with a grant.

Back home in Nigeria, my most significant giving is for scholarships to young people covering primary, secondary, or university education. Scholarship opportunities are pivotal in nurturing a new generation of leaders, as they democratize access to education, allowing talented individuals from diverse backgrounds to realize their full potential. I am a living testimonial to the difference that scholarships can make. Part of the funding for my undergraduate studies at Nsukka came from a very competitive scholarship scheme championed by Shell Plc, the British multinational oil and gas company.

My Harvard MBA program was partly funded by

a loan from Barclays Bank UK and partly covered by a scholarship from an HBS Fellowship. Without a doubt, my MBA has given me one of the highest returns on investment that I have ever earned. Financial aid does not only alleviate the burden of tuition fees and other educational expenses but also empower students to focus on their studies and personal development without the constant stress of financial constraints. By providing access to quality education even for those who cannot afford it, scholarships help with social mobility and can reduce inequality. As the beneficiaries grow and thrive, they are likely to pay it forward, helping others in turn and perpetuating a cycle of upliftment and generosity.

As our careers progressed, my siblings and I made it a practice to keep our mother's philanthropy alive with regular projects in the same community where she led women's groups. We built a mini stadium in her honor, we regularly finance medical assistance programs, and we contribute to the scholarship program that the king of our community established. We also contribute actively to the community programs organized by the community's women's association. Additionally, the Oteh Oteh Foundation, founded in honor of our beloved parents, provides various other forms of support to the underprivileged.

Throughout history, philanthropy has been a powerful force for societal change, driven by remarkable individuals whose generosity and vision have left an indelible mark on the world. Andrew Carnegie, the steel magnate, famously dedicated his fortune to establishing libraries, universities, and cultural institutions, believing in the transformative power of education. John D. Rockefeller's philanthropic legacy includes the creation of the Rockefeller Foundation, which has funded groundbreaking medical research and public health initiatives. In more modern times, Bill and Melinda Gates have redefined global philanthropy through their foundation's extensive work in eradicating diseases, improving education, and reducing poverty. These luminaries, among others, have not only contributed vast financial resources but have also inspired countless others to use their wealth and influence to address some of humanity's most pressing challenges, embodying the spirit of giving and the pursuit of a better world.

Nigeria, despite its challenges, is blessed with wealthy individuals who understand the value of giving back. I have also been inspired by several great Nigerian philanthropic initiatives, such as the Tony Elumelu Foundation (TEF) with a US$100 million commitment, which works on empowering young African entrepreneurs through the provision of seed funding, mentorship, and training, fostering economic growth and innovation across the continent. The TEF has empowered over 18,000 entrepreneurs across fifty-four African countries.[229] The Dangote Foundation, established by Africa's wealthiest man, Aliko Dangote, has also made significant investments in health, education, and disaster relief, notably contributing to the fight against malnutrition and providing scholarships to underprivileged students.[230]

I equally admire the philanthropic work of Folorunsho Alakija through her Rose of Sharon Foundation, which focuses on empowering widows and orphans by providing them with business grants, scholarships, and housing.[231] Femi Otedola also makes significant contributions to education, health, and poverty alleviation. His charitable foundation, the Femi Otedola Foundation, has funded numerous projects, including financing the cancer center at the Lagos University Teaching Hospital.[232] The Abdul Samad Rabiu Initiative and its annual US$100million commitment to Africa Fund for Social Development will also support initiatives in education, healthcare and social development, particularly complementing the efforts of governments in Nigeria and other parts of sub-Saharan African.[233]

The synergy between compassionate leadership and philanthropy creates a powerful force for positive change. Compassionate leaders understand that their success is intertwined with the well-being of the communities they serve, and they recognize the importance of contributing to the greater good. By integrating compassion into their leadership philosophy, leaders not only drive impactful philanthropic efforts but also set a profound example for others to follow, demonstrating that true leadership encompasses a commitment to elevating humanity and nurturing a more equitable and compassionate world.

14

The Unfinished Business

"We are perishing for want of wonder, not for want of wonders."
— G.K. Chesterton

The period since the end of World War II (WW2) has been the longest period of peace and prosperity humanity has ever known, despite threats from the 2008 global financial crisis and the 2020 COVID-19 pandemic. Since the conclusion of the war in 1945, global reduction in poverty has been phenomenal, with the most significant progress occurring in the last few decades. The World Bank estimates that over 1.2 billion people have been lifted out of extreme poverty since 1981. China's economic reforms and rapid growth have enabled over 800 million people to lift themselves out of poverty, which represents two-thirds of the global reduction in extreme poverty during this period.[234]

This era of unprecedented global prosperity has been intermittently challenged by major crises. The 2008 global financial crisis led to severe economic disruptions, contributing to a temporary rise in poverty and economic instability. More recently, the COVID-19 pandemic further threatened global economic progress, causing significant setbacks in poverty-reduction efforts and economic growth. The pandemic exacerbated inequalities and pushed millions back into poverty, with estimates suggesting that up to 97 million people could have been pushed into extreme poverty due to the pandemic.[235] Despite these setbacks, the post-WW2 period remains unmatched in terms of its extended peace and relative stability, which has fostered substantial economic growth and poverty reduction, according to the Global Peace Index and other measures of global conflict.[236]

Institutions such as the United Nations were established to promote peace and prevent the recurrence of global conflicts, fostering a sense of collective security and shared responsibility. Although this period witnessed the emergence of the Cold War, the resultant geopolitical tensions did not escalate into a full-scale international conflict, and did not therefore disturb the prolonged period of relative stability.

Additionally, the Marshall Plan was launched to help rebuild war-torn Europe, leading to the resurgence of strong economies and the creation of the European Union, which also played a crucial role in maintaining peace and fostering economic development in continental Europe and beyond. The Bretton Woods Conference laid the foundation for the modern global financial system, establishing institutions such as the IMF and the World Bank, which have been instrumental in promoting economic stability and development worldwide. The latter half of the twentieth century saw remarkable economic growth, particularly in the Western world, and the rapid development of emerging economies in Asia, thus lifting millions out of poverty and enhancing their quality of life.

Technologically and socially, the post-war period has been transformative. Innovations in science and technology have revolutionized industries, healthcare, and communication, shrinking the world into a global village. The information age, driven by the advent of the internet, has democratized access to information and connected people across continents, while social movements have advanced civil rights, gender equality, and human rights, fostering more inclusive and equitable societies like never before in the history of humanity. The long peace has allowed humanity to focus on these advancements, paving the way for a future of continued progress and collaboration.

The post-WW2 era of prosperity has, however, not been even. It has been characterized by profound inequality and uneven development across different regions – mostly between the Global North and Global South. High-income countries, particularly in North America and Western Europe, experienced rapid industrialization and economic prosperity, leading to substantial improvements in living standards. In contrast, many developing nations, in Africa, Latin America, and parts of Asia, struggled to achieve similar progress. According to World Bank records, the global income gap widened significantly, with the GDP per capita of high-income countries growing at an average annual rate of 2.5% from 1960 to 2015, compared to just 1.1% for low-income countries.[237] This disparity resulted in stark differences in poverty rates, access to education, healthcare, and infrastructure, perpetuating cycles of poverty and underdevelopment in the Global South. The uneven distribution of post-war economic gains underscored the need for targeted development policies and international cooperation to address these persistent inequalities.

To address these development needs, the Sustainable Development Goals (SDGs), adopted by the United Nations in 2015, aim to address a broad spectrum of global challenges that hinder sustainable development and human well-being. One of the primary challenges is poverty eradication, recognizing that over 700 million people still live in extreme poverty, struggling to meet basic needs such as food, water, and shelter.[238] The SDGs also set out to tackle hunger, aiming to ensure food security and improved nutrition for all in a world where approximately 820 million people suffer from chronic hunger.[239] Furthermore, the SDGs seek to ensure good health and well-being by addressing issues such as child mortality, maternal health, and epidemics such as HIV/AIDS, tuberculosis, and malaria. Education is another critical area, with goals set to provide inclusive and equitable quality education, ensuring that all children and adults have access to learning opportunities.

Beyond social issues, the SDGs focus on environmental sustainability, recognizing the urgent need to address climate change, protect ecosystems, and ensure the sustainable use of natural resources. Goals related to clean water and sanitation aim to provide universal access to safe and affordable drinking water while promoting sustainable management of water resources. Affordable and clean energy goals focus on ensuring access to modern, sustainable energy for all. The SDGs also emphasize the importance of sustainable economic growth, decent work, and innovation, advocating for resilient infrastructure and inclusive industrialization. Additionally, they address inequalities within and among countries, aiming to reduce disparities based on income, gender, age, race, and other factors, while promoting peaceful and inclusive societies with justice for all.

SDG investment gaps

Meeting the SDGs by 2030 requires unprecedented levels of investment, underscoring the critical financing needs that span across various sectors and regions. According to the United Nations Conference on Trade and Development (UNCTAD), achieving the SDGs will necessitate an estimated annual investment of US$5 trillion to US$7 trillion globally.[240] This substantial funding requirement encompasses a wide array of critical areas, including infrastructure, healthcare, education, and climate action. UNCTAD further notes that developing countries alone face an annual SDG financing gap of about US$4 trillion, up from US$2.5 trillion in 2015.[241] This highlights the urgent need for world class capital markets, the mobilization of private sector resources, innovative financing solutions, and enhanced international cooperation to bridge this massive shortfall. Moreover, the COVID-19 pandemic which diverted resources toward immediate health and economic responses, and away from long-term development goals, further exacerbated the financing challenges. UNCTAD notes that the US$4 trillion annual investment needs are less than 1% of total global financial assets, estimated at US$440 trillion according to 2021 data from the Bank of International Settlements (BIS).[242]

The Organisation for Economic Co-operation and Development (OECD) reports that official development assistance (ODA) remains a vital source of funding for many low-income countries, yet it alone is insufficient to meet the SDG targets.[243] Enhanced global financial architecture, including debt relief initiatives and increased development aid, alongside innovative financing mechanisms from the capital markets, such as green bonds and social impact bonds, are imperative to ensure sustained progress.

Capital markets, with their expansive reach and deep pools of liquidity, offer an unparalleled opportunity to attract private sector investment into SDG-aligned projects. For example, green bonds, social impact bonds, and sustainability-linked loans, can tap into the growing appetite among investors for socially responsible and environmentally sustainable investments. This not only helps bridge the financing gap, but also aligns the interests of investors with the long-term goals of sustainable development, fostering a more resilient and inclusive global economy.

Since the adoption of the SDGs in 2015, there has been a significant surge in the issuance of green bonds, social impact bonds, and sustainability-linked loans, reflecting a growing commitment to sustainable finance. According to the Climate Bonds Initiative, the global climate bond market experienced remarkable growth, with annual issuance increasing from just US$42 billion in 2015 to over US$870 billion in 2023.[244] As of March 2024, the cumulative issuance of green bonds had surpassed US$4.4 trillion across 43,000 instruments, driven by strong investor demand and heightened corporate and governmental focus on environmental sustainability. This dramatic increase highlights the critical role of green bonds in financing projects that address climate change and environmental protection, aligning with SDG goals.

Sustainability-linked loans, which tie borrowing costs to the borrower's performance on sustainability metrics, have also gained traction. According to *The Asset*, annual issuance of sustainability-linked loan issuance soared from virtually zero in 2015 to approximately US$300 billion in 2023, although down from a peak of about US$500 billion in 2021.[245] This growth underscores the increasing importance of incorporating environmental, social, and governance (ESG) criteria into financial decisions, encouraging companies to adopt more sustainable practices in line with the SDGs. These trends demonstrate the financial sector's critical role in advancing sustainable development through innovative financial instruments.

Furthermore, capital markets can stimulate greater collaboration between the public and private sectors. Public-private partnerships (PPPs) can play a pivotal role in scaling up investments, as governments can provide initial funding and policy support to de-risk projects, making them more attractive to private investors. Additionally, innovative financial mechanisms such as blended finance can combine public and private capital to enhance the viability and impact of SDG initiatives. By fostering such synergies, capital markets can amplify the efforts to close the SDG financing gap, ensuring that the global community moves closer to achieving the 2030 SDGs.

According to the Global Impact Investing Network (GIIN), the impact investing market, with a current size of US$1.16 trillion, has "evolved significantly and continues to mature in a world that is slowly emerging from the COVID-19 pandemic and fraught with economic and racial inequities."[246] As of 2023, investor allocations to impact strategies have increased, with significant growth in public markets, housing, and technology. Surprisingly, however, when it comes to actual asset allocation by geography, the regions of the world that require the most help get the least allocation. GIIN's 2023 survey of asset managers showed that, in 2023, the greatest proportion was allocated to the United States and Canada (29% of impact AUM), followed by Western, Northern, and Southern Europe (23%), sub-Saharan Africa (10%), and the rest of the world (38%) – including 3% in the Middle East, 5% in Southeast Asia, and 8% each in South Asia, Latin America, and the Caribbean.

Africa's unfinished business

Achieving the SDGs by 2030 presents a challenge of gigantic proportions for Africa, with massive investment gaps that need to be addressed. According to UNCTAD, Africa faces an annual SDG financing gap of about US$200 billion to US$300 billion.[247] This funding shortfall spans critical areas such as infrastructure, healthcare, education, and climate action. The AfDB estimates that the continent needs around US$130 billion to US$170 billion annually for infrastructure development alone, yet current investment levels are only around US$67 billion, leaving a substantial gap.[248] These figures highlight the urgent need for increased financial flows from both domestic and international sources to bridge the investment gaps and accelerate progress toward the SDGs.

As in other developing regions of the world, the COVID-19 pandemic exacerbated the challenges Africa faces. The IMF notes that the pandemic could push an additional 49 million Africans into extreme poverty, underscoring the critical need for investment in social protection systems and economic recovery initiatives.[249] To meet the SDGs, Africa will require a concerted effort to mobilize resources, including enhanced domestic revenue generation, increased foreign direct investment, and innovative financing mechanisms such as blended finance and public-private partnerships. Addressing these investment gaps is essential to ensuring that Africa can achieve sustainable and inclusive growth, improve living standards, and build resilience against future shocks.

It is worth repeating that Africa's wealth of resources, if harnessed effectively, can significantly contribute to meeting the SDGs. According to the United Nations Economic Commission for Africa (UNECA), Africa holds over 90% of the world's known reserves of platinum group metals and 75% of the value in diamonds, making it a crucial player in the global precious metals market.[250] The continent is also home to 80% of the world's manganese, a key component in steel production, and 70% of global phosphates, essential for agricultural fertilizers. Additionally, Africa possesses 80% of the world's coltan, critical for electronics, 40% of gold reserves, and 60% of cobalt, vital for battery technology. It also harbors significant deposits of chromium, uranium, bauxite, copper, iron ore, lithium, zinc, and lead. This rich resource base, coupled with its growing young population, underscores Africa's strategic importance in the economy of the future. By leveraging these resources through sustainable exploitation and equitable distribution of revenues, African nations can fund essential infrastructure projects, healthcare systems, and educational programs, thereby advancing multiple SDGs simultaneously.

In addition to its famed mineral wealth, Africa holds 39% of the world's renewable potential. Our continent possesses immense potential for renewable energy generation, with its vast solar, wind, and hydro resources significantly underutilized compared to global figures. The continent has about 60% of the world's best solar resources, yet it currently generates less than 1% of global solar electricity.[251] According to a study commissioned by the IFC, Africa possesses wind resources capable of meeting its entire electricity demand 250 times over. The study, which assessed the continent's technical wind potential, revealed that Africa could generate more than 59,000 gigawatts of wind energy – more than sixty times the current global installed wind capacity.[252] Despite this vast potential, wind power remains largely underutilized in Africa, with the continent accounting for less than 1% of the world's installed wind capacity. Hydropower also remains largely untapped despite the continent's extensive river systems. This disparity underscores the need to accelerate investment to begin tapping into Africa's renewable energy resources fully.

In terms of human resources, the World Bank reports that Africa's population is expected to double by 2050, with over 60% of its people under the age of 25.[253] This demographic dividend presents a tremendous opportunity to drive economic development through a skilled and educated workforce. Investing in quality education, vocational training, and healthcare can empower this young population, fostering innovation, entrepreneurship, and productivity. Such investments will not only contribute to economic growth but also to social stability and improved living standards, directly supporting SDGs related to education, decent work, and economic growth.

Africa's natural resources extend beyond minerals and human capital, encompassing vast agricultural lands. The Food and Agriculture Organization (FAO) highlights that Africa possesses 60% of the world's uncultivated arable land, offering immense potential for agricultural development and food security.[254] Sustainable agricultural practices can enhance food production, reduce poverty, and ensure nutrition, aligning with SDGs on hunger, poverty, and sustainable agriculture.

Infrastructure deficiencies significantly hinder Africa's economic potential, impeding the ability to achieve the SDGs. Over 600 million Africans, or 43% of the population, lack access to electricity, contrasting sharply with near-universal access in Europe and North America.[255] Africa's per capita electricity consumption stands at just 450 kWh annually, a fraction of the 6,800 kWh in the European Union and 12,000 kWh in the United States.[256] In addition, Sub-Saharan Africa's road network is underdeveloped, with only 204 kilometers of road per 1,000 square kilometers, compared to the global average of 944 kilometers. Only 25% of these roads are paved, far below the standards of China, France, Germany, and the United States. The continent's rail infrastructure is also inadequate, with fewer than 75,000 kilometers of operational rail lines, compared to over 202,000 kilometers in Europe and 260,000 kilometers in the United States.[257]

Africa's ports and air transportation further worsen these challenges. African ports handle only about 4% of global container traffic, despite the continent's 20% share of the global population. The average time to clear goods through African ports is twenty days, significantly longer than the three to five days in Europe and Asia. Air traffic through Africa constitutes just 2.1% of the global total, with only 21% of international traffic being intra-African. Less than 20% of African airports can accommodate large, wide-body aircraft, limiting the continent's connectivity and hindering its ability to compete globally. Additionally, only 40% of Africans have internet access, which restricts information, education, and economic opportunities. Addressing these infrastructure gaps is critical for Africa to unlock its vast potential and ensure sustainable and inclusive growth.

Capital markets are crucial drivers of capital formation, enabling the efficient allocation of financial resources across the economy. Research consistently highlights how capital markets facilitate the mobilization and deployment of capital, fostering capital formation within an economy. A 1998 paper by Levine and Zervos in the *Journal of Finance* demonstrates that well-functioning capital markets significantly enhance capital accumulation by providing firms with access to equity and debt financing, which are essential for investment and expansion.[258] Similarly, a World Bank report underscores that countries with developed capital markets experience higher rates of capital formation, as these markets offer diverse financial instruments and investment opportunities that attract both domestic and international investors.[259]

A natural consequence of sustained capital formation is the accumulation of physical assets such as machinery, buildings, and infrastructure. Capital markets played an important role in bringing transformative telecommunications infrastructure to Africa, with companies such as MTN, as the early players, leveraging the capital markets to raise money needed for their major projects. The Global System for Mobile Communications (GSM) network expansion across Africa has been instrumental in bridging the digital divide. Initiated in the late 1990s, the expansion saw significant investments from capital markets, including notable funding through bonds and equity offerings by major telecommunications companies. This infrastructure overhaul has drastically increased mobile connectivity across the continent, with mobile phone subscriptions in Africa growing from 16 million in

2000 to over 1.2 billion by 2022, as reported by the International Telecommunication Union (ITU).[260] This surge in connectivity has not only revolutionized communication but also stimulated economic growth by enabling access to mobile banking, e-commerce, and digital services, thus driving significant advancements in various sectors.

Investment in digital infrastructure is crucial for enabling transformative technologies and enhancing connectivity, as it lays the foundation for the digital economy's growth. Africa needs these investments to transition the continent from the current dominance of slow, 3G networks and leapfrog 4G into 5G. While 3G technology remains the most prevalent in the region, the adoption of 4G has accelerated due to rising demand for faster speeds, particularly among younger Africans. In the coming years, the adoption of 4G is projected to more than double, reaching 45% by 2028, according to the GSM Association. Meanwhile, 5G technology is gaining traction, though initial deployments are concentrated in urban areas and industrial zones where the technology is most needed. By 2030, 5G is expected to contribute US$11 billion to the sub-Saharan African economy, representing over 6% of the total economic impact of mobile technology.[261]

In West Africa, MainOne raised substantial capital to build and deploy undersea cables stretching across the Atlantic Ocean, linking West Africa to global internet networks. In 2010, the company secured US$240 million in funding through a combination of private equity and debt instruments to support the construction of its high-capacity submarine cable system. The funding came mostly from Nigerian banks, Africa Finance Corporation, and the AfDB. This ambitious project not only provided West Africa with a robust and reliable internet backbone, but also dramatically increased bandwidth capacity, reduced latency, and lowered internet costs for millions of users.

By enhancing connectivity, companies such as MainOne are facilitating significant technological advancements and economic growth across Nigeria and the broader West African region. Businesses and consumers benefit from improved access to cloud services, e-commerce, and digital communication tools, which have catalyzed innovation and fostered economic development. MainOne's undersea cable network has also attracted global technology companies seeking to tap into the growing African market, further boosting the region's digital economy. In 2022, Equinix, an American multinational listed on NASDAQ, which is the largest global data center and colocation provider in the world, acquired MainOne for US$320 million.[262]

These world class projects should inspire Africa to redouble efforts to harness the power of capital markets to address its significant infrastructure deficits. Just as successful initiatives have transformed transportation networks and communication systems in other regions, Africa has the potential to also leverage capital markets to fund essential developments in road networks, railways, aviation, and telecommunications. These investments are not merely about improving physical infrastructure but also about fostering economic growth, enhancing connectivity, and driving innovation. Capital markets offer a powerful mechanism to mobilize the substantial financial resources required for such transformative projects. By tapping into these markets, African nations can attract both domestic and international investors, ensuring that the necessary funds are secured to build and modernize infrastructure across our beautiful continent.

The expansion of the high-speed fiber optic network in South Korea has been a model of capital market-driven infrastructure development. South Korea's ambitious plan, funded through a combination of public and private capital, involved the issuance of bonds and significant equity investments. The project has created one of the world's most advanced broadband networks, with average internet speeds exceeding 200 Mbps by 2020, according to Akamai's *State of the Internet* report. The high-speed network has profoundly impacted South Korea's economy, enhanced digital connectivity and fostered growth in tech-driven industries.

In the 1860s, the construction of the Transcontinental Railroad in the United States was financed through the sale of bonds and stocks to investors. The capital raised allowed for the completion of the railroad, which connected the eastern and western parts of the United States, facilitating trade, commerce, and the movement of people. This infrastructure project spurred economic development across the country by opening up new markets and resources.

In a similar more recent example in the United Kingdom, the Crossrail project in London, one of Europe's largest infrastructure projects, raised a significant portion of its funding through bonds. The UK government and Transport for London issued bonds to finance the construction of the new Elizabeth Line, which extended the rail network across London by 100 kilometers.[263] It passes through forty stations from Heathrow to Abbey Wood and Shenfield in the east. The project has raised billions of pounds through bond issuances, attracting domestic and international investors.

The new Elizabeth Line has significantly transformed the daily lives of London residents and invigorated economic activities across the United Kingdom. By seamlessly connecting key areas of London with its surrounding regions, the Elizabeth Line has drastically reduced commuting times and alleviated congestion on existing transport routes. For instance, travel between central London and Heathrow Airport has been cut to just thirty-five minutes, making it far more convenient for both business travelers and tourists. This enhanced connectivity has not only improved the quality of life for residents but has also stimulated local economies by increasing access to various commercial and retail areas, boosting consumer spending, and supporting job creation. Additionally, the project has facilitated greater regional integration, enabling businesses to operate more efficiently across a broader geographic area and attracting investment into previously underserved locations.

Halfway around the world, in 2002, Sydney Airport was privatized and sold to a consortium of investors led by the Australian global financial services group,

Macquarie Group. The privatization process involved significant funding through capital markets, with investors purchasing shares in the newly formed Sydney Airport Corporation. The capital raised allowed for extensive upgrades and expansions, including terminal improvements, new runways, and enhanced passenger facilities. These investments have helped Sydney Airport become one of the leading airports in the Asia-Pacific region, supporting tourism and trade. Indeed, when UK-based insurance company, All Clear Travel Insurance, analyzed more than 1,800 airports in early 2024, they ranked Sydney International Airport in the top five of the most luxurious airports in the world.[264]

In yet another example, China Merchants Port Holdings, a leading port operator in China, frequently raises capital through equity markets. In 2017, the company raised approximately HKD 15 billion (USD 1.9 billion) through a rights issue.[265] The funds were used to finance the acquisition and development of port assets both within China and internationally. This equity financing helped the company expand its operations and improve port infrastructure. Still in China, the Tianjin Port Development Holdings issued green bonds to finance environmentally sustainable projects within the port. The proceeds from these bonds were used to fund initiatives aimed at reducing carbon emissions, improving energy efficiency, and enhancing environmental protection measures at the port. This approach not only raised capital but also aligned with global sustainability standards, attracting investors focused on responsible investments.

Nigeria's unfinished business

Nigeria, the world's most populous black country, presents a contrasting picture when compared to the BRICS countries – Brazil, Russia, India, China, and South Africa – in terms of economic development. As of 2023, Nigeria's GDP was down to approximately US$363 billion (from a peak of US$574 billion in 2014), according to the World Bank, compared to the colossal economies of China and India, whose GDPs were approximately US$17.8 trillion and US$3.55 trillion, respectively.[266] The smallest member of the BRICS grouping, South Africa, with a GDP of about US$378 billion, maintains a higher per capita income and a more diversified industrial base than Nigeria.[267] This underscores the significant challenges Nigeria faces, including reliance on oil exports, limited industrialization, and substantial infrastructure deficits, which impede its economic development relative to its BRICS counterparts.

In terms of the Human Development Index (HDI), Nigeria lags significantly behind the BRICS nations. According to the United Nations Development Programme's (UNDP) Human Development Report 2023/2024, Nigeria's HDI was 0.548, placing it in the low human development category and ranking 157th out of 189 countries. In contrast, the BRICS countries fare better with higher HDI scores: China (0.788), Brazil (0.760), Russia (0.821), India (0.650), and South Africa (0.717).[268] This highlights the country's pressing need for substantial investments in human capital development to enhance education, healthcare, and overall quality of life.

Furthermore, Nigeria's economic diversification remains limited compared to the more varied economies of the BRICS countries. While oil exports account for over 80% of Nigeria's export earnings, countries such as China and India have been more successful in diversifying their economies.[269] According to the World Bank, manufacturing contributes around 29% to China's GDP and 17% to India's, while Nigeria's manufacturing sector contributes a mere 9%.[270] This lack of diversification makes Nigeria's economy more vulnerable to global oil price fluctuations, affecting its overall economic stability and growth prospects.

Despite the strong foundation established and the notable progress made over the past fifteen years, Nigeria's capital markets continue to lag significantly behind those of the BRIC countries. According to data from the World Bank and SIFMA, as of July 2024, Nigeria's stock market had a market capitalization of just US$27 billion, a mere 7% of the country's GDP. In contrast, during the same period, Brazil's stock market capitalization was approximately US$864 billion, representing 68% of GDP; South Africa's was US$1.2 trillion, or 348% of GDP; India's stood at US$5.5 trillion, equating to 130% of GDP; and China's market capitalization reached US$10 trillion, or 65% of GDP. Developed markets are even more advanced: the United States' stock market capitalization is around US$49 trillion, which is over 194% of GDP; the United Kingdom's market capitalization totals US$3 trillion, or 100% of GDP; and Japan's market capitalization is US$6.2 trillion, approximately 146% of GDP.[271]

Market Depth Statistics as of July 2024 (WEF, World Bank, Bank for International Settlements)

Country	Total Market Capitalization		Bond Market size	Number of Domestic Listed Companies
	(in billion US$)	(as a % of GDP)	(in billion US$)	
United States	54,000	194.5	51,300	4,642
China	10,088	65.1	20,900	11,497
Japan	6,246	146.2	11,000	3,865
India	5,458	130	1,300	5,376
France	3,894	84.9	4,400	457
United Kingdom	2,183	100	4,300	1,646
Brazil	864	68.4	2,400	361
South Africa	1,230	348.3	320	237
Nigeria	26	7	43	173

The disparity becomes even more apparent when comparing the number of listed companies and trading volumes in Nigeria's capital market to those in the BRIC nations. As of 2023, the Nigerian Stock Exchange had 173 listed companies, while Brazil had over 361, South Africa had 237, India boasted of more than 5,000, and China had over 11,000. Additionally, Nigeria's bond market is significantly smaller compared to its global counterparts. The United States and China alone account for 55% of the global bond market, with other countries such as Japan, France, and the United Kingdom also maintaining robust and liquid bond markets.

Housing

One of the critical areas where Nigeria's capital market could have a significant impact is housing. The impact of capital markets on housing is deeply felt by many, as nothing compares to the profound experience of entering one's first home. A home is far more than just a physical shelter; it serves as a sanctuary where cherished memories are created, a haven of comfort and security, a place where dreams are nurtured, and love is shared. For most individuals, a home is the central focus of their lives, where personal stories unfold, and true well-being is achieved. Whether acquiring a home through a lengthy mortgage process, receiving government support, or – for the fortunate few – paying in full from personal savings, housing is intricately linked to capital markets in today's world.

Nigeria continues to face a severe housing deficit, with current estimates indicating a shortfall of around 28 million housing units.[272] This gap has been growing at an alarming rate due to rapid urbanization and population growth, with the United Nations projecting that Nigeria's urban population will double by 2050.[273] According to the World Bank, addressing this deficit requires at least 700,000 new housing units annually, yet the country is currently only producing about 100,000 units per year.[274] The financial implications are considerable, with the Federal Mortgage Bank of Nigeria (FMBN) estimating that bridging this housing gap would require over US$400 billion in investment.[275] With the 220 million population growing at 2.5% annually, there must be a sense of urgency to find ways to provide affordable housing that meets UN and WHO standards for habitability, safety, and comfort.

Addressing Nigeria's significant housing deficit will require deepening our capital market and elongating the yield curve to thirty years and beyond. A deeper capital market can provide mortgage lenders with access to long-term capital essential for financing long-term home loans. This extended yield curve serves as a benchmark, enabling lenders to secure long-term funding at more stable rates, which in turn can be used to issue mortgages for home buyers.

Establishing a vibrant market for mortgage-backed securities (MBS) is vital for enhancing liquidity within the mortgage lenders. By bundling individual mortgages into securities, lenders can sell these MBS to investors, thereby freeing up capital on their balance sheets to issue additional mortgages. This process mirrors the success seen in advanced economies, where MBS have been instrumental in expanding housing markets by providing a steady flow of capital. For instance, in the United States, the development of a sophisticated MBS market has facilitated increased homeownership rates and more dynamic housing markets.

The MBS market in Nigeria is still in its nascent stages. Despite the country's significant housing deficit and growing demand for housing finance, the MBS market has yet to achieve substantial depth and liquidity sufficient to unleash the capital to fill these deficits. Initiatives by the Nigerian Mortgage Refinance Company (NMRC), leveraging the regulatory framework in place, such as securitization rules of the SEC, are aiming for greater access to affordable housing finance. These initiatives should be better supported and scaled up by the local bond market.

On the supply side of housing, we should support developers and builders to tap capital markets by issuing new equity or approaching private equity to raise the necessary funds to undertake large-scale housing projects. Or they may issue corporate bonds to raise long-term debt to finance large housing projects without immediate repayment pressures, allowing the developers to complete and sell properties before paying off the debt. Capital markets can similarly facilitate the provision of large-scale loans to real estate developers, often syndicated by multiple financial institutions to spread risk.

Still on the supply side, government policy and support can unlock significant amounts of capital. In many countries with deep capital markets, it is common for local governments to issue municipal housing bonds to finance affordable housing projects. These bonds are often tax-exempt, making them attractive to investors. Increasingly, governmental and other entities are issuing green bonds to finance eco-friendly housing projects, targeting socially responsible investors.

Nigeria must accelerate progress in the securitization

space, supporting financial institutions to pool mortgages and sell them as securities to investors, freeing up capital for banks to underwrite even more home loans. These mortgage-backed securities provide the added benefit of providing Nigerians with diversified investment opportunities in addition to providing liquidity to the housing finance system by enabling lenders to convert illiquid mortgage loans into liquid assets, facilitating continuous lending activity.

For many of these initiatives, the United States is a good example for us to emulate in Nigeria. The housing industry in the United States performs exceptionally well compared to other parts of the world in large part due to its robust capital markets. It benefits from a well-developed mortgage financing system, which provides accessible home loans to a broad spectrum of buyers. According to the SIFMA, the United States mortgage-related securities market, including both residential and commercial mortgage-backed securities, amounted to approximately US$10.8 trillion in outstanding securities as of 2023.[276] This deep pool of capital facilitates extensive mortgage lending, enabling financial institutions to offer various loan products to homebuyers.

As mentioned earlier, institutions such as Fannie Mae and Freddie Mac are vital to maintaining liquidity and stability in the mortgage market. They achieve this by purchasing mortgages from lenders, thereby facilitating more extensive lending. The availability of diverse mortgage products, including fixed-rate and adjustable-rate options, caters to various financial needs and makes homeownership more accessible to a broad range of individuals. The homeownership rate in the United States was approximately 65.9% in 2023, which is higher than in most countries with similar cultural and economic development levels.[277] Interestingly, the highest homeownership rates globally are found in Central and Eastern Europe, where cultural factors play a significant role. Romania, for instance, boasts an impressive homeownership rate of around 96%, a result of its historical context and government policies promoting property ownership. Other countries with notable homeownership rates include Croatia, Hungary, and Slovakia, with approximately 90%, due to favorable conditions for buyers and a strong cultural preference for ownership.

The vast majority of people aspire to become homeowners, viewing property not only as a sound investment but also as a crucial tool for wealth creation. The dream of owning a home represents more than just acquiring real estate; it symbolizes a significant personal milestone and a physically tangible achievement. However, various impediments often obstruct this path, such as high property prices, the availability of capital, and rising living costs. For many, these barriers can seem insurmountable, causing frustration and discouragement despite their earnest efforts and aspirations.

Why is it that a young Belgian entering the workforce may find it much easier to own a home before she turns thirty, while a professional in Nigeria may spend over thirty years in their career without owning a home? What is the main differentiator between a small apartment in downtown Brooklyn and a palatial country home in my village in Nigeria? In *The Mystery of Capital*, famous economist Hernando de Soto attempts to answer these questions. In June 2003, I had the pleasure of attending the Annual Euromoney Global Borrowers and Bond Investors Forum in London, where Hernando de Soto delivered a compelling presentation on his groundbreaking research published in *The Mystery of Capital*. His insights into the importance of formal property rights and the profound economic impact of transforming "dead capital" into viable assets were nothing short of revelatory. As he eloquently described how formalizing property ownership could unlock vast economic potential, I was struck by the relevance of his findings to countries such as Nigeria.

He argues that the ease of transferring ownership is a critical determinant of property value and economic utility. In cities such as New York, the formal property system is well-established, allowing for transparent and efficient transfer of ownership. This system includes clear documentation, reliable land registries, and legal frameworks that facilitate buying, selling, and mortgaging property for a loan to start a business, for example. The ease of transferring ownership in such a structured environment enhances the liquidity and value of the property, making it a more significant asset in the formal economy. This formal recognition and fluid transferability contribute to increased property investment and economic activity.

In contrast, homes in Cairo often face challenges due

to informal property systems where ownership transfer is complicated by unclear or incomplete documentation. This lack of formal property records makes it difficult to sell, buy, or use the property as collateral for loans. The rigidity and inefficiency in transferring ownership in such informal contexts can severely limit the property's economic potential and value. Similarly, comparing city and village homes using the same reasoning, city properties benefit from established legal frameworks and efficient transfer processes, whereas village homes may be hindered by informal ownership structures. This discrepancy affects not only property values, but also access to financial resources and economic opportunities, underscoring the broader impact of formal property systems on economic growth and stability.

Hernando de Soto also presents compelling real-life examples to present the findings from his study. He describes how, in Peru, the lack of formal property documentation prevents individuals from leveraging their assets for economic purposes. For instance, he notes that, in Lima, a substantial portion of the city's real estate exists outside the formal legal system, rendering these properties "dead capital." Conversely, in the United States, the formal property system allows individuals to use their property as collateral, facilitating access to credit and investment. De Soto also contrasts the situation in Egypt, where informal property systems leave much of the population without legal recognition of their assets, with the U.S., where formal property rights contribute to robust economic growth and capital accumulation. Through these examples, de Soto demonstrates how formal property rights are crucial for transforming assets into economic capital and fostering broader economic development.

De Soto's analysis suggests that the secret to prosperous capitalism is not merely the existence of assets, but the ability to convert them into capital through a recognized legal framework. His work challenges policymakers and development experts to rethink their approaches, advocating for the creation of inclusive legal systems that recognize and formalize property rights for all citizens. By doing so, de Soto believes that developing nations such as Nigeria can harness their latent wealth, stimulate economic growth, and empower millions out of poverty.

Reforming Nigeria's Land Use Act is crucial for unlocking the full potential of the capital market to transform the housing sector in Nigeria. Currently, the process of transferring property rights is cumbersome and inefficient, largely due to the requirement for state governor approval, which can significantly delay transactions. This bureaucratic bottleneck hinders the smooth functioning of property markets, impeding the ability of the capital market to mobilize resources effectively for housing development. According to the World Bank's *Doing Business* report for 2020, it takes an average of seventy-one days to register property in Nigeria, compared to just fifteen days in South Africa, and five days in the United Arab Emirates, where wealthy Nigerians love to purchase real estate.[278] Such delays can deter investment and stifle the growth of the housing sector, as investors and developers face uncertainty and inefficiencies.

The current system, which requires state governors to approve property transactions, adds an additional layer of complexity and delay. Governors, who are often occupied with a multitude of other pressing issues, may not be able to address property transactions promptly, further exacerbating delays. By streamlining the process and making property rights more easily transferable, Nigeria could enhance the efficiency of its capital markets to stimulate significant investment in housing. Simplified property rights transfer would not only facilitate quicker transactions but also attract both domestic and international investors. This reform is essential for Nigeria to leverage its capital markets in driving the growth and development of its housing sector, ultimately contributing to broader economic progress.

How Nigeria can close the gaps

I am optimistic about Nigeria's immense potential to not only catch up to the BRICs countries and achieve the SDGs, but to build one of the most prosperous countries in the world. Nigeria is endowed with an abundance of natural resources that can enable it to become a formidable player in the global economy. In addition to its immense wealth of hydrocarbons, with over 37 billion barrels of proven oil reserves and approximately 202 trillion cubic feet of natural gas, Nigeria is rich in solid minerals that remain largely untapped, presenting vast opportunities for economic diversification and development. The nation possesses large deposits of minerals such as tin, limestone, coal, gold, and iron ore. For instance, Nigeria's iron ore reserves are estimated at over 3 billion metric tons, while its gold reserves are believed to hold significant potential for economic exploitation. Leveraging these mineral resources through sustainable mining practices and investment can spur industrial growth, create jobs, and generate revenue, contributing to a more diversified and resilient economy.

In addition to its mineral wealth, Nigeria's agricultural potential is immense, supported by extensive arable land and a favorable climate. Agriculture already accounts for about 25% of Nigeria's GDP and employs roughly 70% of the workforce. The country is a leading producer of several key crops, including cassava, yams, and sorghum. However, only about 40% of the arable land is currently under cultivation, underscoring a significant opportunity to boost agricultural productivity and achieve food security. By investing in modern farming techniques, irrigation systems, and value-added processing, Nigeria can enhance its agricultural output, reduce dependency on food imports, and bolster rural incomes.

Furthermore, Nigeria's human capital is the centerpiece of its economic potential. With a population exceeding 220 million, approximately 60% of which is under the age of twenty-five, Nigeria boasts of a vast pool of energetic and innovative talent.[279] Investing in education, vocational training, and healthcare can harness this demographic dividend, fostering a skilled workforce capable of driving technological advancements and entrepreneurial ventures. By capitalizing on its abundant natural and human resources, Nigeria has the potential to transform its economy, achieve sustainable development, and improve the quality of life for its citizens, positioning itself among the leading economic powerhouses in the world.

Conclusion

In tracing the root of my lifelong involvement in the world of finance, I have shared stories of my upbringing, starting at the age of eight, when my parents introduced me to the magic of saving and investing, and taught me that there was no substitute to hard work, because success does not come by accident. Indeed, the phrase "hard work does not kill," was more or less a mantra I grew up with. My parents also provided me an opportunity to live the talk in small ways, for example, they taught me to work as a cashier in their small business during holidays. The lessons were useful foundations that I built on as I grew older, which helped me in becoming a finance professional.

Working in global financial markets made me acutely aware of the power of capital markets. People who live in countries where such markets are well developed can afford mortgages to buy comfortable homes and enjoy reliable, world class infrastructure, such as consistent electricity, flights between major cities, and clean public environments. They also have access to quality healthcare and education. People in the developing world, on the other hand, often lack the basic necessities of life because their capital markets are not robust or developed enough to support such quality living standards.

I have in some way explored key concepts, including the time value of money, the definition of capital as long-term money, and the concept of compounding, which exemplifies the ability of money or wealth to accumulate and grow geometrically. I have also attempted to trace the history and reviewed the research supporting these concepts as well, broken down the components, participants, products, and policies that make up the sophisticated financial ecosystem, including the interplay between banking and capital markets and the ecosystem that supports startups to become global household names such as Apple and Google. Through the examples and anecdotes I have shared, I hope a clear picture has emerged of the critical role that capital markets play in sustaining society's prosperity.

My journey back home after over two decades of working outside Nigeria was more or less an obligation I felt I owed myself and, indeed, my country. It made no sense to me to desire a developed country if I refused to seize a good opportunity to help drive its development. I accepted the challenge to return home and lead the reform of Nigeria's capital market following a severe crash that decimated investor confidence during the 2008 financial crisis. I have detailed the many steps I took to prepare for this challenge, including securing a peer review of the Nigerian capital market by the U.S. SEC, leveraging the strengths of the existing legal framework, and reforming the rulemaking process at the SEC. In my earliest actions after taking the helm of Nigeria's capital markets, I communicated a categorical zero-tolerance policy, making it clear to the market community that there was a "new sheriff" in town. Our other early actions included conducting fit and proper inspections to remove "bad actors," replacing the leadership of the stock exchange, strengthening the SEC, including bringing in young professionals, and improving the regulatory regime.

I have also outlined our many market development initiatives, such as expansive financial literacy programs, the introduction of new products such as REITs, ETFs, securitization, and non-interest products, as well as the registration of new platforms for trading securities. Additionally, we explored the impact of capital markets beyond finance, highlighting how they promote good governance in the public sector and enhance corporate governance in the private sector. We reviewed the different domestic and international partnerships, including collaborations with IOSCO, the IFC, the World Bank, ICAEW, CFA Institute, and others, that enabled us to achieve success in our reforms.

Throughout the book, my leadership philosophy has been a recurring theme. I firmly believe that strong leadership is essential to building the capital markets that can unlock the same value for the developing world as seen in advanced countries. I shared the significant influence my parents had on my leadership style, which is anchored in the four Cs that form the core of my philosophy – character, compassion, competence, and courage. These principles have enabled me to thrive in the challenging environment of public service in Nigeria, where I had to confront stiff opposition from lawmakers and others determined to undermine our reform agenda.

Lastly, I have articulated how the unfinished business at the global, continental, and national levels continues to hinder our ability to tackle some of humanity's most pressing challenges. I will conclude with four recommendations that serve as a call to action. If we thoughtfully place all hands on deck and implement these recommendations, we will begin to replicate the living standards of advanced economies across the developing world.

Accelerate the development of world class capital markets across the developing world

Knowing the transformative power of capital markets in bridging development finance gaps and elevating living standards, my foremost recommendation is for leaders to prioritize supporting the development of world class capital markets in the developing world.

These markets are essential for effectively bridging the financing gaps and accelerating progress toward achieving the SDGs.

Developing countries must spearhead the advancement of their capital markets rather than depending solely on external development aid. Countries should empower their respective capital markets by reviewing their existing legislation and regulatory frameworks to ensure alignment with the IOSCO principles. Additionally, enhancing the independence and effectiveness of financial regulators, alongside strengthening enforcement mechanisms and safeguarding investor protection, are crucial steps. By implementing these measures, countries can lay the foundation for building robust, world class capital markets that foster economic growth and reduce reliance on foreign assistance.

Development partners should consider radically increasing the budget dedicated to supporting the development of capital markets. World Bank research confirms that countries with deeper capital markets experience higher economic growth rates, improved financial stability, and better resilience to economic shocks, all of which are crucial for sustainable development.[280] Capital markets have proven their ability to mobilize vast resources, as seen in advanced economies, where robust financial systems channel investments into critical sectors. By establishing well-regulated and efficient capital markets, developing nations can attract both domestic and international investors, providing a much-needed influx of capital to fund infrastructure, healthcare, education, and renewable energy projects.

We have seen further empirical evidence of capital markets driving such sustainable development. For instance, green bonds are funding a wide array of environmental projects, from renewable energy installations to sustainable agriculture. Supporting the growth of capital markets in the developing world will also foster financial inclusion, innovation, and job creation. Therefore, it is essential for global leaders to join forces with leaders in these countries, supporting them to establish robust regulatory frameworks, enhance market infrastructure, and invest in related capacity-building initiatives.

Convene a renewed global focus on financial literacy

Leaders must prioritize promoting financial literacy worldwide, with a particular focus on the developing world, as it is foundational to economic empowerment, wealth creation, and sustainable development. Financial literacy equips individuals with the knowledge and skills to make informed decisions about their finances, enabling them to effectively manage resources, save for the future, and invest wisely. According to the World Bank, enhancing financial literacy in developing countries can significantly increase economic participation while fostering a culture of savings and investment that underpins economic growth. By empowering individuals with financial knowledge, we can create a more inclusive financial system where people have the confidence and capability to participate and invest locally, unlocking new domestic sources for financing development priorities.

Financial literacy is important even within developed countries. A survey by Standard & Poor's found that only 33% of adults globally are financially literate, with even lower rates in developing regions.[281] This gap highlights the urgent need for targeted financial education programs that can bridge this knowledge divide. Financial literacy initiatives can help individuals understand the benefits of formal banking systems, capital markets, microfinance, and digital financial services, thereby expanding access to credit, insurance, and investment opportunities. Moreover, these programs can foster entrepreneurial skills, enabling small business owners to manage their enterprises more effectively, contributing to economic diversification and job creation.

Promoting financial literacy also aligns with broader sustainable development goals. Financially literate populations are better equipped to participate in the formal economy, leading to increased tax revenues and more robust economic systems. Furthermore, by understanding and accessing financial services, individuals can improve their resilience to economic shocks and reduce their vulnerability to poverty. For women and marginalized groups, financial literacy can be a powerful tool for empowerment, promoting gender equality and social inclusion. Therefore, it is imperative for global leaders to champion financial literacy initiatives, recognizing them as vital investments in the human capital that drives sustainable development and economic prosperity across the globe.

Financial literacy programs can be deployed through a multipronged approach that leverages various platforms and partnerships. Schools should be supported to integrate financial education into their curricula, ensuring that students gain essential financial skills from a young age. Community centers and local governments can offer workshops and seminars tailored to different age groups and financial needs, from basic budgeting and saving techniques to more advanced topics such as investing and retirement planning. Leveraging digital technology, online courses, mobile apps, and social media campaigns can reach a broader audience, providing accessible and interactive financial education resources. Collaborations with financial services institutions and governmental and nongovernmental organizations can also enhance the reach and effectiveness of these programs, ensuring that even the most underserved communities are reached.

Renegotiate Africa's place in the new world

Africa stands as a treasure trove of natural resources, from its abundant arable land to its enviable deposits of rare earth minerals, essential for powering the new world of sustainability and driving the global transition to renewable energy. Among these valuable resources, cobalt, nickel, and lithium play a pivotal role in the production of batteries for electric vehicles (EVs) and energy storage systems. In addition, elements such as neodymium, praseodymium, dysprosium, and terbium are essential for producing high-tech products such as smartphones, electric vehicle batteries, wind turbines, and various military technologies. The continent's abundant rare earth resources have attracted considerable global interest, particularly as demand for green technologies and renewable energy solutions continues to rise. The Democratic Republic of Congo holds 70% of the world's known cobalt resources. Madagascar and South Africa possess significant nickel reserves. Zimbabwe and other countries have found lithium in substantial quantities.

Africa's rich endowment of these rare earth minerals must be leveraged to reposition the continent not as the world's mine, but as host for the leading high-tech industries that produce our smartphones, computers, electric batteries, and the technologies upon which the new world of sustainability depends.

Harness the African demographic dividend

Africa boasts the youngest population in the world, with over 60% of its inhabitants under the age of twenty-five.[282] According to the United Nations, the median age across the continent is approximately 19.7 years, significantly lower than the global median age of 30.4 years. By 2050, Africa's population is projected to double, reaching around 2.5 billion, with young people continuing to make up a substantial proportion.[283] This demographic trend underscores the immense potential for economic growth and development if investments are made in education, job creation, and healthcare to harness the capabilities of this youthful populace. With the right investments, it can be a demographic dividend. But with neglect and a lack of coordinated intervention, it can become a demographic time bomb.

Africa's demographic dividend presents an unparalleled opportunity for economic transformation and sustainable development. To harness this potential, investments in education and skills development are paramount. By prioritizing quality education and vocational training, Africa can equip its youth with the knowledge and competencies required to thrive in the modern economy. Emphasizing STEM (science, technology, engineering, and mathematics) education, as well as digital and financial literacy, will prepare our young ones for the jobs of the future. Additionally, strengthening higher education institutions and creating pathways for continuous learning will ensure that the workforce remains adaptable and capable of driving economic growth and technological advancement.

Creating an enabling environment for job creation is equally crucial to harnessing Africa's demographic dividend. Governments and private sector entities must collaborate to develop industries that can absorb the burgeoning workforce, focusing on sectors with high-growth potential such as technology, artificial intelligence, renewable energy, agriculture, and manufacturing. Promoting entrepreneurship through access to finance, mentorship, and supportive policies will empower our young people to create their own employment opportunities and contribute to economic diversification. Moreover, investing in healthcare and social protection systems will ensure a healthy, resilient, and productive population. By leveraging the energy, creativity, and innovation of its youth, Africa can transform its demographic dividend into a powerful engine for inclusive and sustainable economic development, positioning the continent as a dynamic player on the global stage.

All Hands on Deck

The challenges facing humanity at global, regional, and national levels are indeed profound. But there is no doubt that, with an *all hands-on-deck* approach, we are capable of not only surmounting them, but ultimately creating a prosperous world for all.

Notes

1. United Nations Development Programme, "Human Development Index (HDI)" (UNDP, no date), https://hdr.undp.org/data-center/human-development-index#/indicies/HDI
2. Wikipedia, "List of countries by road network size" (updated 2024), https://en.wikipedia.org/wiki/List_of_countries_by_road_network_size
3. International Monetary Fund (IMF), *Sovereign Wealth Funds: A work agenda* (IMF, 2008), www.imf.org/external/np/pp/eng/2008/022908.pdf
4. R. Downie, "This is the 8th wonder of the world, according to Albert Einstein. And utilizing it correctly can help make saving for retirement an absolute breeze," *The Motley Fool* (March 16, 2024), www.nasdaq.com/articles/this-is-the-8th-wonder-of-the-world-according-to-albert-einstein.-and-utilizing-it
5. T. Franck, "Buffett's Berkshire Hathaway hits $1 trillion market value, first U.S. company outside of tech to do so," *CNBC* (August 28, 2024), www.cnbc.com/2024/08/28/buffetts-berkshire-hathaway-hits-1-trillion-market-value-first-us-company-outside-of-tech-to-do-so.html

6. G. Baid, *The Joys of Compounding: The passionate pursuit of lifelong learning* (Columbia Business School Publishing, 2019)

7. S.R. Covey, *The 7 Habits of Highly Effective People: Powerful lessons in personal change* (Free Press, 1989)

8. J. Clear, *Atomic Habits* (Random House Business, 2018)

9. P.A. Samuelson, "A note on the measurement of utility," *Journal of Political Economy*, 45/5 (1937), 617–628

10. Knology, *2021 Annual report* (Knology, 2022), www.datocms-assets.com/15254/1663873687-2021-annual-report.pdf

11. OECD, *Infrastructure Investment and the Time Value of Money* (OECD Publishing, 2020)

12. G. Gary, *The Main Determinants of Inflation in Nigeria* (IMF, 1995)

13. N.G. Mankiw, *Principles of Macroeconomics*, 7th edition (Cengage Learning, 2014)

14. S. Fischer, "The role of macroeconomic factors in growth," *Journal of Monetary Economics*, 32/1 (1993), 49–72

15. S. Edwards, "Exchange rate regimes, capital flows, and economic performance," *Journal of International Economics*, 27/3–4 (1989), 167–182

16. P. Krugman and M. Obstfeld, *International Economics: Theory and policy*, 8th edition (Pearson, 2009)

17. M. Housel, *The Psychology of Money: Timeless lessons on wealth, greed, and happiness* (Harriman House, 2020)

18. Alstom, "Alstom successfully launched a 7-year €700 million senior bond issue" (October 8, 2019), www.alstom.com/alstom-successfully-launched-7-year-eu700-million-senior-bond-issue

19. The Legatum Prosperity Index annually ranks countries based on twelve metrics and annually shows countries with high rankings on security usually have higher overall ranking. The 2023 ranking is available at: https://prosperity.com.

20. G.W. Brown, M.J. Chow, D. Fisher and L. Yi, *Employment Dynamics at VC-Backed Companies in the United States: 1990 to 2020* (NVCA, Venture Forward, and the University of North Carolina Kenan Institute of Private Enterprise, 2023), https://nvca.org/employment-dynamics

21. W. Chen, M. Mrkaic and M.S. Nabar, *The Global Economic Recovery 10 Years after the 2008 Financial Crisis* (IMF, 2019), www.imf.org/en/Publications/WP/Issues/2019/04/26/The-Global-Economic-Recovery-10-Years-After-the-2008-Financial-Crisis-46711

22. J.B. Say, *A Treatise on Political Economy* (Grigg & Elliott, 1803)

23. A. Marshall, *Principles of Economics*, 8th edition (Macmillan, 1890)

24. M. Hargrave, "Capital: Definition, how it's used, structure, and types in business," *Investopedia* (updated July 11, 2024), www.investopedia.com/terms/c/capital.asp

25. A. Smith, *An Inquiry into the Nature and Causes of the Wealth of Nations* (W. Strahan and T. Cadell, 1776)

26. K. Marx, *Das Kapital*, F. Engels edition (Regnery Publishing, 1996)

27. J.M. Keynes, *The General Theory of Employment, Interest, and Money* (Macmillan, 1936)

28. T. Piketty, *Capital in the Twenty-First Century* (The Belknap Press of Harvard University Press, 2014)

29. R. Spendelow, "Capital markets" (Corporate Finance Institute, no date), https://corporatefinanceinstitute.com/resources/career-map/sell-side/capital-markets/capital-markets

30. A. Hayes, "*Capital markets:* what they are and how they work," *Investopedia* (updated June 13, 2024), www.investopedia.com/terms/c/capitalmarkets.asp

31. Federal Reserve Bank of St. Louis, "Understanding capital markets?" (2019), www.stlouisfed.org/education/tools-for-enhancing-the-stock-market-game-invest-it-forward/episode-1-understanding-capital-markets

32. Ibid.

33. LexisNexis, "Capital market definition" (2024), www.lexisnexis.co.uk/legal/glossary/capital-market

34. E.F. Fama and K.R. French, "Dissecting anomalies," *Journal of Finance*, 56/1 (2001), 125–155

35. J. Fernando, "*Bonds: How they work and how to invest,*" *Investopedia* (updated May 3, 2024), www.investopedia.com/terms/b/bond.asp

36. World Bank, *Global Financial Development Report 2015/2016: Long-term finance* (World Bank Publications, 2015), https://documents1.worldbank.org/curated/en/955811467986333727/pdf/99100-PUB-REVISED-Box393195B-OUO-9-until-9-14-15.pdf

37. H. Schafer and H. Stutz, "Bond market development in emerging economies," *Journal of Emerging Markets Finance*, 5/2 (2020), 45–62

38. Bank for International Settlements (BIS), "The internationalization of bond markets," *BIS Quarterly Review* (2021)

39. O. Gelderblom and J. Jonker, "Completing a financial revolution: The Finance of the Dutch East India trade and the rise of the Amsterdam capital market, 1595–1612," *The Journal of Economic History*, 64/3 (2004), 641–672

40. R.C. Michie, *The London Stock Exchange: A history* (Oxford University Press, 1999)

41. C.R. Geisst, *Wall Street: A history*, 2nd edition (Oxford University Press, 2004)

42. G.L. Gastineau, "Exchange-traded funds: An innovative investment tool," *The Journal of Portfolio Management*, 27/3 (2001), 88–94

43. Real Estate Investment Trust Act of 1960 (U.S. Statutes at Large, 74 Stat. 998)

44. M.A. Segoviano and M. Singh, "Counterparty risk in the over-the-counter derivatives market," IMF Working Paper WP/08/258 (2008)

45. A. Davda, "The power of the retail investor," *Forbes* (March 18, 2024), www.forbes.com/councils/forbesfinancecouncil/2024/03/18/the-power-of-the-retail-investor

46. Schroders Wealth Management, "The rise of the retail investor" (2020)

47. U.S. Securities and Exchange Commission, *Staff Report on Equity and Options Market Structure Conditions in Early 2021* (U.S. SEC, 2021), www.sec.gov/files/staff-report-equity-options-market-struction-conditions-early-2021.pdf

48. Nigerian Stock Exchange, *Annual Report and Accounts* (2008)

49. Nigerian Stock Exchange, *Annual Report and Accounts* (2023), https://ngxgroup.com/investor-relations

50. C. McIntyre, S. Alsubaihin, et al., *The Tide Has Turned* (Boston Consulting Group, 2023), www.bcg.com/publications/2023/the-tide-has-changed-for-asset-managers

51. A.K. Basil and D. Barbuscia, "BlackRock assets hit record $10.5 trillion as market surges," *Reuters* (April 12, 2024), www.reuters.com/markets/us/blackrocks-first-quarter-profit-rises-higher-fee-income-2024-04-12

52. Vanguard, "About Vanguard" (no date), www.nl.vanguard/professional/about-vanguard

53. A. Massa and E. Harrison, "Schwab's $7 trillion empire built on low rates is showing cracks," *Bloomberg* (March 27, 2023), www.bloomberg.com/news/articles/2023-03-27/schwab-s-7-trillion-empire-built-on-low-rates-is-showing-cracks

54. S. Tunji, "Nigeria borrowed N7.71 trillion, not N24.33

trillion in Q1 2024 – DMO," *Nairametrics* (2024), https://
nairametrics.com/2024/06/26/nigeria-borrowed-n7–71
-trillion-not-n24–33-trillion-in-q1–2024-dmo

55. U.S. Securities and Exchange Commission, "Accredited
Investor – Updated Investor Bulletin" (U.S. SEC, 2019)

56. European Parliament and Council, "Directive 2014/65/EU on
Markets in Financial Instruments (MiFID II), Articles 4(1)
(10) and 4(1)(11)," *Official Journal of the European Union* (May
15, 2014)

57. JPMorgan Chase & Co., 2023 Investor Day presentation
(JPMorgan Chase, 2023)

58. The Vanguard Group, *Vanguard 2023 Annual Report: Vanguard
500 Index Fund* (Vanguard, 2024), https://fund-docs
.vanguard.com/q400.pdf

59. Fidelity Investments, "We are Fidelity: By the numbers" (no
date), www.fidelity.com/about-fidelity/our-company

60. Charles Schwab Corporation, "Schwab reports second quarter
results" (July 18, 2023), https://pressroom.aboutschwab
.com/press-releases/press-release/2023/Schwab-Reports
-Second-Quarter-Results/default.aspx

61. U.S. House of Representatives Committee Repository,
"Testimony of Kenneth C. Griffin, CEO of Citadel LLC"
(2021), https://docs.house.gov/Committee/Calendar
/ByEvent.aspx?EventID=111207

62. T. Maloney, "Citadel Securities gets the spotlight," *Bloomberg*
(April 6, 2021), www.bloomberg.com/news/features/2021
-04-06/citadel-securities-feels-the-heat-of-the-political
-spotlight

63. Kevin, "The Biggest and the Best," *Funds Europe* (March 30,
2023), https://funds-europe.com/the-biggest-and-the-best/

64. IFRS Foundation, "Who uses IFRS accounting standards?"
(2023), www.ifrs.org/use-around-the-world/use-of-ifrs
-standards-by-jurisdiction

65. Federal Reserve Bank of St. Louis, "Total assets, all
commercial banks" (FRED, updated October 18, 2024),
https://fred.stlouisfed.org/series/TLAACBW027SBOG

66. European Central Bank, "Total assets/liabilities reported
by credit institutions in the Euro area (stocks), Euro
area (changing composition), Quarterly" (ECB, updated
September 26, 2024), https://data.ecb.europa.eu/data
/datasets/BSI/BSI.Q.U2.N.R.T00.A.1.Z5.0000.Z01.E

67. G. Teare, "Global funding data analysis: AI drives venture

growth in 2023," *Crunchbase News* (January 4, 2024), https://news.crunchbase.com/venture/global-funding-data-analysis-ai-eoy-2023

68. Crunchbase, "Glossary of funding types" (2024), https://support.crunchbase.com/hc/en-us/articles/115010458467-Glossary-of-Funding-Types

69. Ibid.

70. Ibid.

71. G. Teare, "Global startup funding in 2023 clocks in at lowest level in 5 years," *Crunchbase News* (January 4, 2024), https://news.crunchbase.com/venture/global-funding-data-analysis-ai-eoy-2023

72. J. Mancini, "Steve Jobs sold his Volkswagen bus for $1,500 so he could create the first Apple computer – Just four years later, Apple was worth $1 Billion," *Benzinga* (January 19, 2024), www.benzinga.com/general/24/01/36695175/steve-jobs-sold-his-volkswagen-bus-for-1-500-so-he-could-create-the-first-apple-computer-just-4-year

73. M. Helft, "Apple overtakes Exxon as most valuable US company," *The New York Times* (August 9, 2011)

74. A. Gara, "Apple is first public company worth $1 trillion," *Forbes* (August 2, 2018)

75. K. Leswing, "Apple becomes first U.S. company to reach $2 trillion market cap," *CNBC* (August 19, 2020)

76. Yahoo Finance, "Apple Inc. (AAPL) stock price, quote and news," *MarketWatch* (2024)

77. National Venture Capital Association (NVCA), *Venture Impact: The economic importance of venture capital-backed companies* (IHS Global Insight, 2009)

78. STIP Compass, "Defense Innovation Fund" (2023), https://stip.oecd.org/stip/interactive-dashboards/policy-initiatives/2023%2Fdata%2FpolicyInitiatives%2F99994967

79. Enterprise Singapore, "Invest in startups" (no date), www.enterprisesg.gov.sg/Grow-Your-Business/partner-with-singapore/Innovation-and-Startups/invest-in-startups

80. CB Insights, "The future according to GV, Alphabet's most active venture capital arm" (November 19, 2019), www.cbinsights.com/research/gv-google-ventures-investments

81. Intel Capital, "Portfolio" (2021), www.intelcapital.com/portfolio

82. Salesforce Ventures, "Reinventing the way the world works" (no date), https://salesforceventures.com/companies

83. Although this depends on various factors, including the

issuer's creditworthiness, market conditions, and the overall economic environment

84. International Monetary Fund (IMF), *World Economic Outlook: Challenges to steady growth* (IMF, 2018), www.imf.org/en /Publications/WEO/Issues/2018/09/24/world-economic -outlook-october-2018

85. E.F. Fama, "Efficient capital markets: A review of theory and empirical work," *Journal of Finance*, 25/2 (1970), 383–417

86. L. Mills, "Can stock prices reliably predict recessions?" *Business Review* (Sep/Oct 1988)

87. R. Roll, R.A. Schwartz and M. Subrahmanyam, "Price discovery and exchange listings," *Journal of Finance*, 64/6 (2009), 2725–2751

88. C.M. Jones, O.A. Lamont and R.L. Lumsdaine, "The structure of mutual fund fees," *Review of Financial Studies*, 11/1 (1998), 107–139

89. International Monetary Fund (IMF), *World Economic Outlook: Challenges to steady growth* (IMF, 2018), www.imf.org/en /Publications/WEO/Issues/2018/09/24/world-economic -outlook-october-2018

90. Bank for International Settlements, *Annual Economic Report 2021* (BIS, 2021), www.bis.org/publ/arpdf/ar2021e.pdf

91. World Bank, *Global Financial Development Report 2017/2018: Bankers without Borders* (World Bank, 2018), https:// openknowledge.worldbank.org/server/api/core /bitstreams/549fc090-e101-5519-ab84-94e3d28c1650/content

92. Nigerian Exchange Group, "Corporate overview" (NGX, no date), https://ngxgroup.com/about

93. V.A. Odozi, "The Indigenization Decree of Nigeria: An overview of its objectives and impact," *Journal of African Studies* (1991)

94. A.O. Olukoshi, "The politics of structural adjustment in Nigeria," *African Journal of Political Economy*, 21 (1993), 178–179

95. Debt Management Office (DMO) Nigeria, *Annual Report and Statement of Accounts* (DMO Nigeria, 2003)

96. L.S. Sanusi, "The Nigerian banking industry: What went wrong and the way forward" (Bank for International Settlements, 2010), www.bis.org/review/r100419c.pdf

97. Central Bank of Nigeria (CBN), *Annual Report: The Nigerian banking industry* (CBN, 2006), https://dc.cbn.gov.ng/cbn _annual_report

98. Securities and Exchange Commission, Nigeria, *Making World Class a Reality* (SEC Nigeria, 2009)

99. Nigerian Stock Exchange (NSE), *Annual Report and Financial Statements 2007* (NSE, 2008)

100. A.R. Sorkin, *Too Big to Fail: The inside story of how Wall Street and Washington fought to save the financial system – and themselves* (Viking Press, 2009)

101. D. Ellis, "Stocks crushed: Worst day on Wall Street since Black Monday," *CNN Money* (September 29, 2008)

102. Financial Crisis Inquiry Commission (FCIC), *The Financial Crisis Inquiry Report: Final report of the National Commission on the causes of the financial and economic crisis in the United States* (FCIC, 2011), www.govinfo.gov/content/pkg/GPO -FCIC/pdf/GPO-FCIC.pdf

103. L.S. Sanusi, "The Nigerian Banking Industry: What went wrong and the way forward" (Bank for International Settlements, 2010), www.bis.org/review/r100419c.pdf

104. The act was later repealed in 1825 owing to its restrictive impact on legitimate business formation

105. Securities Investor Protection Corporation (SIPC), "What SIPC protects (SIPC, no date), www.sipc.org/for-investors /what-sipc-protects

106. Financial Conduct Authority (FCA), *FCA Handbook* (2023), www.handbook.fca.org.uk/handbook

107. Securities and Futures Commission (SFC), *Annual Report 2022 –2023: Investor protection* (2023), www.sfc.hk/en /Published-resources/Corporate-publications/Annual -reports/2022-2023

108. U.S. Department of Justice (DOJ), "Press Release: Bernard L. Madoff sentenced to 150 years in prison for multi-billion-dollar Ponzi scheme" (2009)

109. U.S. Securities and Exchange Commission (SEC), *Investigation of Failure of the SEC to Uncover Bernard Madoff's Ponzi Scheme – Public Version* (2009), www.sec.gov/news /studies/2009/oig-509.pdf

110. International Organization of Securities Commissions (IOSCO), "About IOSCO" (no date), www.iosco.org/v2 /about/?subsection=about_iosco

111. U.S. Department of Justice (DOJ), "Justice Department, Federal and State partners secure record $13 billion global settlement with JPMorgan for misleading investors about securities containing toxic mortgages" (Office of Public

Affairs, November 19, 2013), www.justice.gov/opa/pr
/justice-department-federal-and-state-partners-secure
-record-13-billion-global-settlement

112. U.S. Department of Justice (DOJ), "Bank of America to pay
$16.65 billion in historic Justice Department settlement
for financial fraud leading up to and during the financial
crisis" (Office of Public Affairs, August 21, 2014), www
.justice.gov/opa/pr/bank-america-pay-1665-billion-historic
-justice-department-settlement-financial-fraud-leading

113. U.S. Securities and Exchange Commission, "Securities and
Exchange Commission v. WorldCom Inc., Civil Action
No. 02-CV-4963 (SDNY) (JSR)" (2002), www.sec.gov
/enforcement-litigation/litigation-releases/lr-18219

114. Office of Public Affairs, "Goldman Sachs charged in foreign
bribery case and agrees to pay over $2.9 billion" (October
22, 2020), www.justice.gov/opa/pr/goldman-sachs-charged
-foreign-bribery-case-and-agrees-pay-over-29-billion

115. J.C. Coffee, Jr., "Law and the market: The impact of
enforcement," *University of Pennsylvania Law Review*, 156/2
(2007), 229–311

116. International Monetary Fund (IMF), *World Economic Outlook:
Crisis and recovery* (International Monetary Fund, 2009)

117. Bank for International Settlements (BIS), *Quarterly Review:
International banking and financial market developments* (BIS,
2012), www.bis.org/publ/qtrpdf/r_qt1209.pdf

118. C. Duffield, "Nigeria's Iron Lady takes on fraudsters," *BBC
News* (July 1, 2010), www.bbc.com/news/10464725

119. N. Tattersall, "Nigeria graft police probe gala dinner for
Obama," *Reuters* (September 19, 2008), www.reuters.com
/article/world/nigeria-graft-police-probe-gala-dinner-for
-obama-idUSBAN225720

120. U.S. Securities and Exchange Commission (SEC), "MIDAS:
Market Information Data Analytics System" (June 28, 2024),
www.sec.gov/securities-topics/market-structure-analytics
/midas-market-information-data-analytics-system

121. D. Novak, "The power of employee recognition," *Harvard
Business Review* (2016)

122. Gallup, "State of the global workplace: Employee
engagement insights for business leaders worldwide"
(October 8, 2013), https://news.gallup.com/opinion
/gallup/171632/gallup-releases-new-insights-state-global
-workplace.aspx

123. World Bank Group, "Young Professionals Program (YPP): About the program" (no date), www.ifc.org/en/about /careers/wbg-young-professionals-program

124. African Development Bank (AfDB), "Young Professionals Program (YPP)" (no date), www.afdb.org/en/about-us /careers/young-professionals-program-ypp

125. I. Nwachukwu and B. Augie, "NSE misses $1 trillion market value target," *BusinessDay Nigeria* (December 6, 2016), https://businessday.ng/exclusives/article/nse-misses -1-trillion-market-value-target

126. WFE Focus Team, "NSE launches state-of-the-art data centre," *Focus* (October 2017), https://focus.world -exchanges.org/articles/nse-launches-state-art-data-centre

127. Nigerian Exchange Group, "NSE Demutualisation update" (2021), https://ngxgroup.com/demutualisation-update

128. Securities and Exchange Commission Nigeria, *Annual Report and Financial Statements 2010* (2010), https://sec.gov.ng /about/annual-reports

129. R. Tomas, "America is educating a nation of investors," *The Economist* (June 20, 2024), www.economist.com/united -states/2024/06/20/america-is-educating-a-nation-of -investors

130. T. Kaiser and L. Menkhoff, "Financial education in schools: A meta-analysis of experimental studies," *Economics of Education Review*, 78 (2020), https://doi.org/10.1016 /j.econedurev.2019.101930

131. EFInA, *Access to Financial Services in Nigeria Survey 2010* (October 19, 2021), https://efina.org.ng/publication/access -to-financial-services-in-nigeria-survey-2010

132. EFInA's periodic surveys are currently funded by the Bill & Melinda Gates Foundation. During my time at the SEC the surveys were sponsored by the United Kingdom's Foreign Commonwealth Development Office.

133. EFInA's 2023 survey showed that we missed this target. The level of financial inclusion is now down to 32% but still well above the 20% target we set in 2010.

134. J. Haynes, *Nollywood: The creation of Nigerian film genres* (University of Chicago Press, 2016)

135. M. Sassoon, "Nollywood: The next big thing" (BU College of Communication, May 1, 2023), www.bu.edu/com/articles /nollywood-the-next-big-thing

136. S. Busari, "Nigeria's 'Lionheart' disqualified from Oscar

race for having too much English," *CNN* (November 5, 2019), https://edition.cnn.com/2019/11/05/africa/lionheart -disqualified-from-the-oscars/index.html

137. A. Akingbulu, "Media and culture in Nigeria: A case study of Wale Adenuga's Superstory," *Journal of African Media Studies*, 2/1 (2010)

138. *Eye on Nigeria's Capital Market* (CNBC Africa, 2013)

139. P.E. Orbanes, *Monopoly: The world's most famous game and how it got that way* (Da Capo Press, 2006)

140. S.B. Shanklin and C.R. Ehlen, "Extending the use and effectiveness of the Monopoly® board game as an in-class economic simulation in the introductory financial accounting course," *American Journal of Business Education*, 10/2 (2017), 75–80

141. R.A. Baron and J.M. Ward, "Educational games in economics: The role of Monopoly in financial literacy," *Journal of Economic Education*, 46/2 (2015), 152–167

142. Federal Ministry of Information and National Orientation, Nigeria, "End-of-year world press conference addressed by the Supervising Minister of Information/Minister of State II Foreign Affairs" (December 31, 2014), https://fmino.gov .ng/end-of-year-world-press-conference-addressed-by-the -supervising-minister-of-informationminister-of-state-ii -foreign-affairs

143. United Nations Security Council, *Report of the Analytical Support and Sanctions Monitoring Team on Boko Haram's Activities in Nigeria* (UNSC, 2014), https://main.un.org /securitycouncil/en/sanctions/1267/monitoring-team /reports

144. M. Segun, "Those terrible weeks in their camp: Boko Haram violence against women and girls in northeast Nigeria," *Human Rights Watch* (October 27, 2014), www.hrw.org /report/2014/10/27/those-terrible-weeks-their-camp/boko -haram-violence-against-women-and-girls

145. Securities and Exchange Commission Nigeria, *CIS Registration and Market Trends Report* (2024), https://sec.gov .ng/weekly-net-asset-value-data-for-cis

146. Ibid.

147. P. Ungersboeck and C. Runkel, "Asset Management Corporation of Nigeria (AMCON): Asset management," *The Journal of Financial Crises*, 3/2 (2021), 618–640

148. The NGX Premium includes Access Holdings Plc, Dangote

Cement Plc, FBN Holdings Plc, United Bank for Africa
Plc, Lafarge Africa Plc, Zenith Bank Plc, MTN Nigeria
Communications Plc, and Seplat Energy Plc

149. B. Albrecht, "The best-performing ETFs of the month,"
Morningstar Canada (June 6, 2024), www.morningstar.ca/ca
/news/250072/the-best-performing-etfs-of-the-month.aspx

150. PricewaterhouseCoopers, *ETFs 2028: Shaping the future*
(PWC, 2024), www.pwc.at/de/publikationen/pwc-etf-2028
-shaping-the-future.pdf

151. Morningstar, "Active vs. Passive funds by investment
category" (March 21, 2024), www.morningstar.com
/business/insights/blog/funds/active-vs-passive-investing

152. J. Bogle and R. Ferri, "Exchange-traded funds: A review
of the literature," *Journal of Financial Economics* (2019);
referenced in https://econpapers.repec.org/article
/kapfmktpm/v_3a34_3ay_3a2020_3ai_3a2_3ad_3a10.1007
_5fs11408-020-00349-1.htm

153. Nareit, *Global REIT Approach to Real Estate Investing: 2023
edition* (REIT.com, 2023), https://www.reit.com/sites
/default/files/2023–04/2023_Global_REIT_Brochure.pdf

154. Nareit, "REITs and the economy" (2022)

155. Nareit, *Economic Impact of REITs: An analysis of their
contributions to the real estate sector* (2020)

156. N.G. Miller and D. Geltner, "REITs and real estate market
outcomes: An analysis of regional impacts," *Journal of Real
Estate Research*, 40/2 (2018), 223–2449

157. Securities and Exchange Commission Nigeria, *Annual Report
and Financial Statements 2012* (2012), https://sec.gov.ng
/weekly-net-asset-value-data-for-cis

158. Securities Industry and Financial Markets Association
(SIFMA), "US Mortgage-Backed Securities Statistics"
(October 3, 2024), www.sifma.org/resources/research/us
-mortgage-backed-securities-statistics

159. E.M. Gunter and N.W. Kraemer, *Default, Transition, and
Recovery: 2023 annual global leveraged loan CLO default and
rating transition study* (S&P Global, 2023), www.spglobal
.com/ratings/en/research/articles/240627-default
-transition-and-recovery-2023-annual-global-leveraged-loan
-clo-default-and-rating-transition-study-13160502

160. HM Treasury and The Rt Hon George Osborne, "UK
Government issues first Islamic Bond" (June 25, 2014),

www.gov.uk/government/news/government-issues-first
-islamic-bond

161. Islamic Financial Services Board (IFSB), *Islamic Financial Services Industry (IFSI) Stability Report 2022* (2023), www .ifsb.org/wp-content/uploads/2023/10/Islamic-Financial -Services-Industry-Stability-Report-2022_En.pdf

162. M. Damak, "Sukuk outlook 2024: Cautiously optimistic" (S&P Global, 2024), www.spglobal.com/ratings/en /research/articles/240115-sukuk-outlook-2024-cautiously -optimistic-12964886

163. J. Diamant, "The countries with the 10 largest Christian populations and the 10 largest Muslim populations" (Pew Research Center, 2019), www.pewresearch.org/short-reads /2019/04/01/the-countries-with-the-10-largest-christian -populations-and-the-10-largest-muslim-populations

164. C. Ohuocha, "Nigeria to issue first sovereign sukuk in 2014 – Regulator," *Reuters* (October 2, 2013), www.reuters.com /article/nigeria-sukuk-idINL6N0HS2UE20131002

165. Aluko and Oyebode, "Understanding sukuk in Nigeria," *Lexology* (April 26, 2022), www.lexology.com/library/detail .aspx?g=cfa138a0-d5c2-44af-ac44-d5ba78ee7118

166. C. Ohuocha, "Nigeria starts sale of 100 bln naira debut sovereign sukuk," *Reuters* (September 14, 2017), www .reuters.com/article/business/finance/nigeria-starts-sale-of -100-bln-naira-debut-sovereign-sukuk-idUSL5N1LV45W

167. Malaysia International Financial Centre (MIFC), "Malaysia continues to lead the global Sukuk market" (MIFC, 2023), www.mifc.com/-/epicentre-february-2023-malaysia -continues-to-lead-the-global-sukuk-market

168. Lotus Capital, "Lotus Halal Equity Exchange Traded Fund" (no date), www.lotuscapitallimited.com/individual -investors/lotus-halal-equity-etf/

169. FMDQ Group, *FMDQ Monthly Market Report April 2024* (2024), https://fmdqgroup.com/wpfd_file/fmdq-markets-monthly -report-april-2024

170. Financial Stability Board (FSB), "OTC Derivatives Market Reforms: Implementation progress in 2022" (2023), www.fsb.org/2022/11/otc-derivatives-market-reforms -implementation-progress-in-2022

171. Ibid.

172. AFEX, "About us: Expanding across Africa" (2023), www .afex.africa/company/about-us

173. African Private Equity and Venture Capital Association (AVCA), "British International Investment commits US$265mn to address food security" (2023), www.avca.africa/news-insights/member-news/british-international-investment-commits-us-265mn-to-address-food-security

174. A recent post on LinkedIn can be found at www.linkedin.com/in/arunma-oteh/recent-activity/comments

175. M.R. Iskander and N. Chamlou, *Corporate Governance: A Framework for analysis* (World Bank Group, 2000), https://documents1.worldbank.org/curated/pt/831651468781818619/pdf/30446.pdf

176. At the NSE market closing on April 17, 2024, a Seplat share was priced at 3,370 naira, above the IPO price of 576 naira

177. A. Salaudeen, "Why Africa's biggest telecoms company is listing on the Nigerian Stock Exchange," *CNN* (May 16, 2019), https://edition.cnn.com/2019/05/16/africa/mtn-nigerian-stock-exchange-listing-intl/index.html

178. B3, "Listing segments" (no date), www.b3.com.br/en_us/products-and-services/solutions-for-issuers/listing-segments/novo-mercado

179. Brazilian Stock Market data is available on financial data platforms like Yahoo Finance or MarketWatch

180. International Finance Corporation (IFC), "Governance and performance in emerging markets" (March 11, 2019), www.ifc.org/en/insights-reports/2019/governance-and-performance-in-emerging-markets

181. Organisation for Economic Co-operation and Development (OECD), *G20/OECD Principles of Corporate Governance* (OECD Publishing, 2015), www.oecd.org/en/publications/g20-oecd-principles-of-corporate-governance-2015_9789264236882-en.html

182. Anap Foundation, "Mr Atedo N A Peterside CON" (2024), www.anapfoundation.com/the-founder-and-advisory-board/mr-atedo-n-a-peterside-con

183. "SEC gives ETI Plc 7 days ultimatum to reverse sack of Do Rego," *Proshare*, (January 12, 2014), https://proshare.co/articles/sec-gives-eti-plc-7-days-ultimatum-to-reverse-sack-of-do-rego

184. W. Wallis, "Ecobank chief to forego bonus in bid to quell unease," *Financial Times* (September 2, 2013), www.ft.com/content/7368671c-13e9-11e3-9289-00144feabdc0

185. M. Mpoke Bigg, "Ecobank board removes CEO following

months of turmoil," *Reuters* (March 11, 2014), www.reuters
.com/article/business/ecobank-board-removes-ceo
-following-months-of-turmoil-idUSBREA2A1OQ

186. W. Wallis, "Ousted Ecobank CEO awarded $15m
damages," *Financial Times* (January 15, 2015), www.ft.com/
content/862a4620-9cd4-11e4-adf3-00144feabdc0

187. A. Hayes, "AIM: What the Alternative Investment Market
is and how it works," *Investopedia* (updated April 26, 2024),
www.investopedia.com/terms/a/alternative-investment
-market.asp

188. I. Nwachukwu, "Alternative securities market: What
stakeholders said at the launch," *Business Day* (April
25, 2013), https://businessday.ng/news/article/alternative
-securities-marketwhat-stakeholders-said-at-the-launch

189. The Quoted Companies Alliance, "How many companies
move from AIM to the Main Market and from the Main
Market to AIM?" (2019), www.theqca.com/news-insights
/how-many-companies-move-from-aim-to-the-main
-market-and-from-the-main-market-to-aim

190. Nigerian Exchange Group, *Strengthening the Competitiveness
of African economies* (2020), https://ngxgroup.com/nse
-migrates-four-companies-from-asem-to-growth-board

191. World Bank Group, *World Development Report 2014: Risk and
opportunity – managing risk for development* (2013), https://
openknowledge.worldbank.org/entities/publication
/8b0ce20f-98e5-5a1b-a069-9ddc42addc76

192. G. Bekaert, C.R. Harvey and C. Lundblad, "Growth volatility
and financial liberalization," *Journal of Financial Economics*,
86/1 (2007), 72–100

193. Securities and Exchange Commission Nigeria, *Annual
Report and Financial Statements 2015* (2015), www.sec.gov.ng
/files/Annual%20reports/SEC%20ANNUAL%20REPORT
%20AND%20ACCOUNTS%202015.pdf

194. R.M. Stulz, "Globalization, corporate finance, and the cost of
capital," *Journal of Financial Economics*, 59/1 (1999), 3–29

195. World Bank, *Global Financial Development Report 2014* (2014),
https://blogs.worldbank.org/en/allaboutfinance/fresh
-press-global-financial-development-report-2014

196. Securities and Exchange Commission Nigeria, *Annual Report
and Financial Statements 2010* (2010), https://sec.gov.ng/files
/Annual%20reports/SEC%20ANNUAL%20REPORTS%20&
%20ACCOUNTS%202010_lite.pdf

197. International Finance Corporation, "IFC to Launch $1 Billion Local-Currency Bond Program to Support Nigeria's Capital Markets" (August 12, 2013), www.proshare.co /articles/ifc-to-launch-1-billion-local-currency-bond -program-to-support-nigerias-capital-markets

198. International Monetary Fund (IMF) *Global Financial Stability Report, April 2021: Preempting a legacy of vulnerabilities* (2021), www.imf.org/en/Publications/GFSR /Issues/2021/04/06/global-financial-stability-report-april -2021

199. A.R. Ghosh and J.D. Ostry, "Maturity Transformation and debt sustainability: The role of currency in emerging markets. IMF Working Paper No. 16/81" (2016)

200. World Bank, "International debt statistics" (no date), www .worldbank.org/en/programs/debt-statistics/ids

201. International Finance Corporation (IFC), *IFC Annual Report 2021: Meeting the moment* (2021), www.ifc.org/en/insights -reports/2021/ifc-ar-2021-download

202. World Bank, *Recent Developments on Local Currency Bond Markets in Emerging Economies* (2020), https://documents1.worldbank.org/curated /en/129961580334830825/pdf/Staff-Note-for-the-G20 -International-Financial-Architecture-Working-Group -IFAWG-Recent-Developments-On-Local-Currency-Bond -Markets-In-Emerging-Economies.pdf

203. African Development Bank (AfDB), "AfDB issues its inaugural local currency bond in the Nigerian capital market" (July 18, 2014), www.afdb.org/en/news-and-events/afdb-issues-its-inaugural-local-currency-bond-in-the-nigerian-capital-market-13376

204. "MTN Nigeria completes N200B bond issuance," *Business Today Nigeria* (November 4, 2021), https://businesstodayng .com/mtn-nigeria-completes-n200b-bond-issuance

205. Proshare, "Lafarge Africa Plc redeemed its n26.4 billion series 1 bond due on June 15, 2019" (June 19, 2019), https:// proshare.co/articles/lafarge-africa-plc-redeemed-its-n26 .4-billion-series-1-bond-due-on-june-15-2019

206. FMDQ Group, "Fidelity Bank Plc ₦100.00bn Bond Issuance Programme" (no date), https://fmdqgroup.com/exchange /programme/fidelity-bank-plc-₦A6100-00bn-bond -issuance-programme

207. World Bank, *International Financial Reporting Standards:*

A *practical guide* (2024), https://documents.worldbank
.org/en/publication/documents-reports/documentdetail
/099719108282411390

208. M.E. Barth, W.R. Landsman and M.H. Lang, "International accounting standards and accounting quality," *Journal of Accounting Research*, 46/3 (2008), 467–498

209. C. Kim, S. Li and L. Zhang, "Corporate tax avoidance and stock price crash risk: Firm-level analysis," *The Accounting Review*, 86/4 (2011), 1271–1315

210. European Commission, *Study on the Economic Impact of IFRS Adoption on European Capital Markets* (2013)

211. The World Bank, *Reserves Advisory and Management Program (RAMP)* (2021), https://thedocs.worldbank
.org/en/doc/745221572017478325-0340022019/original
/brochureramp2019.pdf

212. F. Luthans and B.J. Avolio, "Authentic leadership theory and practice: Origins, effects, and development," *Journal of Leadership and Organizational Studies*, 10/1 (2003), 20–40

213. In 2022, the Nigerian National Bureau of Statistics estimated Nigeria's population at 216,783,381: https://nigerianstat.gov
.ng/elibrary/read/1241422

214. JP Morgan, "Nigeria's government bonds added to JP Morgan GBI-EM Index" (2012)

215. National Pension Commission (PenCom), *Nigeria's Pension Reform and the Growth of the Pension Industry* (2012)

216. Ibid.

217. Securities and Exchange Commission Nigeria, *Annual Report and Financial Statements 2014* (2015)

218. Central Bank of Nigeria (CBN), *CBN Economic Report Second Quarter 2013* (2013), www.cbn.gov.ng/out/2013/rsd/cbn
%20economic%20report%20for%20the%20second%20
%20quarter%20of%202013.pdf

219. O. Umoru, S. Pam et al, "Imperative of mainstreaming the Nigerian capital market master plan into national economic development policy," *Nigerian Journal of Securities Markets*, 1/1 (2016), 41–53, https://sec.gov.ng/nigerian
-journal-of-securities-market

220. Securities and Exchange Commission Nigeria, *The Nigerian Capital Market Master Plan 2021–2025* (2021), https://sec.gov
.ng/nigerian-capital-market-masterplan

221. P. Egwuatu, "Law makers' intervention in capital market attracts mixed reactions," *Vanguard Nigeria* (December

20, 2010), www.vanguardngr.com/2010/12/law-makers %E2%80%99-intervention-in-capital-market-attracts-mixed -reactions

222. "EFCC to arraign Hembe, Azubogu over N44m bribery," *Premium Times* (May 10, 2012), www.premiumtimesng.com /news/5041-efcc_to_arraign_hembe_azubogu_over_n44m _bribery.html

223. Economic and Financial Crimes Commission (EFCC), "You have case to answer, court tells Hembe, Azubogu," (June 26, 2013), www.efccnigeria.org/efcc/news-and-information /news-release/531-4-095-sec-fraud-you-have-case-to -answer-court-tells-hembe-azubogu

224. "Hembe accused Oteh of offering him N30 million bribe," *Premium Times* (March 20, 2012), www.premiumtimesng .com/news/4299-hembe_accused_oteh_of_offering_him _n30milion_bribe.html?tztc=1

225. "Nigeria's financial regulator Arunma Oteh suspended," *BBC News* (June 12, 2012), www.bbc.com/news/world -africa-18412132

226. K.A. Ericsson, R.T. Krampe and C. Tesch-Römer, "The role of deliberate practice in the acquisition of expert performance," *Psychological Review*, 100/3 (1993), 363–406

227. E.B. Collins and C.J. Collins, "The effects of preparation on decision-making and performance," *Journal of Management*, 33/4 (2007), 683–707.

228. A'L Bundles, *On Her Own Ground: The life and times of Madam C.J. Walker* (Scribner, 2001)

229. Tony Elumelu Foundation, "Our impact pillars" (no date), www.tonyelumelufoundation.org/our-impact-pillars

230. Dangote Foundation, "About the foundation" (no date), www.dangote.com/foundation/about-foundation

231. Rose of Sharon Foundation, "About RoSF" (no date), https:// theroseofsharonfoundation.org/about-us

232. A. Ogbu, "Otedola: The evolution and revolution of his philanthropy," *ThisDay* (April 14, 2023), www.thisdaylive .com/index.php/2023/04/14/otedola-the-evolution-and -revolution-of-his-philanthropy

233. S. Ozo, "BUA group establishes $100M Africa Endowment Fund," *Voice of Nigeria* (March 24, 2021), https://von.gov.ng /bua-group-establishes-100m-africa-endowment-fund

234. World Bank, *Poverty and Shared Prosperity 2020: Reversals*

of fortune (2020), www.worldbank.org/en/publication /poverty-and-shared-prosperity-2020

235. UN Development Programme, *COVID-19 and Human Development: Assessing the crisis, envisioning the recovery* (2020), https://hdr.undp.org/content/covid-19-and-human -development-assessing-crisis-envisioning-recovery

236. Institute for Economics and Peace, *Global Peace Index 2023 Report* (2023), www.economicsandpeace.org/reports

237. World Bank, *Global Monitoring Report 2015/2016: Development Goals in an era of demographic change* (World Bank Publications, 2016)

238. World Bank, *World Development Indicators 2020* (World Bank Publications, 2020)

239. FAO, IFAD, UNICEF, WFP and WHO, *The State of Food Security and Nutrition in the World 2018: Building climate resilience for food security and nutrition* (FAO, 2018), https:// openknowledge.fao.org/server/api/core/bitstreams /f5019ab4-0f6a-47e8-85b9-15473c012d6a/content

240. UN Trade and Development, *Financing for Sustainable Development Report 2024* (UNCTAD, 2024), https://unctad .org/publication/financing-sustainable-development-report -2024

241. UN Trade and Development, "SDG investment is growing, but too slowly: The investment gap is now $4 trillion, up from $2.5 in 2015," *SDG Investment Trends Monitor*, 4 (2023), https://unctad.org/publication/sdg-investment-trends -monitor-issue-4

242. The IMF estimates this could actually have been as high as US$450 trillion in 2021

243. Organisation for Economic Co-operation and Development (OECD), *Global Outlook on Financing for Sustainable Development 2021: A new way to invest for people and planet* (OECD Publishing, 2020)

244. Climate Bonds Initiative, *Sustainable Debt: Global state of the market 2023* (2024), www.climatebonds.net/files/reports/cbi _sotm23_02h.pdf

245. L. Tang, "Sustainability-linked bonds, loans sink in 2023," *The Asset* (January 13, 2024), www.theasset.com/article-esg /50731/sustainability-linked-bonds-loans-sink-in-2023

246. D. Hand, S. Sunderji and N.M. Pardo, *2023 GIIN Impact Investing Allocations, Activity and Performance* (GIIN, 2023),

https://s3.amazonaws.com/giin-web-assets/giin/assets/publication/research/2023-giinsight-impact-investing-allocations-activity-and-performance-c1.pdf

247. UN Trade and Development, *World Investment Report 2022: International tax reforms and sustainable development* (UNCTAD, 2022), https://unctad.org/webflyer/world-investment-report-2022

248. African Development Bank, "African Economic Outlook 2022" (2022), www.afdb.org/en/documents/african-economic-outlook-2022

249. D. Gerszon Mahler, C. Lakner et al., "The impact of COVID-19 (Coronavirus) on global poverty: Why Sub-Saharan Africa might be the region hardest hit," *World Bank Blogs* (April 20, 2020), https://blogs.worldbank.org/en/opendata/impact-covid-19-coronavirus-global-poverty-why-sub-saharan-africa-might-be-region-hardest

250. United Nations Economic Commission for Africa, *Towards a Common Investment Area in the African Continental Free Trade Area* (UNECA, 2021), www.uneca.org/commoninvestmentarea

251. International Renewable Energy Agency, "Renewable capacity statistics 2020" (IRENA, 2020), www.irena.org/publications/2020/Mar/Renewable-Capacity-Statistics-2020

252. International Finance Corporation (IFC), "New analysis shows onshore wind potential across Africa enough to power the entire continent many times over" (November 2, 2020), www.ifc.org/en/pressroom/2020/new-analysis-shows-onshore-wind-potential-across-africa-enough-to-power-the-entire-continent-many-times-over

253. A.G. Zeufack et al., *Africa's Pulse: An analysis of issues shaping Africa's economic future* (World Bank Group, 2020), https://documents.worldbank.org/en/publication/documents-reports/documentdetail/799911586462355556/an-analysis-of-issues-shaping-africas-economic-future

254. Food and Agriculture Organization of the United Nations, *The Future of Food and Agriculture: Trends and challenges* (FAO, 2014), https://openknowledge.fao.org/server/api/core/bitstreams/2e90c833-8e84-46f2-a675-ea2d7afa4e24/content

255. International Energy Agency, "Africa energy outlook 2019"

(IEA, 2019), www.iea.org/reports/africa-energy-outlook
-2019

256. World Bank Group, "World development indicators: Electric power consumption (kWh per capita)" (2020), https://databank.worldbank.org/source/world-development-indicators/preview/on

257. C.M. Briceno-Garmendia and V. Foster, *Africa's Infrastructure: A time for transformation* (World Bank Group, 2009), https://documents.worldbank.org/en/publication/documents-reports/documentdetail/246961468003355256/africas-infrastructure-a-time-for-transformation

258. R. Levine and S. Zervos, "Stock markets, banks, and economic growth," *Journal of Finance*, 53/6 (1998), 2231–2256

259. World Bank, *Global Financial Development Report 2017/2018: Bankers without Borders* (World Bank Publications, 2018), www.worldbank.org/en/publication/gfdr/gfdr-2018

260. International Telecommunication Union, *Measuring Digital Development: Facts and figures 2023* (ITU, 2023), www.itu.int/en/ITU-D/Statistics/Pages/facts/default.aspx

261. GSMA, *The Mobile Economy Sub-Saharan Africa 2020* (2020), www.gsma.com/r/mobileeconomy/sub-saharan-africa

262. Equinix, "Equinix Enters Africa, Closing the US$320 Million Acquisition of MainOne" (April 5, 2022), www.equinix.com/newsroom/press-releases/2022/04/equinix-enters-africa-closing-the-us-320-million-acquisition-of-mainone

263. UK Government and Transport for London (TfL), *Elizabeth Line Benefits Framework* (2022), https://tfl.gov.uk/corporate/publications-and-reports/elizabeth-line-benefits-framework

264. R. Wallace, "The world's most luxurious airports" (AllClear Travel Insurance, updated August 2, 2024), www.allcleartravel.co.uk/blog/worlds-most-luxurious-airports

265. "China Merchants Port Holdings Co Ltd," *Financial Times* (no date), https://markets.ft.com/data/equities/tearsheet/profile?s=144:HKG

266. World Bank, "GDP (current US$) – Nigeria" (World Bank Data, no date), https://data.worldbank.org/indicator/NY.GDP.MKTP.CD?locations=NG

267. World Bank, "GDP (Current US$) – South Africa" (World Bank Data, no date), https://data.worldbank.org/indicator/NY.GDP.MKTP.CD?view=bar&locations=ZA

268. United Nations Development Programme, *Human*

Development Report 2023–24: Breaking the gridlock: Reimagining cooperation in a polarized world (UNDP, 2024), https://hdr.undp.org/system/files/documents/global-report-document/hdr2023-24reporten.pdf

269. National Bureau of Statistics (NBS), "Foreign Trade in Goods Statistics (Q2 2023)" (2023), https://nigerianstat.gov.ng/elibrary/read/1241466

270. World Bank, "Manufacturing, Value Added (% of GDP) – China, India, and Nigeria" (World Bank Data, 2023)

271. Securities Industry and Financial Markets Association (SIFMA), "SIFMA data and statistics" (SIFMA, no date), www.sifma.org/resources/archive/research/data-and-statistics

272. O. Uduu, "Why Nigeria's housing deficit quadrupled in three decades," *Dataphyte* (June 30, 2023), www.dataphyte.com/housing/why-nigerias-housing-deficit-quadrupled-in-3-decades

273. United Nations Department of Economic and Social Affairs, *World Urbanization Prospects: The 2018 revision* (DESA, 2018), https://population.un.org/wup/Publications/Files/WUP2018-Report.pdf

274. World Bank, "Nigeria: Housing Finance Development Program" (2019) https://documents1.worldbank.org/curated/pt/451061575564485490/text/Nigeria-Housing-Finance-Development-Program.txt,

275. N. Ibrahim, "Real estate sector to experience demand surge in 2022 – Noah Ibrahim, CEO, Novarick Homes," *ThisDay* (2021), www.thisdaylive.com/index.php/2022/02/10/real-estate-sector-to-experience-demand-surge-in-2022-noah-ibrahim-ceo-novarick-homes/#google_vignette

276. SIFMA, *US Fixed-Income Markets: 2023 review & 2024 outlook* (2024), www.sifma.org/wp-content/uploads/2023/12/SIFMA-2024-Capital-Markets-Outlook.pdf

277. U.S. Census Bureau, "Quarterly residential vacancies and homeownership, second quarter 2023" (2023), https://getfea.com/end-use/us-census-bureau-releases-q2-residential-vacancies-and-homeownership-report

278. International Bank for Reconstruction and Development and The World Bank, *Doing Business 2020: Comparing business regulation in 190 economies* (World Bank Group, 2020), https://documents1.worldbank.org/curated/fr/688761571934946384/pdf/Doing-Business-2020-Comparing-Business-Regulation-in-190-Economies.pdf

279. National Bureau of Statistics, Nigeria, *Demographic Statistics Bulletin 2022* (NBS, 2023), www.nigerianstat.gov.ng /pdfuploads/DEMOGRAPHIC_BULLETIN_2022_FINAL .pdf

280. A.F. Carvajal and R. Bebczuk, *A Literature Review: Capital markets development: Causes, effects, and sequencing* (World Bank Group, 2019), https://documents1.worldbank.org /curated/en/701021588343376548/pdf/Capital-Markets -Development-Causes-Effects-and-Sequencing.pdf

281. L. Klapper, A. Lusardi and P. Van Oudheusden, *Financial Literacy around the World: Insights from the Standard & Poor's Ratings Services Global Financial Literacy Survey* (2015), https://gflec.org/wp-content/uploads/2015/11/Finlit _paper_16_F2_singles.pdf

282. H. El Habti, "Why Africa's youth hold the key to its development potential" (World Economic Forum, September 19, 2022), www.weforum.org/agenda/2022/09 /why-africa-youth-key-development-potential

283. United Nations Department of Economic and Social Affairs, "World Population Prospects 2022: Summary of results" (DESA, 2022), https://population.un.org/wpp

Acknowledgments

This book has been long in the making. From the moment I first held a book as a young girl, I rapidly evolved into an avid reader, consuming stories across all genres, fueling my boundless curiosity. This love for reading, combined with my passion for finance, and my experience in international development and capital markets, meant that I have always wanted to tell the story of the value of capital markets to society. In the late 1990s, with support from the Nordic Africa Institute, I co-edited a collection of essays written by young African thinkers, scholars, and leaders. This work was published in 2001 as *African Voices, African Visions*. It explores Africa's development challenges and prospects, covering governance, economics, culture, and social issues. It also offers an optimistic, yet realistic view of Africa's potential, emphasizing the importance of strategic leadership and innovative solutions to uplift the continent. Working on that book further intensified my desire to write one that would highlight the significance of leadership and the transformative power of capital markets in society. Almost a decade later, during my tenure leading capital markets reform in Nigeria, I was even more convinced of the merit of such a book. I must therefore start by extending my deepest appreciation to Nigerians, whose support for our reforms enabled my colleagues and I to survive the fierce opposition of powerful stakeholders. We championed bold and far-reaching reforms that are not only widely recognized for their transformative impact, but also inspired me to share my lifelong lessons on the value of capital markets to society.

Working on that book further intensified my desire to write one that would highlight the significance of leadership and the transformative power of capital markets in society. Almost a decade later, during my tenure leading capital markets reform in Nigeria, I was even more convinced about the merit of such a book. I must therefore start by extending my deepest appreciation to Nigerians, whose support for our reforms enabled my colleagues and I to survive the fierce opposition of some powerful stakeholders. We championed bold and far-reaching reforms, which are not only widely recognized for their transformative impact, but also inspired me to share my lifelong lessons on the value of capital markets to society.

I am grateful to President Umaru Yar'Adua for giving me the honor to serve Nigeria as Director General of the Securities and Exchange Commission (SEC) at such a pivotal time as the period right after the global financial crisis. Leading the transformation of the Nigerian capital markets was an incredible opportunity that allowed me to lay a solid foundation for the emergence of world class capital markets capable of catalyzing lasting prosperity for all Nigerians. President Goodluck Jonathan gave us his full support, including for our decisions that negatively impacted some politically connected persons who relished the status quo. He exemplified true leadership, standing by me personally even when it came at political costs to him. I was also fortunate to serve at a time when many Nigerians of the highest competence and integrity held key positions in government. I am indebted to the ministers and members of the economic management team who helped us ensure that we implemented our reforms effectively.

Many of our successes in reforming the Nigerian capital markets were also made possible through important international partnerships. My colleagues on the Board of the International Organization of Securities Commissions (IOSCO) were a vital source of support, not only offering perspectives on our reforms but also sharing similar experiences from their jurisdictions, whether nascent or developed, small or large. The camaraderie we shared, particularly in the high-stakes environment following the global financial crisis, was invaluable in helping us collectively guide global capital markets toward recovery. I also extend my thanks to the CEOs of regulatory organizations across Africa and the Middle East, who gave me the privilege of leading and representing the region. Representing markets with such diverse complexities taught me a lot about the value of capital markets for meeting the varied needs of different countries and peoples.

The support we received from the United States SEC team was also crucial, and I am especially grateful for their dedication, including sending a team to conduct a peer review of our market. I likewise acknowledge the partnership we enjoyed with the IFC, particularly through the leadership shown by Jingdong Hua, who was then Treasurer of the IFC. Jingdong has been a true evangelist for the value of capital markets, and under him, the IFC issued bonds in Nigerian Naira, walking the talk. The AfDB also deserves commendation for issuing Naira bonds around the same time. Both issuances from triple-A-rate entities bolstered the credibility of Nigeria's capital markets and further deepened our domestic bond market.

I deeply appreciate the cooperation of the Nigerian capital market community, particularly the SEC's Capital Market Committee, whose belief in our vision played a pivotal role in the success of our reforms. They took ownership of many of our reform initiatives, including developing Nigeria's first Capital Market Masterplan, a long-term strategy for capital market growth. I equally commend the dedication of my staff at the SEC, who tirelessly gave their best efforts under intense scrutiny to uphold the highest standards. My former teams at the African Development Bank (AfDB), and the World Bank, along with global market participants who share my belief in the value of capital markets, also deserve recognition. Together, we are continuously working to make these markets work for everyone.

As I think about those who played major roles in inspiring me to tell the stories in this book, I would like to first acknowledge legendary Nigerian-Dutch publisher Chief Joop Berkhout, who visited me at the onset of our capital market reforms and encouraged me to write a book that would resonate with both everyday readers and leaders alike. With over seventy years of publishing experience in Nigeria, Chief Berkhout is rightly called the "father of books" by many Nigerians. My gratitude also goes to Yewande Zaccheaus, whose recent gentle encouragement persuaded me that the timing was right to share my insights. I also appreciate Chinwe Egwim, one of my mentees, for also prodding me to write this book.

When I took the leap to finally begin work on this book, I quickly realized it would be impossible to achieve it within the time constraints, especially with the demands of work, involvement in countless projects, and my commitments to multiple charity and global advocacy initiatives. It is here that I must give special recognition to Samson Pam, my brilliant former staff at the SEC, who worked closely with me to bring this book to life. Sam Pam's remarkable capacity to dig up information and unique ability to recall the many stories from our five years at the SEC enabled me to complete the first manuscript within such a tight timeframe.

Heartfelt thanks go to my sister, Egbichi Akinsanya, whose deep knowledge as an accountant, economist, and former capital market regulator has been priceless. She supported me throughout this project, reading the manuscript meticulously and offering crucial feedback.

Finally, I hope that those too numerous to name will forgive me for not mentioning them individually here. So many people have contributed to the stories shared in this book, and I will be forever grateful to each one of you. Indeed, to everyone who played a role in bringing this book to life, you have my profound thanks.

The Author

Arunma Oteh is a globally acclaimed capital markets expert, business leader, and academic at the University of Oxford. During her career she has regulated capital markets, raised billions globally, pioneered sustainable financing solutions and managed large multi-currency investment portfolios. She has also held leadership roles in global financial institutions, including serving as the Treasurer of the World Bank. She sits on several boards and is the Chairperson of a UK asset manager.

Arunma is passionate about having global impact on key issues for society and co-chairs the Global Task Force on Inequality and Social-related Financial Disclosures (TISFD) and the High-Level Panel on Closing the Crisis Protection Gap. She is the Chairperson of the Royal African Society, and is a board member of King's Trust International. In 2011 she was awarded the national honor of Officer of the Order of the Niger (OON) and has received several global awards.

🌐 www.arunmaoteh.com

in www.linkedin.com/in/arunma-oteh

🇫 www.facebook.com/profile.php?id=100087105100611

❎ @aoteh

📷 @arunmaoteh